Freud's Legacy in the Global Era

Freud's Legacy in the Global Era presents a radically new perspective on Freud's relevance today as a forerunner of the contemporary evolutionary neurosciences also steeped in the tradition of humanistic thought. Carlo Strenger shows how globalization has produced new theoretical, practical and clinical issues for psychoanalysis, which can best be understood by drawing on influences from economics, sociology and philosophy.

Strenger's lively case histories demonstrate a new psychoanalytic viewpoint engaged with surrounding scientific disciplines in an enriching interchange, and open to the fascinating cultural and social developments that shape patients' realities, lives and concerns in a global era.

This book will be of interest to psychoanalysts, psychoanalytic- and psychodynamically oriented psychotherapists and to all mental health professionals interested in the interaction of psychoanalysis and other disciplines from a global viewpoint as well as to lay readers keen to understand the complexity of globalized life.

Carlo Strenger serves as Professor of Psychology and Philosophy at Tel Aviv University, he is a member of the Seminar for Existential Psychoanalysis in Zurich and the Scientific Board of the Sigmund Freud Foundation in Vienna and Senior Research Fellow at the Center for Terrorism Studies, John Jay College, New York, in addition to maintaining a part-time practice in existential psychoanalysis. He is the author of numerous books and papers that have been translated into many languages, and a columnist for leading publications in English and German.

RELATIONAL PERSPECTIVES BOOK SERIES

The Relational Perspectives Book Series (RPBS) publishes books that grow out of or contribute to the relational tradition in contemporary psychoanalysis. The term *relational psychoanalysis* was first used by Greenberg and Mitchell[1] to bridge the traditions of interpersonal relations, as developed within interpersonal psychoanalysis and object relations, as developed within contemporary British theory. But, under the seminal work of the late Stephen Mitchell, the term *relational psychoanalysis* grew and began to accrue to itself many other influences and developments. Various tributaries – interpersonal psychoanalysis, object relations theory, self psychology, empirical infancy research, and elements of contemporary Freudian and Kleinian thought – flow into this tradition, which understands relational configurations between self and others, both real and fantasied, as the primary subject of psychoanalytic investigation.

We refer to the relational tradition, rather than to a relational school, to highlight that we are identifying a trend, a tendency within contemporary psychoanalysis, not a more formally organized or coherent school or system of beliefs. Our use of the term *relational* signifies a dimension of theory and practice that has become salient across the wide spectrum of contemporary psychoanalysis. Now under the editorial supervision of Lewis Aron and Adrienne Harris with the assistance of Associate Editors Steven Kuchuck and Eyal Rozmarin, the Relational Perspectives Book Series originated in 1990 under the editorial eye of the late Stephen A. Mitchell. Mitchell was the most prolific and influential of the originators of the relational tradition. He was committed to dialogue among psychoanalysts and he abhorred the authoritarianism that dictated adherence to a rigid set of beliefs or technical restrictions. He championed open discussion, comparative and integrative approaches, and he promoted new voices across the generations.

Included in the Relational Perspectives Book Series are authors and works that come from within the relational tradition, extend and develop the tradition, as well as works that critique relational approaches or compare and contrast it with alternative points of view. The series includes our most distinguished senior psychoanalysts, along with younger contributors who bring fresh vision.

[1]Greenberg, J. and Mitchell, S. (1983). *Object Relations in Psychoanalytic Theory.* Cambridge, MA: Harvard University Press.

Vol. 1
Conversing with Uncertainty: Practicing Psychotherapy in a Hospital Setting
Rita Wiley McCleary

Vol. 2
Affect in Psychoanalysis: A Clinical Synthesis
Charles Spezzano

Vol. 3
The Analyst in the Inner City: Race, Class, and Culture through a Psychoanalytic Lens
Neil Altman

Vol. 4
A Meeting of Minds: Mutuality in Psychoanalysis
Lewis Aron

Vol. 5
Holding and Psychoanalysis: A Relational Perspective
Joyce A. Slochower

Vol. 6
The Therapist as a Person: Life Crises, Life Choices, Life Experiences, and Their Effects on Treatment
Barbara Gerson (ed.)

Vol. 7
Soul on the Couch: Spirituality, Religion, and Morality in Contemporary Psychoanalysis
Charles Spezzano & Gerald J. Gargiulo (eds.)

Vol. 8
Unformulated Experience: From Dissociation to Imagination in Psychoanalysis
Donnel B. Stern

Vol. 9
Influence and Autonomy in Psychoanalysis
Stephen A. Mitchell

Vol. 10
Fairbairn, Then and Now
Neil J. Skolnick & David E. Scharff (eds.)

Vol. 11
Building Bridges: Negotiation of Paradox in Psychoanalysis
Stuart A. Pizer

Vol. 12
Relational Perspectives on the Body
Lewis Aron & Frances Sommer Anderson (eds.)

Vol. 13
Seduction, Surrender, and Transformation: Emotional Engagement in the Analytic Process
Karen Maroda

Vol. 14
Relational Psychoanalysis: The Emergence of a Tradition
Stephen A. Mitchell & Lewis Aron (eds.)

Vol. 15
The Collapse of the Self and Its Therapeutic Restoration
Rochelle G. K. Kainer

Vol. 16
Psychoanalytic Participation: Action, Interaction, and Integration
Kenneth A. Frank

Vol. 17
The Reproduction of Evil: A Clinical and Cultural Perspective
Sue Grand

Vol. 18
Objects of Hope: Exploring Possibility and Limit in Psychoanalysis
Steven H. Cooper

Vol. 19
Who is the Dreamer, Who Dreams the Dream? A Study of Psychic Presences
James S. Grotstein

Vol. 20
Relationality: From Attachment to Intersubjectivity
Stephen A. Mitchell

Vol. 21
Looking for Ground: Countertransference and the Problem of Value in Psychoanalysis
Peter G. M. Carnochan

Vol. 22
Sexuality, Intimacy, Power
Muriel Dimen

Vol. 23
September 11: Trauma and Human Bonds
Susan W. Coates, Jane L. Rosenthal, & Daniel S. Schechter (eds.)

Vol. 24
Minding Spirituality
Randall Lehman Sorenson

Vol. 25
Gender as Soft Assembly
Adrienne Harris

Vol. 26
Impossible Training: A Relational View of Psychoanalytic Education
Emanuel Berman

Vol. 27
The Designed Self: Psychoanalysis and Contemporary Identities
Carlo Strenger

Vol. 28
Relational Psychoanalysis, Vol. II: Innovation and Expansion
Lewis Aron & Adrienne Harris (eds.)

Vol. 29
Child Therapy in the Great Outdoors: A Relational View
Sebastiano Santostefano

Vol. 30
The Healer's Bent: Solitude and Dialogue in the Clinical Encounter
James T. McLaughlin

Vol. 31
Unconscious Fantasies and the Relational World
Danielle Knafo & Kenneth Feiner

Vol. 32
Getting from Here to There: Analytic Love, Analytic Process
Sheldon Bach

Vol. 33
Creating Bodies: Eating Disorders as Self-Destructive Survival
Katie Gentile

Vol. 34
Relational Psychoanalysis, Vol. III: New Voices
Melanie Suchet, Adrienne Harris, & Lewis Aron (eds.)

Vol. 35
Comparative-Integrative Psychoanalysis: A Relational Perspective for the Discipline's Second Century
Brent Willock

Vol. 36
Bodies in Treatment: The Unspoken Dimension
Frances Sommer Anderson (ed.)

Vol. 37
Adolescent Identities: A Collection of Readings
Deborah Browning (ed.)

Vol. 38
Repair of the Soul: Metaphors of Transformation in Jewish Mysticism and Psychoanalysis
Karen E. Starr

Vol. 39
Dare to be Human: A Contemporary Psychoanalytic Journey
Michael Shoshani Rosenbaum

Vol. 40
The Analyst in the Inner City, Second Edition: Race, Class, and Culture through a Psychoanalytic Lens
Neil Altman

Vol. 41
The Hero in the Mirror: From Fear to Fortitude
Sue Grand

Vol. 42
Sabert Basescu: Selected Papers on Human Nature and Psychoanalysis
George Goldstein & Helen Golden (eds.)

Vol. 43
Invasive Objects: Minds under Siege
Paul Williams

Vol. 44
Good Enough Endings: Breaks, Interruptions, and Terminations from Contemporary Relational Perspectives
Jill Salberg (ed.)

Vol. 45
First Do No Harm: The Paradoxical Encounters of Psychoanalysis, Warmaking, and Resistance
Adrienne Harris & Steven Botticelli (eds.)

Vol. 46
A Disturbance in the Field: Essays in Transference–Countertransference Engagement
Steven H. Cooper

Vol. 47
Uprooted Minds: Surviving the Politics of Terror in the Americas
Nancy Caro Hollander

Vol. 48
Toward Mutual Recognition: Relational Psychoanalysis and the Christian Narrative
Marie T. Hoffman

Vol. 49
Understanding and Treating Dissociative Identity Disorder: A Relational Approach
Elizabeth F. Howell

Vol. 50
With Culture in Mind: Psychoanalytic Stories
Muriel Dimen (ed.)

Vol. 51
Relational Psychoanalysis, Vol. IV: Expansion of Theory
Lewis Aron & Adrienne Harris (eds.)

Vol. 52
Relational Psychoanalysis, Vol. V: Evolution of Process
Lewis Aron & Adrienne Harris (eds.)

Vol. 53
Individualizing Gender and Sexuality: Theory and Practice
Nancy Chodorow

Vol. 54
The Silent Past and the Invisible Present: Memory, Trauma, and Representation in Psychotherapy
Paul Renn

Vol. 55
A Psychotherapy for the People: Toward a Progressive Psychoanalysis
Lewis Aron & Karen Starr

Vol. 56
Holding and Psychoanalysis: A Relational Perspective
Joyce Slochower

Vol. 57
The Play within the Play: The Enacted Dimension of Psychoanalytic Process
Gil Katz

Vol. 58
Traumatic Narcissism: Relational Systems of Subjugation
Daniel Shaw

Vol. 59
Clinical Implications of the Psychoanalyst's Life Experience: When the Personal Becomes Professional
Steven Kuchuck (ed.)

Vol. 60
The Origins of Attachment: Infant Research and Adult Treatment
Beatrice Beebe & Frank M. Lachmann

Vol. 61
The Embodied Analyst: From Freud and Reich to Relationality
Jon Sletvold

Vol. 62
A Relational Psychoanalytic Approach to Couples Psychotherapy
Philip A. Ringstrom

Vol. 63
Cyclical Psychodynamics and the Contextual Self: The Inner World, the Intimate World, and the World of Culture and Society
Paul L. Wachtel

Vol. 64
Traumatic Ruptures: Abandonment and Betrayal in the Analytic Relationship
Robin A. Deutsch (ed.)

Vol. 65
The Cut and the Building of Psychoanalysis, Volume 1: Sigmund Freud and Emma Eckstein
Carlo Bonomi

Vol. 66
Relational Psychoanalysis and Psychotherapy Integration: An Evolving Synergy
Jill Bresler & Karen Starr (eds.)

Vol. 67
The Legacy of Sandor Ferenczi: From Ghost to Ancestor
Adrienne Harris & Steven Kuchuck (eds.)

Vol. 68
Somatic Experience in Psychoanalysis and Psychotherapy: In the Expressive Language of the Living
William F. Cornell

Vol. 69
Relational Treatment of Trauma: Stories of Loss and Hope
Toni Heineman

Vol. 70
Freud's Legacy in the Global Era
Carlo Strenger

Freud's Legacy in the Global Era

Carlo Strenger

Routledge
Taylor & Francis Group
LONDON AND NEW YORK

First published 2016
by Routledge
27 Church Road, Hove, East Sussex, BN3 2FA

and by Routledge
711 Third Avenue, New York, NY 10017

Routledge is an imprint of the Taylor & Francis Group, an informa business

British Library Cataloguing in Publication Data
A catalogue record for this book is available from the British Library

Library of Congress Cataloging in Publication Data
Strenger, Carlo.
Freud's legacy in the global era / Carlo Strenger. — 1st edition.
pages cm
Includes bibliographical references and index.
1. Freud, Sigmund, 1856–1939—Influence. 2. Psychoanalysis. I. Title.
BF173.F85S7685 2015
150.19'52092—dc23 2015007554

ISBN: 978-1-138-84028-7 (hbk)
ISBN: 978-1-138-84029-4 (pbk)
ISBN: 978-1-315-73289-3 (ebk)

Typeset in Times New Roman
by Keystroke, Station Road, Codsall, Wolverhampton

Contents

Introduction

Freud in the Global Era

It is not at all surprising that, seventy-five years after his death, Sigmund Freud's face is vaguely known to most educated people in the free world, in the same way as most of them would recognize the faces of Marx, Darwin and Nietzsche. No cultural historian would even question whether Freud was one of the defining figures of twentieth-century culture. His impact on psychology, psychiatry, sociology, political thought, art and popular culture during that century was enormous. Metaphors he had coined and concepts he had developed were used by most educated citizens of the Western world in daily parlance roughly from the 1930s until deep into the century's last quarter, even if they were unaware that Freud had created them.

Freud's place in the pantheon of Western culture is unquestioned and unquestionable, but the direct influence of his work has been waning over recent decades. The movement he founded – psychoanalysis – has lost the standing it enjoyed from the 1940s until well into the 1970s, an era when it was the dominant force in American psychiatry and highly influential in many European countries. Psychoanalysis today is a relatively insular movement, and its theories are no longer taught in the overwhelming majority of training programs in psychiatry and clinical psychology worldwide. Introductory courses in psychology mention Freud in passing, genuflecting vaguely to a man who was once a towering figure but now does not seem of more importance to most academic psychology than was his great contemporary William James, a man of whom only the initiated have heard and one who did not leave as deep a mark on culture as Freud did.

A few decades ago, the Freud wars (Forrester 1997) were still raging. When journalist Janet Malcolm (1981) published an intimate portrait of the world of New York psychoanalysts in the late 1970s, many ran to buy and read the book – if only to learn a bit more about the mysterious people they were going to see four times a week to talk about their woes. When Jeffrey Moussaief

Masson (1984) published *The Assault on Truth* – about Freud's alleged suppression of the seduction theory of hysteria – the book became a bestseller and generated heated discussion. For many, the question of Freud's veracity or crookedness was still a matter of almost religious significance: for the followers, questioning Freud's motives for rejecting the seduction theory was an assault on the holy grail, because psychoanalytic hagiography had claimed that it was precisely this rejection, based on Freud's self-analysis, that had been the true beginning of psychoanalysis. For his critics, it was proof that psychoanalysis had been unscientific from the very beginning and immoral to boot. The ensuing debate was acrimonious, often uncivilized and, predictably, changed few minds: most of the Freud warriors remained entrenched in their original positions.

Three decades later the situation is very different indeed: in 2010, the well-known French philosopher Michel Onfray published *Le Crépuscule d'une idole* (*The Twilight of an Idol*), in which he claimed that Freud was a charlatan with plenty of character flaws – for example, by rehashing the story of Freud's affair with his wife's sister, Minna Bernays. The book created no more attention in the French press than is to be expected around publications by established authors, but thus far it has been scarcely translated, and it has not generated any attention in other countries. The Freud wars, it seems, have come to an end.

This, I think, is all for the better. Those wars about the utterly pointless question of whether Freud was humanity's liberator or a charlatan, a prophet or a dogmatic authoritarian, were quite irrational from the outset. They were so passionately fought because Freud, for some reason, evoked the hope that there was a benevolent, all-knowing father who could tell us the truth about human nature and how to live our lives. Such an expectation can be based only on the wish for an authority that can always be trusted. It is, after all, completely unreasonable to expect anybody to find the final truth about humanity unless we believe in some form of revelation, for in science there is no such thing as a final, unquestionable truth, as the history of science since the early twentieth century – when age-old certainties were overthrown to change modern cosmology completely – has shown dramatically. And, of course, it is even less rational to become angry when you learn that the theories of a physician and theorist whose thought was shaped in the latter half of the nineteenth century have been superseded in almost every respect a century later.

The problem is that Freud indeed evoked such transference quite often. On the one hand, the psychoanalytic tradition has long tried to turn Freud's work into a bible whose every pronouncement contains some oracular truth, rather than seeing him as a fascinating cultural figure and child of his time – as all human beings, including towering geniuses, are bound to be. On the other hand, some of Freud's detractors – from Karl Popper to Martin Eysenck – depicted him as an almost demonic force that deflected the attempt to study human nature objectively and scientifically for decades, while others – including Jeffrey Masson (1984) – claimed that he was a cruel authoritarian lacking in empathy for women and children. Countless feminist critics pointed out the phallocentricity of his psychology, how little true understanding of women he possessed, and how he perpetuated and took for granted the patriarchal order of the society in which he lived.

Freud, needless to say, was wrong in most of the specifics of his theorizing, because, like every thinker and indeed every human being, he was a man of his time. Frank Sulloway, in his indispensable *Freud, Biologist of the Mind* (1979), has shown in detail how deeply rooted Freud's theories were in the sciences of his time, and how keenly in tune he was with the latest developments of the science of his day – at least until about 1910, when he started to be less interested in ongoing scientific developments. His famed rejection of the seduction theory of hysteria, for example, was due neither to his self-analysis – as psychoanalytic hagiography beginning with Ernest Jones' (1953–1957) monumental three-volume biography had maintained – nor to some dark machinations, as Masson asserted. Sulloway showed that Freud wrote the famous letter to Fliess rejecting the seduction theory three days after he bought, read and annotated an epidemiological study that argued that more than one-third of Vienna's women suffered from hysteria, and Freud simply thought it totally implausible that such a high proportion of women had been sexually molested in early childhood.

Sulloway also demonstrated the degree to which Freud's model of the mind was based on the neurology of his time – a discipline to which Freud had actively contributed in the early years of his career, both in the laboratory and in his work on aphasia that was still considered a standard text decades after it was first published. Freud, it turns out, was much more rational than both his admirers and his detractors claim: he included much of the relevant scientific thought of his time in an edifice that would become one of modernity's most poignant and encompassing interpretations of human existence.

With respect to his failure to address the various social injustices and ailments of his time, particularly the status of women, Freud was definitely not a social revolutionary by temperament: he took the social order for granted and assumed that psychological health required acceptance of that social order. To the extent that he thought the social order needed to be changed – for example, in openness about sexuality – he believed that every change would improve the lot of humanity in small steps, but that there was no utopia to reach. Freud was convinced that there could be no civilization without discontent, and he saw all redemptive visions as infantile illusions that were bound to create needless additional suffering rather than paradise on earth.

Michel Foucault (1966) was right to describe Freud as the founder of a particular form of discourse that shaped twentieth-century culture – a rare occurrence. But this discourse is now receding from public view, because our culture is replacing the language of psychology with the language of biology to understand human beings. Today's headlines are made by discoveries that promise to deepen our understanding of the *biological* foundations of our mental lives and our behavior – a development that Freud would have lauded. Throughout his life he thought that, in time, human nature would be understood through its biological substratum, and his own thinking was shaped by the biology of his time.

The time has come to put aside the wish for an ultimate paternal authority whom we can either always trust for ultimate guidance or must kill in order to find liberty from his tyrannical rule. Freud was neither a prophet nor a demon. He ranks as one of Western culture's great thinkers, alongside Aristotle, Leibniz and Kant. All of these men are indispensable not because of the truth of what they wrote, but because of their towering importance and lasting impact on Western intellectual and cultural history. Freud's influence no longer comprises the impact of his particular theories on today's cultural climate and opinion; it is less direct, yet more lasting. Nobel Physiology Laureate Eric Kandel (2005, 2012) has shown in detail how Freud was a central participant in the revolution that created the contemporary image of human nature now developed in the evolutionary cognitive neurosciences. We will see later in this book that – as opposed to many contemporary psychoanalysts, who decry the rise and prestige of contemporary neuroscience – Freud always believed that psychoanalysis and biology would ultimately have to converge. On a historical scale it does not matter that he got most of the details wrong, because the neurobiology of his time was nowhere close to the knowledge we have today, and his understanding of evolution was primarily Lamarckian.

It is precisely at this moment, when a more dispassionate discussion of Freud's place in the history of modernity has become possible, that we should ask the question: what is Freud's legacy in the era of globalization and neuroscience. We should do so not to dispute, once again, whether Freud is alive or dead, but to understand his place in the history of modernity, and to understand ourselves, as we live in a world that is both deeply similar and radically different from Freud's.

Freud was the great theorist of the new individual who had been created by the Industrial Revolution. Within the space of a century, traditional forms of life had been destroyed completely. In 1780 about four-fifths of Europe's population was rural and one-fifth lived in cities; a century later, the proportions were inverse. Humankind had lived in extended families for most of its prehistory and history, but the nineteenth century tore apart that convention and created the nuclear family that we have come to assume as natural. All traditional cultures had been built on the notion that the individual was but an integral part of a larger whole, supposed to serve and continue traditions reaching far back and based on unshakable authorities. Only the nineteenth century introduced the Enlightenment ideal of questioning all authority that had been developed by a small group of thinkers since the seventeenth century (Gay 1966) into the lives of Europe's and America's bourgeoisie.

The result was a Victorian bourgeoisie torn between tradition and innovation; between social authority as represented by parents and social institutions, and desires, sexual and other, in conflict with this authority (Gay 2002). Because Victorians no longer accepted unquestioned traditions, many of them could no longer rely on the traditional solace offered by religion, and they were also deprived of the comfort given by a long-standing community. The requirements of their careers and the search for opportunity had led many of them to leave their place of origin and rebuild their entire human environment.

To find and maintain a place in bourgeois society, late nineteenth-century Europeans and Americans needed enormous self-discipline. Official sexual morality was strict, particularly for women, and bourgeois culture was flooded with depictions of lives overwhelmed and eventually destroyed by untamable desire – from Flaubert's *Madame Bovary* to Heinrich Mann's *Professor Unrat*, which became even more famous through its film adaptation, *The Blue Angel*, starring Marlene Dietrich (Gay 2002).

Freud created a theory, a mode of listening and writing, that was uniquely suited to understanding the modern individual's soul. The metaphors of the structural model reflected the bourgeois experience that rational self-management (the ego) was under constant threat from untamable impulses (the id) and under constant criticism from internalized strict social authority (the super-ego). His work achieved such prominence and had such impact because it was a grand interpretation of modern human life claiming solely the authority of science. Freud was the embodiment of the Enlightenment ideal of the dispassionate observer who sought hidden laws governing human life and behavior, but he also had the talents of both the novelist and the mythologist: he could describe individual human lives with a novelist's eye, and he could tell a story about the drama of human life with a mythologist's evocative power.

Our world is very different from Freud's, for our generation is involved in and shaped by a social and cultural upheaval no less radical than the Industrial

Revolution. The explosion in communication and computing technologies in the last four decades has changed our lives at a speed that makes that earlier upheaval seem slow and peaceful in comparison. Most of the professions that now populate our cities today did not even exist fifty years ago, while many traditional occupations have disappeared without a trace. Moreover, many of the professions that have nominally survived have changed almost beyond recognition.

What, then, in Freud's legacy is relevant to our late capitalist culture? After all, the free world has changed enormously since Freud's time, when *fin de siècle* members of the middle classes were terrified of themselves because they understood, whether clearly or dimly, that many of their desires ran counter to the taboos of their religions, cultures and families. This seems no longer to be the case in liberal societies of the early twenty-first century. The perversions and sins of yesteryear have become today's legitimate and even celebrated subcultures. Sadomasochism, homosexuality, fetishism and other sexual "perversions" – as they were still called not long ago – are today organized in networks ranging from the LGBT community through the various networks of BDSM to feeders and asexuality.org. Seemingly, then, we have been liberated from the panic of being perverse and condemned for our abominations and can rejoice in the particularities of our specific desires.

It is therefore unsurprising that today's typical psychoanalytic patient's presenting complaints and the structure of their suffering differ strongly from those of previous generations. The classical psychoanalytic patient from Freud's era to the mid-twentieth century was suffocated by taboos well described in Freud's works. They were not supposed to feel anger or hatred towards their parents, and their sexual desires were supposed to fit into a tightly regimented scheme of heterosexual normality. Around the middle of the twentieth century, Theodor Reik, one of Freud's more creative pupils, could still write in a popular psychoanalytic book entitled *Of Love and Lust* (1949) that in successful analytic treatment men's center of pleasure moved from the base of the penis to the glans – while women's, of course, moved from the clitoris to the vagina – adhering to the most conventional prejudices about sexuality of the Victorian period. As a result, many of the pathologies of those times were expressions of disavowed desire, whether sexual or aggressive – pathologies that the practicing clinician is still sure to find today in very conservative communities, such as ultra-orthodox Judaism or pious Islam (as my own experience in supervising students who work with these populations corroborates).

But today's patients seeking psychoanalytic therapy are mostly no longer suffocated by taboos. If anything, they have trouble finding their moorings in the liquid modernity described by the sociologist Zygmunt Bauman (2002, 2007). It should not surprise us that clinical pictures have changed accordingly. Classical hysterics became a rarity in the psychoanalytic consulting rooms of modern societies many decades ago. In the 1960s and 1970s analytic clinicians were ever more confronted with patients who had trouble putting together a functioning life structure. The 1970s therefore brought a spate of publications focusing on narcissistic and borderline personality disorders. For quite some time the prevailing psychoanalytic wisdom was that these were "earlier" disturbances than the classical neuroses; that their etiological roots were not to be found in classical Oedipal conflicts, but in pre-Oedipal dynamics. The leading theorists of the time (Kernberg 1975, Kohut 1971) still aimed to preserve the classic psychoanalytic developmental scheme with its neat developmental stages, and the elegant correlations between how "early" a disturbance was and how difficult treatment would be.

However, during the 1980s and 1990s, a growing number of analytic clinicians and theorists began to suspect that this linear developmental model was simply inadequate, and that the idea that pathologies could be neatly categorized as "earlier" on this developmental scheme the more severe they were did not stand up to either theoretical or clinical scrutiny. In a series of publications, Stephen Mitchell (1988, 1993) showed that many established psychoanalytic categories needed to be deconstructed rather than preserved. Jessica Benjamin (1988, 1995) built a whole developmental perspective based on the core concept of mutual recognition that she brought from her early training in the Frankfurt School of sociology and philosophy. Lewis Aron (1996) gave an overarching picture of the new relational approach, and, together with Stephen Mitchell, started to publish what has become a series of books presenting this school of thought, based on more fluid concepts and more tolerance for paradox and ambiguity.

The established notions of "normal" sexuality and gender conception came under growing critical scrutiny. Before his untimely death, Robert Stoller (1991) came to question the very differentiation between "normal" and "perverse" sexuality that had guided decades of his own work as well as most of the psychoanalytic literature up to that point. Nancy Chodorow (1994) showed persuasively how unconvincing established psychoanalytic categories about sexuality and eroticism were when examined critically, a project she had started in her historical synthesis of psychoanalysis and feminism (Chodorow 1989).

These developments were of great importance, because psychosexual development had been at the core of psychoanalytic theorizing since Freud's early work. These changes in psychoanalytic theorizing reflected profound social and cultural transformations since the 1970s. The gay community had not just come out of the closet but had built considerable political clout, leading to the point in 1980 where the third edition of the *Diagnostic and Statistical Manual of the American Psychiatric Association* (known as *DSM III*), the bible of mental health professionals, no longer included homosexuality as a pathology. The gay liberation movement has since transformed into the LGBT community, which, as its acronym states, represents lesbians, gays, bisexuals and transgenders. Sadomasochism, long considered a pathology, has become a legitimate subculture, currently labeled BDSM to include bondage, domination, sadism and masochism.

Much of the radical change of recent decades is linked to globalization – at this point a widely used buzz term with multiple meanings. We all know that the world has changed dramatically in the last few decades; we all know that the revolution in communication and computing technologies has dramatically changed financial markets, the media landscape, the world's economic system as a whole, the structure of our cities, job security and many other facets of our lives. Economists like Joseph Stiglitz, Amartia Sen and Paul Krugman have described the economic consequences in detail. Sociologists like Saskia Sassen have shown in depth how the economy, social structure and general feel of the world's major cities – which Sassen (2000) calls "global cities" – have been transformed.

But how has globalization impacted our personal lives? What is its influence on our psychology? It is hardly imaginable that changes as profound as those our world has undergone have not transformed our inner lives. We date via the internet; we communicate with our loved ones via texting; we catch up with our friends via Facebook. Our jobs often depend on the decisions made in the headquarters of a company on the other side of the globe; and the value of our homes hinges on decisions made by a bank from another continent. We read books on tablets rather than paper; and we choose our vacation destinations by scrolling through the ratings of people we have never met on TripAdvisor.

And then again: who are "we" and "us"? The world has split into a new class system. At the top there is the new upper class, the half a percent who make enormous amounts of money, drive up property prices in global cities and occupy the ever more expensive business-class seats on planes (Reich 2005). Then there is the much discussed middle class, whose members suffer from the "fear of falling" described so poignantly by the sociologist Barbara Ehrenreich (1989). They know that if they lose their jobs, they may take a tumble into the lower classes without financial assets and mostly without adequate healthcare. Finally, moving down to the bottom rung, there are the swelling ranks of invisible nomads, the tens of millions of human beings who have entered developed countries illegally, devoid of social, political and often human rights, hoping for work that will sustain them and their families.

Psychoanalysis has made some important inroads into treating the lower classes, and some analysts (Altman 2009) have presented courageous explorations of the psychology of these disadvantaged people. But in most countries today, more than ever before the overwhelming majority of people who undergo psychoanalytic treatment pay for it themselves because such treatment is no longer covered by health insurance, and most public health services can no longer afford to provide their patients with long-term therapy.

Typical psychoanalytic patients are members of what the economist Richard Florida (2002) calls the "creative class." As this term implies, their work is devoid of repetitive drudgery. They are less likely than the rest of the population to live where they were born and grew up: they seek out environments that provide them with job opportunities that suit their talents and tastes. They are mostly open-minded and liberal, but they also have high demands, preferring to live in cities that provide a wide variety of cultural institutions, shows and options, whether in music, theater or eating out, as well as a choice of gyms. They have the sort of freedom that was once the preserve of the wealthy upper classes.

The sociologist Dalton Conley (2009) describes the creative class from a different angle. He acknowledges that its members overwhelmingly have academic degrees, fairly creative jobs and incomes that used to be viewed as high, but he shows that they also suffer from the "economic red-shift effect": they feel that the more money they make, the more the goal of prosperity moves further away. They suffer from the pervasive anxiety that they are not doing well enough; that their jobs may not be secure; that their companies, law offices, medical practices or design studios might soon collapse. And they are never convinced that they are doing enough to live a life of significance, as I will show in Part I of this book. Their lives, loves and existential structure have acquired the liquid character described by Zygmunt Bauman (2002, 2007).

Over the last few decades, psychoanalytic thinking has been trying to catch up with a series of social, cultural and economic changes – ignited by communication technologies – that have developed at a faster pace than any previous transformation. Much of the new psychoanalytic literature has focused on the changing world of gender and sexuality (Dimen and Goldner 2010), but there have also been interesting attempts to rethink the relationship between psychoanalysis, spirituality and religion (Spezzano and Gargiulio 2003, Aron and Henik 2013). In this book, I attempt to address a different facet of the impact of the enormously rapid changes in global culture and the world economy on our inner lives. The last three decades have reshuffled, transformed and confused our notions of what it means to live a life of significance. When do we feel that we have a life worth living? What do we have to do in order to be able to say that we are proud of our careers? In previous publications I have argued that recent social, cultural and economic changes have created a new categorical imperative: live a spectacular life (Strenger 2004) – an imperative engraved into our culture by Nike's slogan "Just Do It!" (Strenger 2011a).

As I will show in Part I of this book – "The New Cosmopolitans and Their Discontent" – the emergence of a new upper class that lives spectacularly well and is constantly covered by the global infotainment network has had a powerful impact on the status of professions that were previously safely entrenched within society, including the law, medicine and psychoanalysis itself. The global media floods us with unavoidable accounts, images and videos of global success stories – whether in business, sports, showbusiness or technology – that make the "ordinary" lives of the traditional liberal professions seem pale and insignificant. Connection to the global infotainment system, primarily the internet, has now become part of the self of a new species I call "Homo Globalis" (Strenger 2011a), in the same way as earlier technologies also changed the range of human senses, as Marshall McLuhan famously argued. Homo Globalis' range and reach have, as the name implies, become global for the simple reason that information from around the globe is instantly available worldwide.

Part I of this book is particularly concerned with a subclass of Homo Globalis who are not simply out to make as much money as possible or become famous merely for the sake of being famous. These "New Cosmopolitans" care deeply about the world at large, have universalist values and really want to make a positive difference in the world. However, their lives are becoming ever more difficult because their standards for what counts as making a difference are becoming ever higher, partially due to a cultural atmosphere that perpetuates the myth that there are no limits to what can be achieved with the requisite guts, talent and vision.

The idea that we have gained unfettered freedom and that our possibilities are unlimited is, of course, an illusion. Our culture has replaced fear of perversion with an obsession with living healthily and enjoying a good life. We seek expert advice for everything from child rearing to sex, from weight loss to workout optimization. Most of all, we are preoccupied with how well we are doing, why we are not doing as well as we think we could, or why we are not close to emulating the spectacular successes of celebrities from the worlds of business, sports, film, haute cuisine, politics and design that are relayed to us 24/7 through the global infotainment system via our tablets, phablets and smartphones. Those of us who no longer aspire to theological purity at least expect to live enviable lives worthy of coverage in the endless stream of media devoted to the rich, famous or otherwise noteworthy. The result, as I will show in Part I of this book, is a globally pervasive fear of insignificance, as well as a boom time for "experts" who claim to be able to unlock their clients' full potential – for a fee.

In other words, while *fin de siècle* Western culture was still haunted by all sorts of taboos, the inhabitants of today's developed economies are terrified of living lives that do not measure up to the various icons, ideals and beliefs they are constantly sold by the global infotainment system. We feel that we are not slim enough, do not have the seven habits of effective people, do not combine the tough focus of the successful with the empathic emotional intelligence of the sensitive. We are not having enough fun, but nor do we push ourselves to the limit in our workouts. We should be more knowledgeable about both the latest gadgets and French wine (although, of course, we should consume the latter only in moderation). The proportion of women who currently suffer from a diagnosed eating disorder is high, but not overwhelming. However, a staggering proportion of women (and ever more men) – while behaving within the range of normality – are constantly preoccupied by and feel guilty about their eating habits, anxiously measuring where they stand compared to the prescriptions of all kinds of experts who voice opinions about what they should – and primarily should not – eat.

What, then, could Freud's legacy possibly be for a world that is so spectacularly different from the one that formed him and his vision of human existence? Four leitmotifs contributed to Freud becoming one of the twentieth century's most influential intellectual figures, and I believe they are still highly relevant for our era. First, culturally, he was both an insider and an outsider. Born into a family that was neither cultured nor successful, Freud, like many of his Jewish contemporaries, quickly decided that he needed to escape his father's fate. He therefore embarked on the well-trodden path forged by the previous generation of European Jews: accumulating cultural capital and entering one of the prestigious liberal professions – either law or medicine – proverbially Jewish mothers' preferred occupations for their sons (Slezkine 2004). At the top of his class in the gymnasium, Freud seemed well set on this course by the time he enrolled in his medical studies at Vienna University. And yet, throughout his life, he continued to feel like an outsider from the culture in which he was living. This gave him a perspective that allowed him to see the contradictions, paradoxes and seismic rifts of traditional European society more clearly than those who were more safely rooted within it (Gilman 1988). At its best, psychoanalysis has always had something of this outsider status

– participating in a culture that it tries to understand primarily from within, yet also working at a distance that allows its practitioners to see layers of psyche and culture that are easily missed by others. This insider–outsider perspective is highly relevant for the global era, in which the myths of global power are shaping the psychological life of Homo Globalis.

The second leitmotif is Freud's intimate attachment to modern science and the Enlightenment mentality on which it is based (Gay 1989). He was fortunate to study under one of his generation's leading physiologists, Ernst von Brücke, and hoped to walk in the great man's footsteps. Freud's early research shows that he could indeed have pursued a great career in brain research, but von Brücke advised him to opt for clinical medicine instead as he had no independent means. While Freud heeded this advice, his belief that Darwinian biology was key for any scientific understanding of the human mind would remain a powerful force throughout his work. Among others, it would provide Freud with the ammunition to fight the growing tendency towards racism in medicine and psychiatry, including anti-Semitism – the modern form of Jew-hatred couched in racial language (Gilman 1994a). Freud would come to claim that the whole human species was endowed with a common, biologically based unconscious structure that contained, among others, the polymorphous perversions that were often ascribed solely to Jews. His search for the biological substratum of the human psyche therefore had an ethical component – claiming that the human species was one, and thus promoting universalist Enlightenment values (see Chapter 1). But this search for the biological substratum, often disavowed by many contemporary psychoanalysts as unanalytic, also contributed to Freud's historical importance as one of the founders of the contemporary vision of human nature guiding the paradigm of the evolutionary cognitive neurosciences (Kandel 2012). His commitment to natural science as a frame of reference is crucial in the age of neuroscience: in Part II of this book, we will see how his legacy can be revived by intensified communications with the powerful paradigm of the evolutionary cognitive neurosciences and adjacent disciplines.

The third motif is Freud's keen eye for human drama and his willingness to accept that human lives are invariably messier than official culture acknowledges. As Adam Phillips (2014: ch. 3) has written, Freud was impressed by Charcot's flamboyance, his reckless courage in using intuition where he lacked knowledge, his wealth and the magnetism of his personality. This encouraged Freud to add a creative, artistic dimension to his formerly dry conception of respectable scientific work. (He still felt the need to apologize for this artistic aspect of his work when he ruefully noted that the case studies contained within *Studies on Hysteria* (Freud and Breuer 1895) sounded more like novellas than medical case reports.) Blessed with both a highly developed talent for clinical observation and a novelist's gift for evoking hidden human drama, Freud provided both a diagnosis for the ailments of his time and models for living more truthfully and authentically within the bounds of a given culture. This quality is of particular importance for Freud's legacy in the global era, which all too often is so enamored with quantifiable aspects of the self (see Chapter 2) that it loses the ability to look with a more richly textured and at times ironic perspective at the global mythologies flooding the infotainment system.

The final central motif in Freud's development, which is more pronounced in his later writings on the philosophy of culture and religion, is his radical refusal to harbor illusions about human nature. Famously – and notoriously for some – Freud could see nothing positive in religion. For him, it was nothing but a remnant of childhood wishes for safety and the sense of being at the center of a universe that cares for us. Freud's stature as an Enlightenment thinker (Gay 1989) hinged on insisting on the Enlightenment's call that humankind must liberate itself from self-imposed tutelage and dare to know, among other things, its own nature (see Chapter 1). What made Freud unique was not his Enlightenment ethos but his realization of the depth of the forces of human nature working against human autonomy and rationality, a realization chillingly borne out in world history since Freud's death: the twentieth century saw two major political religions – fascism and communism – rise to power and create destruction and suffering on a scale previously unknown to humanity. This refusal to be drawn into idealized conceptions of human nature is particularly important for the twenty-first century, whose first decade has brought a return of fundamentalist conceptions of monotheism that, at the time of writing, is tearing the Middle East into a chaos of warring factions, sects and tribes that threatens to drag the rest of the world into its maelstrom through global terror networks.

It is this book's contention that Freud's legacy for the global era resides neither in hanging on to any particular aspects of his theory, nor in a ritualistic understanding of his therapeutic tool. His legacy should be to inspire us through his ability to be part of a culture and yet observe it critically; by his unwillingness to accept any explanation that is not at least consistent with the accepted scientific knowledge of our time and refuse any form of obscurantism; by his keen eye for the incoherence, complexity and sheer messiness of human life; and, finally, by his unflinching opposition to illusions about human nature.

One of psychoanalysis's tasks in the global era is to evoke the possibility of a life beyond the gaze of experts who tell us how to live and beyond the popular self-help culture that promises instant hyper-effectiveness and the route to success. Freud provides an interesting model for a therapeutic attitude that tries to understand how culture at any given moment engenders fear in its members and limits genuine autonomy and the possibility of shaping a life according to a freely chosen aesthetics of existence. Freud – outsider and participant–observer of the culture in which he lived – was capable of deciphering the ways in which the civilizational norms of his time could make life a constant series of compromises with which it was often impossible to live.

Contemporary global culture is in desperate need of a perspective informed by Freud's type of irony, openness to incoherence and rejection of obscurantism and cultural myths, because today's global meritocracy is haunted by new dogmas, myths and taboos that have replaced those of Freud's time. As we will see in Part I, the New Cosmopolitans live with myths that are perpetually sold in the worldwide media. Seemingly, these myths are highly empowering: we are told that our potential is endless; that if we only reach deep enough into our true selves and spiritual cores, we can achieve anything – from transforming the world by inventing new technology, or founding an NGO, to running a marathon in under three hours. Meanwhile, we can also be empathetic parents to our children while pushing them gently to the achievements that are demanded of the new upper classes. Speakers sell us this in eighteen minutes or less with gleaming eyes, telling us inspiring stories about how they developed the great insights that turned them into world-transforming leaders. The problem is that most New Cosmopolitans vaguely believe that a good life should indeed look like these inspiring stories that combine creativity with goodness and empathy with financial success; and they live with the constant panic that they are not living up to this glamorous picture of life at the top.

However, as Part II of this book – "Psychoanalysis in the Age of Neuroscience" – argues in detail, psychoanalysis must open up radically if Freud's legacy is to be adapted to our time to find a place in the new intellectual agora and a voice in today's media landscape. We need to be aware of how often institutionalized psychoanalysis lost touch with the critical potential of the analytic attitude. More often than not, as Joyce McDougall (1980) has argued powerfully, psychoanalysis can become an agent of normalization cooperating with society's normalizing pressures rather than helping individuals to find ways of maintaining, in McDougall's felicitous formulation, a measure of abnormality. Moreover, as Adam Phillips (1996) has pointed out, psychoanalysis has often turned itself into a dismayingly conventional etiquette book for good mental behavior. The central reason for this lack of emancipatory discourse and practice is primarily to be found in the institutional structures of psychoanalysis, which Christopher Bollas (in Molino 1998) has accused of killing the spirit of the discipline itself. More than anything, psychoanalysis's self-isolation from the outside world, from academic life and from the wealth of knowledge to be found in other disciplines can be deadening. It is indeed dismaying to see how little most psychoanalytic writers quote anyone other than their fellow psychoanalytic writers.

This was certainly not always the case. Freud himself was involved with the social and natural sciences of his day to an enormous degree and used this knowledge constantly when trying to understand human nature and the culture in which he lived. The great psychoanalytic theorists, including Otto Rank (whose work is now being rediscovered), Erich Fromm and Erik Erikson (who famously contributed to our understanding of the interplay between culture and psyche), always took a wide angle and were conversant with many other disciplines, ranging from anthropology through economics to the biology of their times. While the analytic consulting room was always a central source of their data, ideas and intuitions, they also sought cross-fertilization with other disciplines. This, to me, seems indispensable if psychoanalysis is to have something interesting to say about human life at a particular historical moment.

The psychoanalytic clinician needs to make a concerted effort to understand the intricate interplay between our New Cosmopolitan patients and the ever more complex economic, cultural and social reality that determines their lives. I will therefore argue in Part II that psychoanalysis has no choice but to enrich itself through constant interaction with surrounding disciplines, whether with the social sciences of sociology and economics or at the interface between the social and natural sciences, as in the emerging paradigm of the evolutionary cognitive neurosciences.

Such supplementation is doubly necessary because – as I will show in detail in Chapter 7 – psychoanalysis has virtually disappeared as a cultural force that informs the educated classes (a privileged role it enjoyed for the majority of the twentieth century). But enriching psychoanalysis by interacting with other disciplines is not just an exercise in promoting our tradition. If psychoanalysis were simply irrelevant for the present day, then it should gradually disappear, just as other disciplines – ranging from mesmerism to magnetic cures for hysteria – have in the past. I believe that it *is* relevant, and that it could be an important voice in contemporary culture, but it must find ways to communicate with the world outside psychoanalytic institutes, training programs and journals (see Chapter 10).

Part II is a plea for a psychoanalysis that is open to the richness of knowledge generated by surrounding disciplines. I have found it indispensable to immerse myself into other fields, ranging from sociology and economics through the cognitive neurosciences and contemporary social psychology, in my attempts to understand the forces that shape all of our lives – including, of course, those of our patients. Experts in the contemporary cognitive neurosciences, contrary to the stereotype attached to them by some psychoanalytic writers (Hoffman 2009), are anything but soulless number crunchers. As I will argue in detail later (Chapters 1, 5, 8), researchers like Daniel Kahneman, Daniel Gilbert, Antonio Damasio and Bernard Schwartz provide us with priceless theories and data about how cultural myths limit freedom and misguide many Homo Globalis into chasing happiness at precisely the places where they will not find it.

If psychoanalysis is not to end up as a marginal phenomenon (see Chapter 7), with no cultural impact and an ever-diminishing role in the fields of psychotherapy and mental healthcare, it needs to show how the self can have depth even in the Flat World described by Thomas Friedman (1999, 2005) in his insightful descriptions of the global playing field. But we will not be able to do this unless we learn how to speak in a language that is accessible to more people than those who have spent years in psychoanalytic institutes. Only then will we find ways to reach out to the many who could find relief in the realization that their selves have more depth than the current craze for the quantified self seems to imply.

But how can Freud's legacy be effective in a global culture dominated by Twitter and Facebook? Psychoanalysis is a tradition that has developed through a history of dense and complex texts. It tends to thrive by evoking multilayered meanings, paradox and ambiguity, not via messages that can be condensed into one hundred and forty characters. It does not have the means to uncover new facts about human nature, preferably couched in neurobiological terms that can be demonstrated in quantitative research involving FMRI and even newer technologies, such as optogenetics. As a result, it lacks the appeal of the natural sciences that move from one spectacular discovery to the next – with each and every one eagerly reported by mainstream media – and promise to find chemical, surgical or electronically guided cures for everything from social phobias to depression.

Nevertheless, I think that psychoanalysis still has an important contribution to make to contemporary culture, over and above its clinical applications, so I will try to present an extended example of a psychoanalytic interpretation of the present. Part I presents psychodynamic models of three interrelated phenomena of contemporary life and culture. First, Chapter 2 offers a psychodynamic model of a pervasive global development: the tendency to seek quantitative measures for the significance of life and achievement. I will argue that this search for the quantification of value is an almost inevitable consequence of the globalization of our frame of reference that the new information technologies have brought about. In doing so, I will make extensive use of the results of experimental existential psychology.

Chapter 3 presents my initial encounters with five New Cosmopolitan patients. In telling their stories, I will not try to classify or diagnose them. Instead, I hope that the way they initially told me their stories will provide a sense of the New Cosmopolitan Gestalt – what Wittgenstein called a family resemblance of traits – rather than a sharp definition.

Chapter 4 presents a psychodynamic model based on one of Freud's less quoted works, his book on Leonardo da Vinci (1910). This is used to explore the psychodynamics of one of the most iconic groups of our age and one of the most salient subgroups of the New Cosmopolitans: global entrepreneurs, some of whom, such as Bill Gates, Steve Jobs, Larry Page, Sergei Brin and Mark Zuckerberg, have literally changed the way we live. The problem is that the obsession with quantifiable results has made it difficult to grasp the psychological dimension of the fascinating dynamics of entrepreneurship. Using three extensive case studies, I will try to show that an integration of quantitative research and clinical experience can yield results that are of interest not only to the psychoanalytic community but also to a wider educated public and even to the financial community that has to decide in which ventures to invest.

Chapter 5 attempts to generalize the Gestalt of the New Cosmopolitans, the class defined by their creative contribution to global networks of academia, technology, art and business. I will argue that they are mostly haunted by their desire to make a difference on a playing field that has become virtually unlimited. I will present data from economics and sociology that provide an intelligible context for the New Cosmopolitans' pervasive sense of guilt that they have not done enough to justify their lives.

Throughout the first part of the book, I will argue that objective factors push global culture towards a conception of the self's value that is almost uniquely measured in quantitative terms. The most measurable quantity of all, for millennia, has been wealth, and global culture is replete with scales, lists and ratings of the wealthiest individuals and families worldwide, by nations and by cities. Meanwhile, new measures have evolved for celebrity, influence and power. For those who have no chance of entering any of these lists, there is always the option of participating in a reality show that will make them famous merely for being famous. Finally, those who are unable to make it on to reality shows can measure their popularity by the number of "friends" they have on Facebook and how many "likes" they received for their latest selfie. The self has become a commodity that is traded in the global infotainment system (Strenger 2011a: ch. 2).

This obsession with the quantifiable self is by no means limited to shallow mass culture. Academia, supposedly the bastion of intellectual value per se, now assesses researchers via quantifiable measures too: impact factor of journals where they publish and the number of times their work is cited in the literature. The world of books, once the citadel of high culture, is governed by numbers as well. Publishers survive by identifying the few books that will sell hundreds of thousands of copies, and they are willing to pay six- or even seven-figure advances for such titles. Meanwhile, books that are likely to appeal to smaller audiences have become liabilities rather than assets for the publishing industry, because they are unlikely to recoup even their production costs.

In the ferocious competition for global market share, classical values of Western culture that are central to Freud's thinking and the psychoanalytic tradition are getting lost: individual autonomy, the richness of subjectivity and the uniqueness of historical depth are not amenable to quantification. When members of the species Homo Globalis measure their value through numbers, whether of Facebook "likes" or Google entries, they are bound to lose touch with the richness of subjective experience that alone can give individuals the sense that they are living lives of significance.

The richness of subjective experience, the drama of individuality, relationships, family lives and historical events have been the province of an art form that has characterized Western modernity and spread around the globe throughout the twentieth century: the novel. As Steven Pinker (2011) has argued, the novel has played a crucial role in humanizing first the West and then the rest of the world. It has honed its readers' minds and souls to understand, appreciate and cherish forms of life, experience and subjectivity other than their own, and it has helped them to develop a deeper understanding of their own existence. From Cervantes to Flaubert, from Sterne to Philip Roth, from George Eliot to Zadie Smith and Nicole Strauss, novelists have opened their readers' minds to the wonders of human life. And yet, as Roth (2013) has argued, the novel – except in its escapist form, à la *Fifty Shades of Grey* – is at risk of becoming an endangered species, commanding as little attention as Latin poetry does nowadays.

Psychoanalysis belongs in the same category. One of Freud's most important contributions was to show the human drama behind the silent symptom, the deeper meaning of seemingly useless forms of pathology and the beauty of the human struggle to negotiate the inevitable tension between our inborn biological propensities and the demands of civilization. Hysterics, seen by nineteenth-century psychiatry as suffering from defective genetics, turned out to be telling compelling stories about forbidden desire that were unacceptable to their environment and their own conscious self-concept in the language of neurotic symptoms. Obsessionals turned out to be stuck between their hatred for authoritarian parents and the cultural demand for respect for their progenitors.

The New Cosmopolitans do not seek our help with hysterical symptoms; and if they suffer from OCD, they justifiably prefer a combination of CBT and SSRIs to psychoanalytic treatment. They seek our help because they can no longer bear the tension between their lives as they really are and the mythical expectations generated by the global infotainment system. They want to feel their humanity behind the various personae they adopt in their professional lives, the various social circles (often in different parts of the globe) to which they belong and the fascinating, scintillating, fun-seeking profiles they create and desperately work to maintain on social media. They want to find inner moorings behind the stratagem of self-marketing that they feel forced to practice 24/7. Yet their hectic lives make it impossible for them to commit to the regular sessions in an analyst's consulting room that used to be considered a condition sine qua non for analytic treatment. Like many of my colleagues, I no longer see this as an expression of resistance; instead, I have adapted the setting to the necessities of my patients' work lives.

As a result, some readers of this book may well wonder why I feel that I am working within Freud's tradition, and why I am concerned with his legacy. After all, there is no mention of the Oedipus complex or erotogenic zones in the pages that follow. In fact, few of Freud's concepts are used, only a handful of his works are cited, and the treatments described were mostly held via Skype on schedules determined by the balance between my patients' needs, the necessities of therapeutic continuity and my patients' (and my own) professional pressures, ranging from three or four times a week during certain periods to once a month in others.

I do indeed think that Freud's legacy in the global era cannot consist in offering patients four- to five-times-a-week, on-the-couch analysis – which, in any case, no one has never shown to be superior to face-to-face psychodynamic therapy once or twice a week (Shedler 2010). Many New Cosmopolitans travel too much to allow regular visits to the consulting room even once or twice a week. Skype, Google Hangout and Apple FaceTime have become as ubiquitous in psychodynamic therapy as the proverbial box of tissues used to be. Like many of my colleagues, I conduct at least one-third of my therapeutic sessions through these channels, and it has become part of the ritual of scheduling the next session to ensure that the patient and I establish the correct time difference between their whereabouts and Tel Aviv. The only reminder of Freud's office in this setting is my mouse pad, which resembles the pattern of the rug draped on his couch.

I bought the mouse pad in the shop of the Freud Museum in Vienna, an institution that I love greatly, and on whose scientific advisory board I have served for the last five years. Before the board meetings I often spend some time alone in the rooms that saw the birth and growth of Freud's work, after walking up the steps that hundreds of people from all over the world used on their way to their analytic sessions with Freud. There are many reasons why I have a particular affinity not just for Freud but for *fin de siècle* Vienna. It was where my maternal grandmother, Liane Pappenheim-Ringer, grew up. She was a second cousin of Bertha Pappenheim, better known as Anna O., probably the most famous patient in the history of psychoanalysis, even though Freud never saw her. I often begin courses on psychoanalysis by telling my students about my family connection to Anna O., and invariably add the quip that this gave me just two options – to become a neurotic or to become a psychoanalyst – and that I chose both.

I am particularly fond of the art created in this period. I came to know Mahler's symphonies in my late teens and was struck from the outset by the immense tension between the great tradition to which they belonged and which they completed, and the modernist irony that the composer employed when playing with elements of that tradition. It was only later that I learned that Mahler had seen Freud for a few sessions, which took place during walks in the woods, rather than in the consulting room. I was also drawn to the works of Klimt and Schiele long before I ever saw the originals, many of which are housed in Vienna's various museums. I had read most of Stefan Zweig's novellas by the time I began my journey through Freud's work at the age of sixteen, and soon after I read Robert Musil's grand obituary to the empire that was run from *fin de siècle* Vienna, *Der Mann ohne Eigenschaften* (*The Man without Qualities*).

Wandering through the city, and having a coffee in the Café Central with my wife, I am always struck by the powerful realization of how much *fin de siècle* Vienna is *Die Welt von Gestern* (*The World of Yesterday*), as Zweig entitled the memoir he finished in Brazil before taking his own life. We must never forget how firmly Freud, the man and his work, was planted in this world. Any attempt to define his legacy by the specific terms, concepts and theories of his work is as futile as trying to persuade New Cosmopolitans to lie on a couch covered by a rug five times a week. Attempting to achieve the latter is to turn psychoanalysis into a religion rather than a tradition of thought deeply rooted in the Enlightenment – another intellectual and cultural power definitive of modernity that is central to my personal, intellectual, professional and political identity. Perpetuating the Enlightenment's legacy today does not demand writing in Latin like Spinoza, wearing a wig like Voltaire, or believing in the necessary and a priori truth of Newtonian physics like Kant. Rather, it entails understanding how the Enlightenment's spirit is relevant to the problems, issues and themes of our time.

Freud is one of the Enlightenment's greatest figures, and he deeply identified with its tradition and values. However, this did not prevent him from arguing that most of the early Enlightenment psychologists, such as Locke and Hume, and later ones, such as John Stuart Mill – whose work Freud knew well and had translated – had simplistic and overly optimistic views of human nature. Freud knew that perpetuating the Enlightenment did not involve adhering to the letter of any of its historical originators, but rather continuing to work in their spirit within the context of late nineteenth-century biology, medicine, archeology and anthropology. He also merged many of the insights of romantic philosophy, primarily its emphasis on the irrational aspects of human nature and their crucial function in both human destructiveness and human creativity, into a theory couched in the language of the Enlightenment.

Freud's legacy ranges beyond psychoanalysis, narrowly conceived, certainly by its more conservative institutions, and his heirs are not just to be found in psychoanalytic consulting rooms, but also in neuroscience laboratories, anthropological explorations of the evolutionary origins of religion and the psychodynamic roots of global terrorism and the critical analysis of discourse on gender, identity and sexuality in the humanities. Even if the influence of psychoanalysis in the institutional sense has declined dramatically over recent decades, Freud himself has remained, in W. H. Auden's beautiful phrase, "a whole climate of opinion" (Auden 1939: 91). Freud never hesitated to borrow from and interact with the wider scientific culture of his time, and to integrate it with clinical observation, guided by boundless curiosity enriched by literary imagination. It is in this spirit of critical appropriation, rather than that of religious imitation, that this book offers an interpretation of Freud's legacy in the global era.

Part I

The New Cosmopolitans and Their Discontent

Chapter 1

Sigmund Freud

Fin de Siècle Cosmopolitan

In a letter to one of his first students, Karl Abraham, in 1908 Freud expressed his anxiety that psychoanalysis would remain a purely Jewish national affair (Gilman 1994a: 34). This was one of the reasons why he was so enamored with the Teutonic Carl Gustav Jung, whom he wanted to make his heir. However, Jung, long after his rupture with Freud, would argue that psychoanalysis was indeed a reflection of the specifically Jewish unconscious. Notoriously, in 1928, in a footnote to the *Two Essays in Analytic Psychology*, he wrote: "It is a quite unpardonable mistake to accept the conclusions of a Jewish psychology as generally valid" (quoted in Samuels 2009). And he made his view of the racial unconscious even clearer six years later when he wrote:

> Freud did not understand the Germanic psyche any more than did his Germanic followers. Has the formidable phenomenon of National Socialism, on which the whole world gazes with astonishment, taught them better? Where was that unparalleled tension and energy while as yet no National Socialism existed? Deep in the Germanic psyche, in a pit that is anything but a garbage-bin of unrealizable infantile wishes and unresolved family resentments.
>
> (Jung quoted in Samuels 2009)

Andrew Samuels, a leading contemporary interpreter of Jung, gives a few other examples of the way in which Jung incorporated race into his conception of human nature in general, and Germans and Jews in particular:

> In the same paper, which clarifies the somewhat cryptic language above, Jung asserted (about Jews): "The 'Aryan' unconscious has a higher potential than the Jewish." "The Jew who is something of a nomad has never yet created a cultural form of his own and as far as we can see never will,

> since all his instincts and talents require a more or less civilized nation to act as host for their development." "The Jews have this peculiarity with women; being physically weaker, they have to aim at the chinks in the armour of their adversary." Jung also warned against "applying Jewish categories indiscriminately to Germanic and Slavic Christendom."
>
> (Samuels 2009)

In this clash between Freud and Jung, the much wider cultural and political conflict between universalism and particularism was conducted under the guise of a scientific dispute about the nature of the unconscious. On this level, Freud had one overriding goal: the human psyche needed to be studied objectively; and its phylogenetic structure needed to be deciphered; and this phylogenesis was to be shown as a *universal trait of humankind.*

Freud's thesis that the human psyche is polymorphously perverse by virtue of humanity's phylogenetic heritage is not only an empirical scientific hypothesis; it is also a political and ethical stance. Freud was deeply committed to the Enlightenment's ethical and scientific universalism, and his claim that the human unconscious has universal common traits has a strong political implication: any discrimination along racial lines was not only ethically wrong, but based on bad science. For Freud, there was but one human nature (even though we will soon encounter a strange exception to this). He therefore became one of the great precursors of contemporary evolutionary psychology, and most of all a proponent of a study of human nature fueled by Enlightenment universalism (Kandel 2005, 2012).

One of the pervasive themes in Freud's work was his defense of Enlightenment universalism by ridding the scientific investigation of the human psyche of racial conceptions and irrational prejudice. I will try to demonstrate a strong subterranean connection between two of Freud's projects that, *prima facie*, seem unrelated: his attempt to rid the psychiatry of his time of racial prejudice; and his critique of religion. Freud's universalist ethos, I believe, is very timely in our age, when a resurgence of nationalism and religious fundamentalism threatens the most basic tenets of our civilization.

At the same time, Freud never disavowed his Jewishness; rather, he contributed to the emergence of a specifically modern Jewish identity. What connects him with such figures as Albert Einstein, Franz Boas (the founder of American anthropology), Yehuda Magnes (one of the founders and the first president of the Hebrew University of Jerusalem), the philosopher of culture and science Ernst Cassirer, the political thinker Hannah Arendt and many other Jewish scientists, intellectuals, writers and artists is his profound gratitude to the values of the European Enlightenment. Jews, for many centuries, had been condemned to live an existence "between pariahs and parvenus," in Arendt's (1951, 2006) felicitous phrase. At best, they had the status of *Ausnahme-Juden* and were tolerated because of the financial or commercial services they rendered to kings and countries; but often they had no legal or political rights worthy of the name. Only with the advent of the political and epistemic values of the Enlightenment could Jews, in ever-growing numbers, live as equal citizens in a number of countries.

Yuri Slezkine explains the phenomenally rapid and successful influx of Jews into academia and the sciences in his groundbreaking *The Jewish Century* (2004). For most of their European history, Jews had been denied access to landownership and a variety of occupations, so they had developed a tradition of what Slezkine calls "mercurian" professions, such as trade, finance and law. Hence, once they gained access to the modern universities that developed according to Humboldt's model in Prussia in the early nineteenth century the Jews flooded into the liberal professions with all the pent-up intellectual energy that had long been locked into the physical and cultural ghettoes to which they had been confined.

Slezkine's explanation is certainly valid, but it omits one important aspect of this influx of Jews into academia. The Jews' tradition of learning had been essential to their communities throughout the Diaspora, and the value of thought and logical thinking had been nurtured in those communities for many centuries. Therefore, in the nineteenth century, when the opportunity to gain access to the troves of modern science arose, the value of learning combined with gratitude towards the ethos of the Enlightenment created a unique synergy. Jews owed universalism their dignity as citizens. The idea of knowledge that could be corroborated by universally applicable standards that were to be defined by the philosophy of science was uniquely appealing to a group that had suffered for so many centuries from religious persecution, prejudice and often simple, irrational fear and bigotry.

Freud's Program of Expelling Race from Psychiatry

The nineteenth century had seen spectacular developments in all domains of knowledge. Newtonian physics was supplemented by Maxwell's electrodynamics, and it looked as if natural science was well on the way to deciphering the basic structure of nature. Darwin had provided the missing link needed to bridge the gap between the physical and the biological sciences. In parallel, the development of new historical and philological methods resulted in a veritable explosion of knowledge in the humanities.

Yet, there were problems in the republic of letters and the world of science. The romantic idealization of *Volkstum* found its way into science, in particular medicine and psychiatry (Gilman 1994a). The emerging power of nationalist ideas led many intellectuals to reject the concept of universal reason that had been one of the foundation stones of the Enlightenment project. The German *Volksgeist*, French civilization, the Russian soul, these thinkers argued, were much more concrete embodiments of the actual psyche than the bloodless construct of universal reason (Noll 1994), as Julian Benda, in his classic *The Treason of the Intellectuals* (1926), documented in detail. Suddenly, it was no longer a matter of producing knowledge or contributing to science *tout court*. Now, intellectuals had to advance the German spirit, French knowledge or the Russian soul.

But how could these nationalist ideas be incorporated into the emerging edifice of modern natural science? The answer was through race: a notion that seemed to have scientific respectability gradually became the vehicle through which nationalist ideas were transformed into apparently scientific, biological language. German *Volkstum*, French greatness and Russian spirituality were now all supposedly based on racial foundations. One of the most important notions that emerged during the second half of the nineteenth century was the concept of an Aryan race, allegedly superior to all others in its achievements, nobility and character.

In hindsight it is, of course, impossible to disregard the catastrophic consequences of such race-based thinking. Hence, it is easy to underestimate how respectable the notion of race was in mainstream science in the second half of the nineteenth century, as Sander Gilman (1994a) demonstrated in detail in his groundbreaking work on the prevalence of racial theories in *fin de siècle* medicine. Even at the time, there were some who realized how catastrophic the implications of racial discourse might be. Ernest Renan was among the first to recognize that the combination of the newly emerging passion for nationalism and the mythical constructs of race that went back into Gaelic, Germanic and Slavic pasts could be lethal, and set out to counteract this trend in his classic and justly famous attack on the myths of nationalism. Again in hindsight, it is easy to see how ideologically colored, how scientifically inexact and how unfounded was all of this talk of race in general, and the relative superiority and inferiority of certain races in particular. Jared Diamond (1997) has magisterially shown how all the claims that the West's technological and scientific superiority was due to Europeans' biologically ingrained higher intelligence collapse when they come up against the facts of what is actually known.

Sigmund Freud's work grew into a profession – psychiatry – which gained enormous power in the fabric of the modern state, as Michel Foucault (2006) has shown in a variety of investigations. It was about to become the discipline that would "objectively" describe human nature, scientifically define normality and pathology, and determine the biological foundations of the differences between individuals and groups. I put "objectively" in quotation marks because many of the claims of nineteenth-century psychiatry – ranging from the female propensity towards hysteria, to the Jewish propensity towards hyper-sexuality, to the connection between soil and race that would play such an important role in Jung's thinking – turned out to be thinly disguised attempts to give nationalism, in its new racial form, some sort of scientific respectability. The story of these notions has been recounted primarily in Sander Gilman's (1988, 1994a, 1994b) work and in Noll's (1994) investigation of the intellectual foundations of Jung's research into the German romantic tradition of *völkisch* thought. Gilman (1994a) has also shown convincingly that many of Freud's ideas were designed to counteract the tendency to attach forms of mental illness and psychological dysfunction to racial types.

Freud was particularly concerned with the tendency to stereotype Jews racially, which was ubiquitous in both anthropology and medicine in the second half of the nineteenth century. Jews were supposed to be somewhat effeminate and overly intellectual on the one hand, and overly sexual on the other. They were alleged to have a relatively low moral sense and hence tended to be both sexually and morally perverse and of weak character (Gilman 1994a). All of these stereotypes were taken very seriously and were not only accepted by many Jews themselves (Gilman 1988) but also deeply integrated into their self-image, resulting in the proverbial self-hating Jew. Possibly the most spectacular example of such Jewish internalization of racial stereotypes and the consequent self-hatred is the story of Otto Weininger, a young, very gifted man of Jewish descent and vaulting ambition who saw value in his life only if he could contribute something exceptionally grand to human knowledge. He therefore set out to collate many of the ideas about race and gender that were circulating in psychiatry, biology and general culture into an integrative system based on male and female characterizations. The result of his labors was published under the title *Sex and Character* (Weininger 1903/2005). In Weininger's system, the male principle was intellectual, moral, active, productive and stable, while the female principle was emotional, amoral, passive, reproductive and instable. Races were characterized by the predominance of the male or the female principle. In tune with the zeitgeist, Weininger claimed that the Arian race was predominantly male and therefore naturally creative and powerful, while the Jewish race was predominantly female and therefore passive and reproductive (at best).

Sex and Character did not initially draw much attention. Deeply disappointed by his book's lack of success, Weininger ruthlessly applied his theory to himself: given that he was a Jew, and hence genetically endowed with an overdose of femininity, he would never produce anything of lasting value. Convinced that his life was not worth living, he took this conclusion to its logical end: he rented the room in which Beethoven had died, told the landlady not to disturb him, shot himself, and died in the morning. Paradoxically, shortly after his death, *Sex and Character* finally started to attract attention – partly, perhaps, because of its author's dramatic suicide – and it went on to become a veritable publishing phenomenon, going through more than twenty editions and selling hundreds of thousands of copies.

Freud was quite impressed by Weininger's work, and indeed he played with the idea of universal bisexuality for a few years (Sulloway 1979). But he took both the notion of inborn bisexuality and his notion of the polymorphous perversity of human sexuality in a different direction from Weininger and others who connected them to racial stereotyping. Far from believing that various mixes of masculinity and femininity characterized the different races, Freud argued that bisexuality was a universal trait of the human unconscious, derived from the phylogenesis of the human mind.

His emphasis on the universality of these traits needs to be understood within the context of the pervasive tendency of medicine and psychiatry to attribute racial characteristics to different ethnicities. By claiming that the human psyche per se was polymorphously perverse, Freud wanted to counteract the tendency to recast nationalism in general and, particularly, the rise of anti-Semitism – the racially formulated, new embodiment of hatred of Jews. There is also a deep link between his attempt to expel race from psychiatry and his critique of religion.

Freud's Critique and Psychoanalysis of Religious Epistemology

For some time, it has been fashionable to say that Freud's attitude towards religion has been overly reductive; that he didn't really understand religious experience; that he took religion to be bad science instead of understanding that it is a form of life, and that it is important to see it in a very different context, as a spiritual and communal form of life. Critiquing religion in the context of the more relaxed multicultural point of view that started to evolve in the 1960s seemed politically incorrect. Hence, in this respect, Freud became passé.

But what was Freud's guiding motivation in his critique of religion? What ethos is reflected in his uncompromisingly negative stance towards it? I believe that his views were guided by an ethos that was adopted by a large number of Jewish thinkers in the second half of the nineteenth century and the start of the twentieth.

The Future of an Illusion, Freud's most important text in his critique of religion, is far more a philosophico-political tract than a pure exercise in psychoanalytic thinking. His psychoanalytic elucidation of the psychogenesis of religion is driven by the credo he voices towards the end of the book: "The Voice of Reason is a soft one. But it does not rest until it gets a hearing" (Freud 1927: 55). Freud starts *The Future of an Illusion* by analyzing the functions of civilization. One crucial function of civilization is the protection of the social order and the reining in of human drives, many of which can be destructive. Obviously, religion fulfills some of these functions, and throughout the book Freud points out the major difference between religion and the "laborious acquisition of knowledge." Religion fulfills certain psychological needs that science can never meet for the simple reason that it cannot provide more protection from the powers of nature than is technologically possible, whereas religion's content is driven and shaped by our wishes rather than by the function of reality testing.

Freud's argument is complex and intricate, and I will focus on one aspect that is particularly pertinent to his universalist ethos. In Section 5, he succinctly summarizes what could be called the "epistemology of religious belief." He says that in most religions the main argument for maintaining belief is that it has been passed down through the ages, believed by our ancestors and hence cannot be questioned. He then proposes a psychodynamic explanation for the authoritarian structure of religious epistemology by arguing that the attachment to ancestry is a fixation to the reassuring authority of and protection afforded by parental figures in childhood. As such, it is a wish fulfillment rather than a belief – a fixation to an early reassuring experience felt by everyone that they are the center of the universe, protected by parental figures who are experienced as omnipotent. As our experience of parental protection is more soothing than the essentially conjectural basis of all science and the realistic limitations of technological control, it is more attuned to our desire for total safety than is the enterprise of science.

But humankind pays a heavy price for this reassuring fantasy. Different groups, tribes, nations and religions are loyal to different ancestries; hence, they are attached to beliefs that are bound to clash with those of others in the absence of any means to resolve such clashes in principle. The religious epistemology of blind loyalty to ancestry in the end creates enormous suffering and endless strife.

Freud was by no means the first to criticize the authoritarian structure of traditional religious epistemologies. This critique had been a basic theme of all great epistemological theories ever since the classical Indian and Greek philosophies, and it had been central to every modern Enlightenment critique of religion, from Voltaire and Hume to Schopenhauer, Feuerbach and Nietzsche. Beliefs and values were no longer valued simply because ancestries had held them. This high valuation of critical thought, the assumption that the combined efforts of humans to generate knowledge about the world, is the shibboleth that differentiates all Enlightenment movements from the epistemology of religion as Freud describes it. Most of all, Enlightenment thought does not recognize any prohibition on critical thought and enquiry, because it assumes that such prohibition is likely to inhibit the progress of human knowledge.

In his *Genealogy of Morals* (1888), Nietzsche took this to its logical conclusion: all religious thought, he argued, was based on the idea that an idea's origin (*Ursprung*) determined its value. A god, a prophet or a priest had revealed a truth that derived its dignity from this origin. To this, Nietzsche opposed his project of genealogy, the investigation of the humble provenance (*Herkunft*) of ideas, institutions and beliefs that we believe to be of exalted origin and therefore unassailable (Foucault 1971). Nietzsche's genealogical project pushed the Enlightenment project of investigating all phenomena with the same dispassionate curiosity to the end: even the most revered texts, beliefs and institutions were now amenable to the same biological, psychological and historical investigation as any other object of enquiry.

The Enlightenment determines the value of an idea not by its origin, but by the way it stands up to critical scrutiny. Even ideas that are currently held dear retain their validity only as long as they are not refuted by new evidence. The truth of no idea or statement is guaranteed by its origin; only its constant critical scrutiny in the cooperative venture of human enquiry can provide the hope that the venture known as *episteme* in ancient Greece and science today will gradually approach truth by eliminating error as much as possible.

Obviously, Freud's critique of religion was written in this tradition, and he was not the first to point out the basic, structural opposition between religious and Enlightenment epistemologies. He was also not the first to try to explain the psychological foundation of religion. Such explanations had been suggested many times before, and Schopenhauer and Nietzsche had applied psychodynamic explanatory structures that were quite similar to Freud's. The latter's most important contribution was to provide a psychodynamic explanation of *religious epistemologies* by showing that they were structurally analogous to, and developmentally derived from, early infantile attachments.

In doing so, he reasserted Nietzsche's position that there was a basic, irreducible conflict between religious and Enlightenment epistemologies. For Freud, there was no compromise and no mediation between the Enlightenment credo to "liberate man from self-imposed tutelage" and religions' demands for unquestioned loyalty to ancestry. Demanding respect for beliefs because of their origin was diametrically opposed to the necessity to examine them critically.

This leads us to the strangest and most criticized of Freud's writings: *Moses and Monotheism* (1939). Speculation about Freud's personal motivation for writing this peculiar book has abounded, and some of the analyses are interesting and instructive (Robert 1974, Yerushalmi 1991). Freud himself suffered from many qualms about publishing it at a time when the persecution of Jews had already reached new heights.

I believe that Freud's deepest motivation for writing *Moses and Monotheism* was to defend the universalist ethos that had guided all of his life's work. Behind the historical and scientific inaccuracy of his reasoning, we see a deep drive. Freud, in old age, tries everything to convince his readers that classifying humans according to their biological provenance is wrong. What matters about ideas is not who formulated them, or their provenance, but their validity and their ethical implications.

Edward Said (2003) has made a strong case for interpreting *Moses and Monotheism* as an attempt to dismantle notions of race and ethnicity. Beyond all the speculation and contortions of Freud's argument lies a very simple thesis: Moses, the man who, according to Judaism, led the Jewish people from slavery to freedom, from polytheism to monotheism, was an Egyptian. In other words, he was not a member of one of the Jewish tribes, but the offspring of an African dynasty. While this thesis could certainly hurt the sensibilities of Jews, more importantly it was a frontal attack on the whole idea that there was such a thing as the Jewish race that embodied either the "Jewish genius" (for its defenders) or Jewish depravity and neuroticism (for its critics). The most defining idea of the Jewish tradition – monotheism – was not connected to Jewish ancestry, but rather transmitted by an Egyptian nobleman who tried, through the Jewish tribes, to revive Ekhnaton's failed attempt to introduce monotheism within Egypt itself. Hence, monotheism belongs to neither the Jews nor the Semites.

In biblical terms, all Africans were descendants of Ham; the Semites, as their name suggests, were descendants of Shem; and the Greeks, the founders of a counter-culture to the Jews, were descendants of Yaphet. Freud completely mixed up this neat division: the originator of the Jewish creed was a descendant of Ham; and Freud himself, a Jew (i.e., a "Semite"), was analyzing racial stereotypes with tools developed by the descendants of Yaphet – Western science, which had its historical roots in ancient Greece (Said 2003). It would have suited Freud's agenda very well had he known of the intricate interaction between Greek philosophy and science and parallel advances in ancient India. That would have given him a further reason to deconstruct the ancestral myths connecting ideas and races.[1]

Here, two of Freud's great projects connect: excluding race from psychiatric discourse and critiquing religion. The common theme of these two projects is to deconstruct the notion that origins provide honor, dignity and value. Freud opposed the importance of origins both with respect to human beings and with respect to theories, beliefs and ideas. In the same way as Aryan, Jewish, aristocratic or any other type of ancestry should not be a reason for respecting certain human groups or individuals more than others, the origin of a belief or command should not provide the grounds for its authority.

Freud was intransigent on this. While his undermining of the notion of race in psychiatry was primarily directed against his Germanic environment and its anti-Semitic undertones, his undermining of the specialness of Jews as a race, group or religion was a logical implication of the very same project. For him, there was no way to protect the Jews against the accusation of racial inferiority without, by means of the same argument, denying them any special status because of their provenance or beliefs.

Freud's Jewish Universalist Identity

Freud's deconstruction of myths of origin and his critique of religion are intrinsic to his own Jewish identity, which he addressed in two famous texts. As we have seen, he did not believe that Jews were a race or that they were special in having invented monotheism. In any case, he was as critical towards Judaism as he was towards any other religion. In what sense, then, did he *feel* Jewish? The historically later of the two texts is the preface to the first of his works to be translated into Hebrew, *Totem and Taboo*:

> No reader of [the Hebrew version of] this book will find it easy to put himself in the emotional position of an author who is ignorant of the

1 Strangely, in the third part of *Moses and Monotheism*, Freud argues that Jews are indeed racially distinct, because the genetically transmitted memory of the murder of Moses had made them particularly apt for intellectual (*geistig*) values. This apparent inconsistency with his universalist program is discussed by Biale (2011) and addressed as a dialectical tension between universalism and particularism by Aron and Starr (2013).

> language of holy writ, who is completely estranged from the religion of his fathers – as well as from every other religion – and who cannot take a share in nationalist ideals, but who has yet never repudiated his people, who feels that he is in his essential nature a Jew and who has no desire to alter that nature. If the question were put to him: "Since you have abandoned all these common characteristics of your countrymen, what is there left to you that is Jewish?" he would reply: "A very great deal, and probably its very essence." He could not now express that essence clearly in words; but some day, no doubt, it will become accessible to the scientific mind.
>
> Thus it is an experience of a quite special kind for such an author when a book of his is translated into the Hebrew language and put into the hands of readers for whom that historic idiom is a living tongue: a book, moreover, which deals with the origin of religion and morality, though it adopts no Jewish standpoint and makes no exceptions in favour of Jewry. The author hopes, however, that he will be at one with his readers in the conviction that unprejudiced science cannot remain a stranger to the spirit of the new Jewry.
>
> Vienna, December 1930
>
> (Freud 1930: xv)

Freud describes the complex emotions he felt about this Hebrew translation. He does not apologize for his ethos. He makes it clear that he is critical of religion, repudiates nationalism and emphasizes that his critique of religion will not spare Judaism, the religion of his ancestors. He says very clearly that *Totem and Taboo* does not adopt a "Jewish standpoint."

What, then, could he possibly mean when he says "a great deal of him" remains Jewish? It is easy to dismiss this as nothing but a sentimental utterance, possibly designed to appease the book's readers, who must have been Jewish, as no one else at the time would have chosen the Hebrew edition. But I believe that Freud was doing more than merely paying lip service to his readers. All of his major biographers, from Ernest Jones (1953–1957) to Peter Gay (1989), agree that his Jewishness was essential to his identity. At the time, some Jews were on their way to complete assimilation and were confronted with their Jewishness primarily through their experience of anti-Semitism: most famously, Theodor Herzl; to a large extent, Albert Einstein; and one of the most incisive enquirers into the nature of modern Jewish identity, Hannah Arendt. This was not the case with Freud, however: he never tried to avoid or suppress his Jewishness, partly because of the very lively group of Jewish intellectuals, writers and scientists who lived in *fin de siècle* Vienna. There was no dearth of secular Jews with whom Freud could connect, and they were connected to one another through the precariousness of their situation: on the one hand, they had achieved significant influence in Viennese cultural life; on the other, they knew that anti-Semitic sentiment was rife, as the election of the openly anti-Semitic Karl Lueger as mayor of the city proved beyond any doubt (Schorske 1981).

Freud certainly felt a community of fate with his Jewish brethren in Vienna – in part because their influence did not always open doors for them. Mahler, one of Freud's most famous short-term cases, converted to Catholicism to gain access to the most coveted post in the world of music – the directorship of the Viennese Opera. Freud himself often complained that his ideas were initially rejected because he was Jewish – a claim that has not been substantiated by historical research. Nevertheless, unlike Mahler, he never considered conversion for the sake of acceptance or advancement. The question is whether the "Jewish essence" he mentions comprised nothing but this adversity in advancing in Viennese society.

The key to identifying a positive element in Freud's Jewish identity may be found in the other major text that addresses this question explicitly: the letter he sent to the opening of the Hebrew University in Jerusalem.

> Historians have told us that our small nation withstood the destruction of its independence as a State only because it began to transfer in its estimation of values the highest rank to its spiritual possessions, to its religion and its literature.
>
> We are now living in a time when this people has a prospect of again winning the land of its fathers with the help of a Power that dominates the world, and it celebrates the occasion by the foundation of a University in its ancient capital city.
>
> A University is a place in which knowledge is taught above all differences of religions and of nations, where investigation is carried on, which is to show mankind how far they understand the world around them and how far they can control it.
>
> Such an undertaking is a noble witness to the development to which our people has forced its way in two thousand years of unhappy fortune.
>
> I find it painful that my ill-health prevents me from being present at the opening festivities of the Jewish University in Jerusalem.
>
> (Freud 1925: 252)

In this brief text, Freud connects what he takes to be the essence of Jewish identity throughout most of its history – the "transfer in its estimation of values the highest rank to its spiritual possessions, to its religion and its literature" – and the essence of a university – "a place in which knowledge is taught above all differences of religions and of nations." Finally, he describes the foundation of the "Jewish University" as a "noble witness to the development to which our people has forced its way in two thousand years of unhappy fortune." I believe that Freud is thinking not just of the possibility of a Jewish homeland when he writes of this "development," but of another "transfer in [the Jewish] estimation of values." While Jews had previously prized their religion and literature above all else, the Jews of his time had placed the highest value on the objective investigation of the world – that is, science – which Freud, throughout his life, had seen as humanity's highest achievement. For him, this was not a falsification of Jewishness, as he understood it, but a creative transformation of its essence. Shifting the "possession of spiritual values" from religion to science was a step that all of humanity had to make if it was ever to mature fully and move from the pleasure principle to the reality principle.

In light of this, the following comment is inevitable: "But this is in no way unique to the Jews! Freud thought that all of humanity needed to make this step, so how did this differentiate between Jews and Gentiles?" The particularity of Jewishness was indeed not first and foremost on Freud's mind: for him, humanity's greatest virtue was its ability to transcend "all differences of religions and of nations." Attachment to one's kin is certainly an ineradicable aspect of human nature. Freud knew this and made it a cornerstone of his view of human nature: character was the reflection of our early love attachments, and these could not be erased from the psyche. His large ethical question was the extent to which, as individuals and as a species, humans were capable of transcending these early attachments when it came to formulating their worldview and their ethics. As we have seen, throughout *The Future of an Illusion* Freud insists that overcoming those early attachments, and moving from religion to science, is humankind's only chance to mature fully, and he does not exempt the Jews from this. In the preface to the Hebrew translation of *Totem and Taboo* (Freud 1913/1930), he expresses the hope that the ethos of "unprejudiced science" will find its place in the "new Jewry." Jews, like the rest of humankind, must move towards universalism. This was why, despite his own misgivings about its timing, and his awareness that the argument was rather weak, he felt compelled to write *Moses and Monotheism* in his final years. For him, it was crucial to formulate the decisive argument that both Gentiles and Jews needed to overcome the myth of racial origins against which he had fought all his life, and which was to achieve its most terrible expression, after Freud's death in 1939, during the Holocaust.

Freud in the Era of Globalization

While our world is vastly different from Freud's *fin de siècle* Vienna, some of the problems he dealt with then are very similar with those we are struggling with today, and some of the ways in which he approached them have remained relevant in an interesting way. Even the way in which Freud dealt with his own identity – and identities in general – remains highly relevant.

Freud was of Jewish descent and experienced his Jewishness as a central component of his identity, albeit completely detached from the religion of his ancestors. And throughout his life he merged his Jewishness with the cosmopolitan universalism that was at the core of his thought and his work. In the following chapters we will come to know a global class, the New Cosmopolitans, who are facing questions Freud addressed in an interesting way. How can we be attached to the cultures that formed our minds and souls, yet adhere to a strictly universalist ethics? How can we love the tunes, scents and rituals that have been formative in our upbringing without hating those whose cultures, beliefs and languages are different from our own?

Freud, always the pessimist about human nature, might not have been surprised to hear that, three-quarters of a century after his death, humanity is still far from finding answers to these questions; that racism, religious bigotry and nationalism are on the rise again; and that universalism is severely threatened once more. In the United States, for years white supremacists tried to show that Barack Obama was not really American-born in a thinly disguised attempt to delegitimize the first black president. The issue, obviously, was not really Obama's place of birth, but his half-black and quarter-Muslim ancestry. The Middle East is in the throes of a series of conflicts that have been interpreted as a clash of civilizations by leading thinkers of the stature of Bernard Lewis and Samuel Huntington. Even if we do not accept this interpretation in full, the unconscious of the Middle East (if the metaphor can be forgiven) is undoubtedly structured by the family drama of the three Abrahamic religions. Jews and Muslims are fighting for possession of the Temple Mount or Haram al'Sharif. According to legend, this was where Abraham followed God's command to sacrifice his son, only to be stopped at the very last moment. This biblical story is the epitome of the exaltation of blind obedience: Abraham was willing to commit one of the most horrible acts imaginable to prove his complete submission to God's will.

The paradox and the horrible reality of the myth of origin come to their fullest expression in this conflict. Muslims claim that it was Ishmael, the mythical forefather of the Arabs, who was almost sacrificed on the Temple

Mount, rather than Isaac, the no less mythical forefather of the Jewish people (Posmanik 2009). The irony is that, in a sense, Jews and Muslims are fighting for the dubious honor of being the victims of a trauma that they are both willing to perpetuate for ever. Both religions are prepared to send their sons to their deaths for the possession of a strip of land that, more than anything else, expresses what Freud saw as immature attachment to the authorities of childhood (Strenger 2011b).

Had Freud lived to see this, he might have sighed that the voice of reason does indeed find it very difficult to get a hearing. Yet he would also have insisted that one should never give up hope. He would have pointed out that in the Middle East people kill each other for nothing more than the claim of truth of their respective myths, and he would have seen this as another pernicious consequence of the refusal to mature into universally acceptable standards of truth and the fixation to religious belief. Yet he would have been happy to see psychoanalysis applied to our critical understanding of the Middle Eastern conflict (Bunzl and Beit-Hallahmi 2002).

Freud's universalism accepted only one natural kind for humans: the species of Homo sapiens. He did not think that there were biologically based sub-species within humanity. The unconscious was his metaphor for the biological nature of humans, and its structure was supposed to be universal. All humans have to live with the built-in conflict between the pleasure principle, embodied in the id, and the reality principle, laboriously acquired in the process of maturation and embodied in the ego.

His critique of religion was universalist, too. All humans yearn for a sense of protection and the belief that they have a special, privileged place in the cosmos, and all humans suffer from the insight that we are but a transient species that has evolved by chance on a small planet in one of billions of solar systems in one of countless galaxies. The desire to regain the sense of ontological specialness that characterized our infancy is understandable, but we must by no means give in to this desire: the consequences are too dangerous. History is filled with wars, persecutions and genocides built on the idea that one group is more special, more deserving, than another. It is written in the blood of those killed in the name of religions and other belief systems that tried to restore a pure faith, a pure race or a pure ideology. For Freud, there was but one way to counteract the regressive pull towards claims of racial, ethnic or religious superiority, particularism and specialness: the disinterested study of the nature of humankind, the deciphering of the biologically ingrained forces that push us towards irrationality and inhumanity, and, finally, the realization that all claims to cosmic specialness are but remnants of infantile grandiosity and omnipotence.

Freud's specific theories have, to a large extent, not survived the increase in knowledge since his death. Biology has moved far away from the models in which he was educated and through which he formulated his ideas. As a result, the models of the contemporary cognitive evolutionary neurosciences look radically different from Freud's psychoanalytic theory (Buss 2004). However, as Eric Kandel has shown in detail, Freud's ethos and research program still flourish in those neurosciences. His idea that the evolutionary strata of the mind must be deciphered has become the core of a research paradigm spanning the civilized world. It is fascinating that psychodynamic thinking inspired by the theories of one of Freud's most creative pupils, Otto Rank, has found its way into one of the most interesting research paradigms in evolutionary social psychology, terror management theory (Greenberg et al. 2004), which will play a central role in the explanatory model developed in Chapter 2.

Even Freud's search for the evolutionary roots of religion has turned into a flourishing domain (Atran 2002, Dennett 2005). Current models of the evolutionary psychology of religion have achieved considerable complexity, and they are based on an impressive array of interrelated disciplines, ranging from physical anthropology through comparative religion to cognitive psychology and evolutionary theory. None of the researchers working on the evolutionary roots of religion (or the evolutionary roots of the mind in general) believes that there are black, Asian, Aryan, Jewish or Muslim psychologies. There is human psychology, which, depending on circumstance, leads to a wide variety of cultures, belief systems and religions. But the conflict and yearnings are the same pitfalls of human nature everywhere.

The New Cosmopolitans are, like Freud, heirs of the Enlightenment; like him, they are firmly committed to intellectual and ethical universalism; and, like him, they struggle to live complex identities that unite the particularity of their culture of origin and their cosmopolitanism – which, in turn, is not always well accepted by the more traditional core of their culture of origin. In particular, as we will see, their profound belief that reason can and should prevail over irrational and parochial bigotry often leads to accusations of elitist aloofness or a lack of patriotism or loyalty to their ethnic or religious group, which in turn tends to undermine their sense of existential security.

First, though, we need to develop a clearer picture of how the contemporary world of the New Cosmopolitans radically differs from Freud's *fin de siècle* Vienna.

Chapter 2

The Quantified Self

Psychology and psychoanalysis are today faced with two tasks. The first is to live up to Freud's original program of deciphering the basic, biologically-based structure of the human mind. As Eric Kandel (2012) has shown convincingly, Freud is in many ways the founder of today's vast undertaking of the evolutionary cognitive neurosciences – the attempt to decipher the biological architecture that underlies our psyche. If the metaphor may be allowed, this is research into biological hardware and the basic operating system with which we are born.

The second task is to decipher the applications that contemporary culture uploads into our psyche. Every culture and historical period programs the psyche in its own ways, and these can differ significantly from each other; even within the span of one century Western societies have evolved in profound ways, and psychoanalysis has had to adapt to these changes (Zaretsky 2004). Once we widen our perspective, it becomes clear that the traditional Muslim and Jewish cultures upload very different contents and modes of functioning into the human mind than late modern, urban, secular cultures do.

In this chapter I want to describe the interplay between an aspect of the human psyche that seems to be part of its hard-wired operating system and a very particular cultural configuration that has evolved over the last two or three decades. The hard-wired aspect is the human fear of insignificance – humans' deep-seated fear of dying in general and dying without leaving any sort of mark in particular.

The pornography of the successful life has taken a firm hold on the public imagination, and this pornography is taking the form of the adulation of numbers. The global infotainment system is flooded with rankings of individuals and corporations along several dimensions. First and foremost, of course, is wealth: a person's net *worth* (the expression is itself telling) is a precise number. Then come celebrity and influence. In the age of the internet there are seemingly objective measures for both of these parameters: number of Google entries; number of searches; number of hits.

Some of these rankings are global. *Forbes* has its annual hit parade of the wealthiest and most influential people on the planet. *Time* publishes its often quoted ranking of the most influential people of the year, and these days solves the problem that influence is difficult to quantify by asking visitors to its website to vote on various individuals' importance. Then there is *People* magazine's list of the sexiest and most beautiful. Moreover, each country and even city has its own rankings of the most rich, powerful, popular and cool people in that locality.

These lists have become truly addictive. Two senior editors of influential publications have told me that they feel they have created a monster. One of them, who works for a financial publication that produces a list of "most influential" people, says that he and his staff feel that the list is meaningless. Nevertheless, PR agents of potential nominees lobby the magazine relentlessly on their clients' behalf in the month before the list is published. The other editor works for an influential lifestyle magazine, and explains that he cannot afford to drop the annual lists, because the issues in which they appear sell better than all the others and bring in new subscriptions every year.

But the craze for rankings has also seeped into the strata of those who do not stand any chance of making it into any of the more publicized scales. Today, children and adolescents invest great effort into collecting "friends" and "likes" for their status updates, pictures and videos on Facebook. Seemingly objective wealth, influence, celebrity, popularity and other measures are beginning to define what it means to live a life of significance.

A whole industry has evolved to prep and train us from early childhood to make it into the valued rankings. Sociologist Eva Illouz's (2008) groundbreaking studies have shown the extent to which popular psychology has taken on the role of creating emotional "competence" and "guiding" consumers through their various life-roles, including everything from work to child-rearing to sex. This advice is often based on shaky empirical evidence and packaged into simple three- or seven-step programs that are designed to make people cheerful, communicative, effective, creative and loving at the same time.

Illouz (2008) has made a strong case that popular psychology served the needs of culture at large throughout the twentieth century: it kept reformulating the ideals of mental health to adapt to changing circumstances, starting with early research about management optimization and ending with the theory of emotional intelligence. In doing so, it has served the needs of corporations who need employees who work hard without complaint and help to maintain the organization's peace and quiet; and it has served the needs of the clients who want nothing but to function well in an environment that will provide them with status and a good income.

Over the last few decades the demand for high-functioning hard-workers has been well disguised by a powerful cultural myth: each human being has an inner self with untapped potential (Strenger 2011a). If this potential is unleashed, the person will become highly effective, very successful and yet feel that life is not hard work, but one big experience of self-actualization. In other words, great success, supposedly, is not achieved by hard work and risk-taking; rather, it is a function of tapping sufficiently deeply into the inner self's unlimited potential, which can be unleashed in brief seven-step programs or crash courses in positive thinking.

The defining slogan of the era is "Just Do It!" Like Michael Jordan – the icon most closely associated with Nike, the brand that coined the slogan – we can all become legendary. We simply need to reach deep enough into ourselves. Doing so is the new categorical imperative: the new super-ego's demand is to be a successful self-actualizer (Laurent 2011). Because this myth is so powerful, we tend to think that if we have not realized it in our lives, something must be wrong with us.

This myth is, of course, devoid of any empirical foundation. In fact, the economic literature shows the precise opposite (Sassen 2000, Reich 2005, Conley 2009): social mobility today is substantially *lower* than it was fifty years ago; and the best predictor of economic success is simply the socioeconomic status of the family into which a child is born. The idea that reaching deep into our inner selves and thinking positively will turn us all into immensely successful self-actualizers is nothing but a chimera. The most probable life course is that those born into society's lower strata will stay there (Keller 2005). And the phenomenally popular seven-step guides to ultimate success are, as Tiede (2001) has shown, nothing but contemporary versions of snake oil. They lead only to repeated failure to achieve the promised miraculous transformation from ordinary human being into vaulting success story.

What can psychoanalysis offer as an alternative? Simply arguing that a life lived in depth is better than a life lived along measurable parameters ends up being a matter of claim and counter-claim. In order to build a case for psychoanalysis's multilayered embracing of complexity, in order to show that the emphasis on quantifiable elements of life and achievement is bound to create misery rather than fulfillment, psychoanalysis must find fruitful ways to state its case in a non-defensive manner that is accessible not only to the scientific community but to the wider, educated audiences who most need to hear this message.

In this endeavor, the cognitive neurosciences could be powerful allies. From the very beginning, psychoanalysis has attempted to understand human phenomena rather than simply judge them, and this has been its greatest forte. This is why I believe that psychoanalysis can find valuable allies among the contemporary cognitive neurosciences for its task of deciphering the global deification of the quantified and ranked self. Some highly influential research that has been done in the cognitive sciences could be marshaled to buttress the psychoanalytic insistence on the irreducibility of the subjective dimension.

The Hedonic Treadmill

Nobel Laureate Daniel Kahneman is best known for his work on biases in decision-making, which has become central to the emerging field of behavioral economics. But he is also a founder of and major contributor to the field of hedonic psychology, which studies the nature of human well-being and the factors that contribute to or detract from it.

One of Kahneman's most influential concepts is the "hedonic treadmill" (Kahneman and Deaton 2010). The basic idea is simple and powerful: human beings tend to set goals they believe will increase their happiness in the long run. Many of these goals are economic in nature: we believe that if we can afford a larger apartment, or a larger car, or to travel business class, then this will make us happier. Kahneman's original hypothesis was that any material goal achieved tends to become the new baseline of our psychological balance: within just a few months, our level of happiness returns to its previous level. So we are forever running on a hedonic treadmill without ever going anywhere.

This thesis has been taken in some very interesting directions by a number of researchers. One of the persistent beliefs of our culture is that the more choice we have, the happier we become. However, this has been shown to be untrue: being flooded with choices tends to generate misery rather than happiness, and it makes it very difficult for human beings to enjoy their lives and possessions (Schwartz 2004, Gilbert 2007). In other words, not only does serious academic psychology not support the myths of the craze for quantification; its research results actually undermine them.

Kahneman's original hypothesis has since been refined: levels of happiness can and do change, to some extent, depending on life circumstance, individual variables and age (Kahneman 2003). Furthermore, Kahneman has readjusted his original estimate of the income beyond which material wealth no longer impacts well-being. Nevertheless, his research (Kahneman and Deaton 2010) shows that higher income has a greater impact on a person's *evaluation* of life than on actual moment-to-moment happiness. Kahneman and Deaton (2010) have also argued that there are strong indications that relative wealth is more important than absolute wealth.

This raises a very interesting point: if the impact of wealth and achievement is relative, the frame of comparison becomes crucial. And this frame, the economist Robert Reich (2005) argues, has changed dramatically due to the impact of globalization, primarily because this has created a new upper class composed of the senior executive levels of multinational companies and the firms that provide them with legal, financial and media services. Reich calls the members of this new upper class "global symbolic analysts," and they have been doing extremely well financially over the past few decades. Their success stories are among the favorite topics of the global infotainment system, capturing the public imagination, even though they make up less than half a percent of the population. Add to this the fact that they have had a dramatic impact on the cities in which they concentrate – called "global cities" by Saskia Sassen (2000). They have driven up property prices enormously, and the economies of these places are ever more focused on catering to their needs and desires.

These research results lead to an interesting paradox: globalization has changed the frame of reference of everyone who is connected to the global infotainment; it has led a growing number of people to redefine their expectations of what it means to be successful while simultaneously positioning ninety-nine and a half percent of them outside of that bracket.

Experimental Existential Psychology and the Need for Meaning

These results can be integrated into a psychodynamic model that has become very influential in contemporary social psychology and has its historical roots in the psychoanalytic tradition. Otto Rank's later work suffered a form of excommunication from the psychoanalytic literature after his break with Freud in the early 1920s. Paradoxically, though, this work has become increasingly influential in academic psychology through a rather circuitous route. Rank's *Psychology and the Soul* (1930), *Art and Artist* (1932) and *Beyond Psychology* (1948) develop one central idea: the human psyche is incapable of truly accepting a fact that our evolving neo-cortex has exposed us to – our mortality. Rank's work analyzed the various defense mechanisms by which we try to deny what we know in the domains of religion, culture and art.

The ideas of the anthropologist Ernest Becker, particularly his last two books – *The Denial of Death* (Becker 1974) and the posthumously published *Escape from Evil* (Becker 1975) – reformulated some of Rank's core ideas of existentialism in a way that was closer to evolutionary biology. Becker argues that evolution has created an impossible situation for the human species. Like all other animals, we are terrified of anything that might lead to our death; but unlike other animals, we *know of our death.* Yet we simply cannot bear this knowledge. Becker's momentous hypothesis is that *the denial of death is one of the strongest motivators of the human species.* But how can we deny something that we know? The primary answer is that, in order not to feel exposed to the naked terror of death, humans buy into worldviews that have two functions: first, they provide us with meaning by telling us what we are here for and how to structure our lives; second, they protect us by giving us the experience of being part of a larger whole. Belonging to a uniquely valuable group (tribe, religion, nation, profession or race), as defined by the worldview, makes us eon ipso valuable and thus bolsters our self-esteem. The central tenet of existential psychology is that only an animal that knows that time is limited can – and must – ask the question: "Do I live a life worth living?" (Jacques 1965). Only such an animal is preoccupied with the question of whether life as a whole is good, valiant and successful (Becker 1971, 1974). This question camouflages unbearable terror that is generated by our awareness of the passage of time and death.

Cultures and their worldviews provide us with what Becker has called "symbolic immortality." Each worldview is based on the premise that the group and its mission on earth are there to stay, beyond our own individual death. By contributing to the larger group, its task on earth and its continuity, we feel that something of us will survive our physical death. This mitigates the sense of feeling like an insignificant speck in a universe that is indifferent to us.

As Otto Rank argued in his major later works (1930, 1932, 1948), this theme is one of the deepest in all of mythology. The heroes of all myths face doubts. Each of them feels that they have a calling, but they do not know whether they can live up to their destiny. The drama of the psychological birth of the hero is facing fear, doubt and hesitation; knowing that reaching for the stars entails the risk of failure, ridicule and even injury or death; and knowing that, by not trying, the possibility of greatness is forfeited. Greek mythology has the great advantage of shining a bright light on themes that have been relegated into the unconscious by modern culture. Its heroes are all motivated by the desire for immortal fame. They are even willing to die physically for the possibility that all future generations will tell the tale of their bravery.

In the late 1980s a new research paradigm of social psychology and the theory of motivation and personality based on Becker's ideas emerged – experimental existential psychology (EEP) – which turned Becker's intriguing idea into a testable empirical theory with quite spectacular success (Greenberg et al. 2004). Terror management theory (TMT) (Pyszczynski et al. 2003), one of the most successful paradigms of EEP, has established beyond any doubt that humans invest enormous energy into denying death, and that this denial is one of the most powerful motivators of the human psyche: we cannot really accept that we will die. The findings of EEP confirm the centrality of this most basic theme of Greek mythology. Our fear of death, of insignificance, of vanishing into nothingness is so tremendous that many people are willing to die for the symbolic immortality that heroism bestows upon us (Rank 1932).

This is also one of the most basic functions of self-esteem: the fear of insignificance is crucially lowered if we are recognized as significant by our own culture. One experiment conducted in EEP has corroborated this repeatedly (Greenberg et al. 2004). The experimental group is given a boost to their self-esteem by some positive feedback on their performance of a task, whereas the control group is not. All of the subjects are then shown stimuli involving some mortality salience. The two groups are then tested for worldview defense. As the researchers predicted, the group whose self-esteem was bolstered makes less use of worldview defense than the control group.

Such experiments show that when we feel valued within our cultural framework, we are less afraid of dying. Like the Greek heroes, we feel that our contribution to the larger whole to which we belong, our culture, is leaving a mark that might well outlast our physical lives. Yet, this is usually not an explicit thought. We do not think consciously every time we feel good about ourselves that we might be remembered beyond our deaths. We simply feel good about ourselves and strengthened. We unconsciously equate what we do as a contribution to a whole that is larger than ourselves, and we want to feel that we are appreciated for that. This reflects our need for the symbolic immortality that Becker studied so extensively. It is the deepest motivating factor in the quest for fame and extraordinary achievement.

EEP is of particular interest for psychoanalysis because it is a psychodynamic paradigm. Its core hypothesis is that the human psyche cannot fully accept mortality, and that it has three major anxiety buffers to maintain the sense of symbolic immortality described by Becker: close and significant attachments comprise the first tier; self-esteem (that is, feeling valued by our culture for who we are and for our contribution to that culture) is the second tier; while the third tier is provided by a cultural worldview that organizes our experience, tells us what it means to live a valuable life and thus imbues our lives with meaning.

TMT's connection to psychoanalysis is more than historical: it deals with some of the central questions that preoccupy psychoanalysis both theoretically and clinically. TMT researchers have studied the intricate relation between attachment, self-esteem and existential meaning and have experimentally demonstrated that there is an intimate connection between the individual feeling safely embedded in a cultural system and self-esteem. This squares well with clinical observation: we often observe patients trying to overcome personal loss (i.e., loss of attachment) by turning to religious or ideological meaning systems that provide them with a sense of safety.

There are several interesting similarities between EEP's core theory and some major psychoanalytic theories. Becker always emphasized that symbolic immortality is based on an illusory structure because, in the end, every individual will die; and this cannot be changed by attachment, self-esteem or cultural continuity. Nevertheless, the human psyche cannot survive without the illusions provided by culture. This echoes one of D. W. Winnicott's most basic claims: that the human psyche needs a space of illusion, a transitional space for its survival. Winnicott specifically placed the whole domain of culture within this space – art, religion and ideology – and his work showed in detail how this space of culture evolves developmentally when the infant bridges the subjective and the objective world through transitional space. Throughout his life, Winnicott investigated the complex balance between the space of illusion that is necessary to stay alive and the psyche's ability to accept the external world as independent of the subject.

EEP's emphasis on the crucial function of cultural meaning systems also resonates strongly with one of the most basic motifs in Kohut's self-psychology. Kohut (1971) emphasized that a healthy psyche cannot survive without what he called the "pole of ideals": the images, ideals and values that provide the psyche with a sense of direction and a structure that tells us what is important in life. Without a safely established pole of values, the self cannot maintain cohesiveness, and the individual will experience fragmentation and meaninglessness.

While exploring the affinities between Winnicott, Kohut and EEP is fascinating and likely to yield some important insights, doing so would lead us too far afield. The task at hand is to combine the results of hedonic psychology, behavioral economics and the results of EEP into an interpretive framework that will allow us to understand some of the psychological implications of globalization.

The Psychodynamics of the Globalized Individual

Students of globalization have emphasized two irrevocable implications of the process through which every point of the globe has been connected to every other, not only through economic and ecological ties, but through the powerful network of the global infotainment system, which allows access to information, entertainment, images, videos and sounds from anywhere in the world. The first of these implications, as we have seen, is that self-esteem management has become incomparably more difficult. If the frame of comparison of every achievement is now global, it is almost inevitable that the achievements of the overwhelming majority of humanity will be dwarfed by the global success stories pulsating through the infotainment system.

The second implication is that it has become far more difficult to feel protected by a cultural tradition. Every religion, every form of art, every form of social life is now seen as but one possible way of giving meaning to life. The implications of this are staggering: EEP has shown how difficult it is for us to accept that whichever cultural meaning system provides us with meaning and symbolic immortality is just one of many ways of seeing the world and living life. How, then, can we maintain psychic equilibrium when we know that our culture is merely one among many?

The political scientist Benjamin Barber (1995) has claimed that the rise of fundamentalism in all three monotheistic religions can be explained by the impact of globalization: Judaism, Christianity and Islam have developed fundamentalist variations that simply deny the importance of any other culture on earth, and they have retreated into the demand for a purified version of their own religion that expels all foreign influence. Historian of religion Karen Armstrong (2000) has proposed a similar thesis and has documented the rise of fundamentalism as a reaction to globalization in detail. This squares well with the experimental results generated by EEP: time and again, it has shown that, under duress, human beings become less capable of tolerating difference and flatly reject any ideology, religion or culture other than their own. Fundamentalism reflects this hardening of boundaries and our inability to live in a universe of multiple cultures writ large.

But, for our purpose, an alternative mode of dealing with the relativizing of all cultural frames of reference is crucial. If no cultural tradition can claim absolute validity, is there a way to define value that is, so to speak, unassailable? Global capitalism has provided a potential answer: the only value that remains unassailable is provided by numbers. Mathematics is a cultural constant: no matter what your culture, two plus two always equals four, and one billion is always greater than one million. Quantification has become the Archimedean point that is not shaken by globalization. If value can be quantified, the psyche can find a resting point in the maelstrom of competing conceptions of the good life. We could finally claim that A is more valuable than B if we established that A is numerically larger than B; and we would no longer have to worry about this conception of value being threatened or invalidated by a competing culture or value system.

We seem to be arriving at a psychodynamic explanation of the craze for ranking and quantification described above. Wealth and celebrity can be quantified, and they seem to provide an unassailable means through which to determine value: if A is wealthier or better known (i.e., more influential) than B, then A is more valuable than B. We no longer have to bother with judgements of quality or worry that others will invalidate such judgements; only quantity matters.

This conception has reached far into the domain of culture. The literary world has become obsessed with bestseller lists. Publishers and authors now crave a place in them – and not only for the obvious financial reasons. Amazon has provided an alternative to traditional measures like the *New York Times* bestseller list. Furthermore, its users are encouraged to review and rank books. As a result, several numbers now define a book's "value": its sales ranking; the number of reviews it has received; and its average approval rating between one and five stars.

Even academia has moved progressively into purely quantitative measures of a researcher's impact and standing. The first of these is the impact factor of the journals in which they have published, with that impact factor itself being quantitative: it is the average number of citations of articles contained in the journal. The second measure is how often a researcher has been cited in the scientific literature. Ideally, we should end up with a single number that measures a researcher's standing, and such single measures have indeed been proposed by a number of rating agencies, including Thomson Reuters, and are readily accessible via computer programs such as Publish or Perish.

The logic of this development is seemingly unassailable, even though the results may border on the absurd: for instance, it is easy to claim that Justin Bieber, the celebrity teen singer catapulted into stardom by YouTube, is much more valuable than J. S. Bach, whose Mass in B-minor has been viewed and downloaded far less than any of Bieber's songs. Similarly, it could be said that Dan Brown's *The Da Vinci Code* is one of the most valuable pieces of literature ever produced.

The absurdity of such conclusions is dwarfed by the existential implications of the total quantification of value: every self would be reduced to a tradable entity in the global infotainment system; and the value of each individual would be an amalgamation of several quantifiable parameters, ranging from number of Google entries, to wealth, to ranking in a specific field (such as position on the ATP's list of top tennis players or chart placing on *Billboard*'s Hot 100).

Today, the optimization of rankings is big business. Some companies specialize in optimizing a product's, individual's or company's position in Google searches; others manage Facebook pages in order to generate as many followers as possible. While this may be seen as a legitimate development in the general competition for market share, the question is whether the change in ranking genuinely reflects a change in intrinsic value. If the interpretive hypothesis presented above is correct, the reason for this phenomenon runs deep and is rooted in some crucial implications of the process of globalization that has changed the world radically within the space of a few decades.

The next chapter paints five portraits of what I call New Cosmopolitans, a group that has emerged over the last few decades. On the one hand, they have developed a cosmopolitan ethics; on the other, they are haunted by the demand to prove that they have lived significant lives. The categorical imperative of New Cosmopolitans is no less than *transform the world* (Rothkopf 2008), and the phenomenal acceleration of technological development has turned this imperative into a real possibility. If Google could transform the internet and the organization of human knowledge, if Facebook facilitated uprisings against dictatorial regimes, if illnesses that used to be death sentences can now be cured, the sky now seems to be the limit. The following chapters explore how this global horizon of seemingly limitless possibilities impacts the inner lives of the New Cosmopolitans.

Chapter 3

Five New Cosmopolitans in Search of Meaning

This chapter will present the initial therapeutic sessions of five typical New Cosmopolitans.[1] The psychoanalytic clinician will immediately notice that all of them differ substantially from most of the patients we used to treat in the past. First and foremost, none of them spent most of their time in Tel Aviv, the city where I live and work. The two academics among them – Jeff and Naomi – were in Tel Aviv for sabbaticals and research projects. An international news network posted Ella to the city, but it was clear that she would not stay in Tel Aviv in the long run. Ben, a high-tech entrepreneur, had a home in the city, but he spent at most about one-third of his time there. Mark, the managing partner of an investment fund, was only ever in Tel Aviv for a few weeks at a time, to assess startups.

Four of these New Cosmopolitans contacted me from outside Israel and scheduled their first meeting for their next visit to the city. It was clear to all of them that, if we subsequently embarked on a therapeutic journey, most of that journey would be conducted on Skype. None of them had any doubts that this was feasible; and I had accumulated four years of experience with this tool, so I was similarly confident. I had first used Skype because some of my Israeli patients – academics, CEOs of high-tech startups and some artists – spent a good deal of time out of the country. For instance, one academic took a sabbatical abroad, and one CEO had to relocate to the US West Coast in order to develop his startup. At that stage I had not considered taking on patients who were based abroad, but by the time the five New Cosmopolitans contacted me, a few years later, several of my colleagues were already treating patients primarily via Skype.

1 The case examples are composites based on actual patients. All identifying characteristics, including occupation, gender and provenance, have been changed to preserve privacy.

I have chosen to focus on Jeff, Naomi, Ben, Ella and Mark's initial sessions because – even though they had very different personalities, backgrounds and occupations – I think that the New Cosmopolitans' Gestalt emerges through their presentation of their existential problems and psychic pain. I will attempt to spell out this Gestalt in more general terms in Chapter 4.

Jeff: the Global Impostor Syndrome

My first impression of Jeff was of a bundle of energy that was hardly contained. He was of medium height and his physique seemed strong, but he was somewhat overweight. I was undecided whether he was studiously casual in his attire or didn't care about slight mismatches: his jeans' and his jacket's colors grated slightly; and his shirt was not tucked into his jeans, which is not unusual in academic circles. His curly, thick hair was unruly. His facial features were strong, slightly fleshy and dominated by amazingly expressive dark eyes.

> Doctor Strenger . . . can I call you Carlo? [I nodded.] Carlo, I've come to see you because I've read you. I am, as I told you, an academic. And I'm thorough. I think I've read almost everything you've published. I hope you don't mind me saying so, but I feel that you did your best work in the 1990s. Your *Individuality, the Impossible Project* really got to me.
>
> I called you because I hope that you are what I believe you to be: a combination of soul and brain. I . . . I don't know how to put this. I . . . I really need help.
>
> My guess is that you've looked me up on Google. So you probably know that I'm considered to be a very successful academic. I'll get straight to the point: I feel that my life has been one big hoax. I'm a con-man. I'm forty-two, and I feel that I've never had a day of decent work of value. I feel like shit. I feel that I can't continue like this.
>
> I don't know whether I'll ever have children. But at this point, I can't even consider having any. How can I raise a son when I don't have anything of true value to give to him? How can I raise children who will have a father who loathes himself?

Huge sobs pulsed through Jeff's big chest. He was shaking violently, crying his heart out.

Usually patients in first sessions are more concerned with maintaining a minimum of composure; they are apprehensive about how they come across. But I wasn't taken aback by Jeff's outburst. I felt deep sympathy for him and my intuition told me that he was neither a drama queen nor mentally ill. It seemed to me that he had already spoken to me so much in his head that he felt he knew me well enough simply to let go.

Then I noticed that the box of tissues that normally sits on the table near the patient had disappeared. Freud, our German shepherd, loves tissues infused with aloe vera, and he had probably run off with the box. The problem was that I didn't have another, so I had no choice but to hand Jeff a roll of toilet paper. "Sorry, Jeff, but our dog ate the tissues. This may not be very stylish, but I hope you're fine with it."

Jeff couldn't help laughing at my embarrassment, then he used the tissue to wipe his tears and blow his nose. He calmed down a bit and said, "Hmm . . . that was a dramatic opening. I didn't plan this. Don't worry, I'm not a nutcase. I'm just in pain."

Jeff is a world-famous political scientist. He had made a name for himself by merging a social psychology theory into a model of political processes, both within individual polities and between countries. In his doctoral research he had claimed that all models of political decision-making were hopelessly flawed because they were overly rationalist; that if you neglected to consider deep existential needs that drove both voters and politicians, you could never understand political processes.

Later, in a series of papers and books, he had impressed the academic community by bolstering his hypothesis with a highly sophisticated statistical analysis of a huge amount of data. Some people thought that he might revolutionize the whole of political science. He held a professorship at one of the most prestigious universities in the United States, which paid him a substantial salary to ward off the constant attempts to lure him elsewhere. They also kept his teaching duties to a minimum to allow him to conduct research projects around the world. Atypically for an academic, he would usually fly in business class from one high-powered conference to the next, before being whisked away by various governments to advise them on the most pressing conflicts around the world.

Jeff was exhibiting a classic case of impostor syndrome. This is quite prevalent among – although not unique to – the New Cosmopolitans. Most of them rarely see any concrete, physical result of their work: instead, they see numbers, graphs, words, websites. This leads many of them to wonder whether what they do is real, or whether they are in fact fooling the world. I told Jeff, "In either case you assume that you're a genius; if not in your academic field, then at least because you are able to fool everybody all the time."

Jeff was bubbly, energetic and expressive; he spoke at phenomenal speed, underscoring each point with expansive gestures. Even after he had stopped crying, he was still quite emotional. His pain was a strong, almost physical presence in the room. And now he looked at me with a combination of disappointment and humor.

> I would have expected more from you, Carlo. I know all about the impostor syndrome, and I don't just think that I'm an impostor. I think the whole game we're part of – and that includes your discipline – is a huge hoax. We feed the world the illusion that we actually understand the phenomena we purportedly analyze. We write papers based on complex statistical analyses, giving the impression that this is science. But you know how minimal the effects are; you know that there is no way we can truly ground our conclusions in our data. There are zillions of alternative explanations.
>
> Somehow we manage to convince taxpayers to fly us around the globe for conferences that are basically rituals of self-congratulation. We celebrate how smart we are, and what we're doing for the world, and we convince everybody that they can't live without us. But you know as well as I do that not much would change if most major social scientists were blown up in one of these conferences!
>
> There are people who do actual science: physicists, chemists, biologists. They don't work on totally minimal effects: they *do* stuff. You can see the end results clearly. A friend of mine in physical chemistry developed a new form of ceramic, and it's now being applied in the production of luxury-car brakes. In twenty years, all brakes will be made of this material because it's lighter, more durable and has much better heat conductivity than steel. Neither you nor I has ever – or will ever – produce something that is as tangible as that. Our castles are made of air, so you never see them crumble. And you shrinks, as the joke famously says, collect the rent from those air castles. All you do is get people to realize after a thousand sessions and a quarter of a million dollars that they should accept that they are who they are. Carlo, you won't be any help if all you have to tell me is that I suffer from impostor syndrome!

Jeff was touching a raw nerve. I am a New Cosmopolitan myself, and I have the same thoughts about the social sciences and the humanities being a major hoax every now and then. And, of course, he was right about therapy. More often than not, it *is* about helping people to accept who they are. So there was no reason to argue:

> Jeff, point very well taken and duly acknowledged. So I, a pseudo-social scientist, ask you, another pseudo-social scientist: given that you know all

> this, what on earth are you doing in my consulting room? You know very well that we shrinks are basically some form of secular priests or rabbis. I always tell my students that we are "meaning-fixers": people come to us with stories about themselves that make them unhappy, and we try to fix those stories. That's what I sell; and you know that. Yet still you're here.

Jeff's eyes gleamed: "You're not exactly reaching deep into your bag of tricks. This is what you teach your first-year students, I guess. Always refocus on the patient. Have him take responsibility for his words and actions."

"But the fact is that you're here, aren't you?"

His face fell again:

> I'm in pain; I'm in bloody pain. If your field was any good, you'd sever some neural connection, then feed something else into my brain, and I'd be out of here in an hour. Given that you guys still basically are in the stage of alchemy, I don't have much of a choice, do I? Just tell me that there is hope. Tell me that one day maybe I'll love a woman. That I'll have a boy I can raise. And that I'll be in less pain!

I felt on safer ground now:

> I can tell you that much with a reasonable degree of certainty as I don't see any obvious psychopathology. People like you – who are basically healthy, have high ego strength, suffer from profound feelings of guilt and have relationship problems – tend to do well in psychodynamic psychotherapy. You have something like a sixty or seventy percent chance of being better in a few years' time. That's not much, but it's something, isn't it?

Jeff grinned. "Given the alternative of a one hundred percent chance of feeling like shit . . ."

I asked him whether he could tell me something about his background. He answered that he had grown up in a small town suburban environment. His parents were both born to immigrants who worked hard to give their children a better life. His paternal grandparents felt it was almost a miracle that their son was able to attend medical school, and Jeff's father never ceased to express his profound gratitude to them for giving him the option of a good life.

> My father's whole life was about doing good. He was a GP, and he never aspired to more. He loved his work; he cared for his patients; he cared for his wife; he cared for his children; he cared for his parents. He was

grateful for the house that we had; he was grateful for having a nice car; he was grateful for the barbecues with the neighbors. He was grateful, period. He was a good person, period.

And I was basically a piece of shit. I hated it all. I hated the barbecues; I hated the niceness of all these people who brought each other blueberry pie; I hated the discussions about baseball. I remember feeling when I was ten that if I was condemned to live my life like this, I'd be better off dying in an accident. All I could dream about was how to get out of there, and by age thirteen I knew that my ticket to the big world was my brain. I was smarter than anybody there, and I knew I had to use that to leave. I was basically counting the minutes.

So here I am. I made it. I got out. I'm here in Israel for a few weeks continuing my research on your bloody Israel–Palestine conflict, knowing that my results won't make any difference. But what the hell! I have a quarter-of-a-million-dollar grant that funds this, because my theory is hot stuff. I have partners here and they run the whole operation. I just fly in and out, speak on CNN and meet senior intelligence officials, diplomats and politicians.

And now I'm busy hating myself. I'm doomed, it seems. Maybe my problem wasn't small town life; maybe I have been born with a dissatisfaction gene that you guys haven't discovered yet.

Jeff's pain was considerable and I wondered what I could do to give him at least a little relief as we neared the end of this opening session. I generally refrain from commenting too much at the end of a first session, but I found myself saying:

I saw that you like dogs – you stopped to pat Freud on the way in. And I assume that you don't think that dogs can be impostors or anything of that sort. Freud wasn't bred to spend his life in an apartment, so we make sure that he has enough time to run, play with other dogs and chase after balls. If we didn't do that, he'd go nuts. He would become aggressive and difficult to handle.

It's not your fault that you were born with a powerful brain. It's like a very strong CPU that's been packed into a small box with not enough cooling. It'll run hot all the time. It's also not your fault that you need space. You can no more choose your temperament than Freud can. You can only learn how to channel it productively.

It seems to me that your main problem is not dissatisfaction. It's a strong propensity to feel overwhelming guilt: you feel guilty that you didn't give your parents the pleasure of feeling that they were giving you a good life in the same way as your father gave that pleasure to your grandfather; you feel guilty for having a life that is so much more interesting than your father's and because you're famous and respected. And as you feel so profoundly guilty, you cannot take the risk of loving, because you think you'll hurt those you love just as you think you have hurt your parents. Let's schedule the next session.

Intelligence and Fate

Jeff's story, like that of every other individual, is unique, so one needs to be very careful about generalizing from it. Yet, if one accepts the existence of the New Cosmopolitans, one assumes that they comprise a Gestalt, a group of people who have certain similarities.

Jeff exemplifies a dynamic that frequently drives individuals to work hard and move beyond the confines of the culture in which they are raised: his supreme intelligence, his natural curiosity and his instinctive dislike of stifling social norms made it almost impossible for him to live the type of suburban existence into which he was born. This is a recurring theme in many New Cosmopolitans' life stories (Strenger 2004). They feel different from their environment because of their innate intelligence. This creates complex character traits: on the one hand, they learn that they are more gifted, at least intellectually, than their peers and often their parents and teachers. But it is easy to overlook that this often condemns them to deep isolation: they tend to have few, if any, peers with whom they can share their interests and passions. They are often seen as brainy nerds, which makes them unpopular as children and adolescents. Because they do not feel that they safely belong to any groups, they tend to feel exposed and vulnerable for the rest of their lives. They are never confident that dominant groups will not turn against them.

This leads most New Cosmopolitans to develop a visceral antagonism to mob situations: they see natural groups as a source of danger and they are always wary of the tendency of groups to attack those who are different. Consequently, New Cosmopolitans typically combine superiority, or even arrogance, with a deep sense of insecurity. Many of them come into their own only when they finally find a network of like-minded people. In Jeff's case, academia provided this safe haven. This also explains why New Cosmopolitans tend to be meritocratic: they want to belong to tribes that demand effort and achievement and reward it, rather than to tribes that are based on territory, ethnicity or simple local belonging.

Naomi: Rebellion, Universalism and Guilt

I first met Naomi at a conference about Israel held in Paris. However, I had known of her before as she was very politically active. She belonged to a Jewish group that claimed that Jews in the Diaspora had both the right and the duty to criticize the Israeli government for immoral policies, primarily the occupation of the West Bank and the building of Jewish settlements there. I also knew that she was a respected figure in literary theory and had written a number of books about the deconstruction of ethnic, religious and gender identities. She had claimed, along with others in her field, that taking such identities too seriously created political and social problems and injustices.

I participated in the conference as a political commentator for Israel's leading liberal newspaper, *Haaretz*, not as a psychotherapist. I was therefore rather surprised when Naomi approached me and asked whether she could speak to me professionally. She explained that she would be traveling to Israel for a sabbatical in six months' time, and wondered whether I could take her into therapy. She had read some of my work and knew that I would be able to conduct the sessions in French. As I had no office in Paris, I suggested an initial Skype talk once I was back in Tel Aviv, which would help us decide whether I was the right therapist for her.

Ten days later, Naomi and I spoke from our respective offices. She was the daughter of two Polish–Jewish Holocaust survivors who had rebuilt their lives in Paris after the war. They were in their late thirties when she was born, and were overjoyed because they had thought they could not have children. They raised her with one major philosophy: after the catastrophe that had just befallen the Jewish people, it was their task – and Naomi's – to continue the struggle for Jewish continuity. They were Orthodox Jews, but quite open-minded, and strongly drawn to the work of an influential French–Lithuanian–Jewish philosopher, Emanuel Levinas. After he moved to Paris in the 1960s, they became part of a circle that studied with him. Naomi was therefore raised as an Orthodox Jew, but with strong ties to Western humanism.

Her conflict with her upbringing began when she studied philosophy and literature at one of Paris's leading universities, where she was exposed to post-colonialist thought. In the 1970s, the Palestinian struggle had become the post-colonial leftist's favorite cause. Naomi heard mordant criticism of Israel as an occupying power. She was told that the whole Zionist enterprise was racist to the core, and that the UN resolution of 1975 that equated Zionism with racism was just and right.

This initiated a very difficult period for Naomi. She had been brought up to support Israel, no matter what, and had viewed Palestinians as inhuman terrorists, having seen Black September murder twelve Israeli athletes at the 1972 Munich Olympics. She had also been raised with the narrative of Jewish history as a tragedy of persecution and suffering. Yet now she was confronted with an alternative narrative of Israel that went against all she believed. She felt that she could not talk to her parents about this. They had gone through too much, and she was afraid that even bringing up these topics would be unbearable for them. So she mustered all her courage and contacted her parent's guru, Emanuel Levinas, who at the time was a walking legend in French intellectual circles. To her surprise and relief, he agreed to meet her at the Sorbonne.

She started to talk to him about her parents, about her background and about what she was now hearing in her studies. She explained that she felt torn. Then, to her dismay, she began to cry uncontrollably. Levinas first sat silently, then told her that he understood precisely what she was saying because his own heart had been torn to pieces. He asked her not to quote him because – on a point of principle – he refused to take any position on current affairs, including criticizing Israel in public. However, he explained that he thought the occupation of the Palestinian territories was wrong, and suggested that Naomi should try to find a way to express her misgivings without delegitimizing Israel's existence per se.

Naomi felt that this meeting was a crucial turning point in her life. She began to seek out Jewish intellectuals who were Zionists and supported Israel, but were critical of the occupation. At the time, a new generation of such intellectuals was beginning to make its mark in France, and she felt that she had found a new group of peers.

Around the same time, she began to have doubts about Orthodox Judaism. She could not accept that Jewish women could not officiate in any ceremony, and that they had to pray in a separate area of the synagogue. She also had trouble with the idea that women were regarded as impure during menstruation and for a week thereafter. In general, she began to feel uncomfortable with having to accept male authority. Eventually, she found a place in a more flexible congregation, where she met her future husband. He was a kind man, a good-looking and caring physician who, she soon realized, would be a doting husband and father.

Before long, she turned her personal concerns about identity and gender into the focus of her academic career. It became her mission to show that various widely accepted forms of identity were but social constructions that stopped human beings from living free lives. She joined forces with a number of postmodern writers who were deconstructing notions of gender, national and ethnic identities around the same time.

It was only after both of her parents passed away that she became deeply involved with Israel. She joined French left-leaning groups that defended the country against delegitimation while forcefully criticizing its policies in the West Bank and the Gaza Strip. "I could never have done this while they were still alive," she explained. "It would have killed them."

This account of Naomi's background took up most of the first session. There were just ten minutes left, so I asked her whether she needed help with something specific. She hesitated for a minute, then said: "I have cheated on my husband for the last twenty years. I have had many, many affairs. I am a moral monster. And yet I can't stop it."

It turned out that this stylish, beautiful, almost aristocratic woman had led a double life for most of her adult life. Although married to a man whom she admired as a human being and cherished as a father and husband, she had almost obsessively pursued countless affairs with a wide variety of men: she was as likely to seduce a hotel bellboy as a successful businessmen. Her affairs rarely acquired any emotional depth, even though some of them continued for years.

Naomi felt terrible. She believed that her obsession had swallowed so much of her energy that she had not been a good mother to her two children (who, at this point, were already young adults). She was sure that they had suffered emotional damage from growing up with a mother whose heart was always elsewhere. She also felt that she had been utterly reckless, and was amazed that she had not been found out. She was a minor celebrity in France, and numerous people must have seen her during her countless furtive meetings with lovers. She ruefully said that she was probably lucky that French culture had always tolerated sexual escapades and that, at least in her circles, it was considered uncivilized to create scandals out of amorous affairs. She was not sure whether her husband knew. He had never confronted her, but she felt that he had become weak and somewhat bitter over the years. She suspected that he had simply accepted her behavior, and she was tortured with guilt over the suffering that this would have caused him.

Towards the end of the introductory session, almost as an aside, Naomi mentioned something that would turn out to be the key to understanding her obsession: not one of her affairs had been with a Jewish man, even though she met many of them in her social and academic circles.

I told her:

> Naomi, you have a complex biography and a complicated identity. I do not know yet why you have felt compelled to do something that you feel

deeply guilty about. We will have to find out what meanings you attach to love, loyalty and desire. We may find out that your conflicts about your political identity and your role as a wife and mother are related to each other. But it will take some time.

Between Family, Tribe and Humanity

Naomi's story is hers alone, but New Cosmopolitans worldwide, whether Christian, Muslim, Jewish or Hindu, experience the unbearable pull between the tribal loyalties that are programmed into our genes and the ethical universalism that reason prescribes. Her story and fate exemplify one of the New Cosmopolitans' deepest dilemmas. Like all human beings, they are born into a particular family, nation, culture and religion. All of these make demands on our loyalty: our nation tells us that we should be proud of its history and culture; our religion tell us to respect its prophets and its authority; our culture tells us that we should define who we are by its language, music and work.

Of course, conflict about nation, religion and tribe are by no means new. Ever since classical drama or the biblical story of Ruth the Moabite, this has been an enduring literary theme. But our historical period is unique in one respect: while the idea of universal human rights has been developing gradually since the Renaissance, after the Second World War the concretization of this program took on new forms. The UN Declaration of Human Rights was humankind's first attempt to build a framework that made individual human rights the touchstone by which every political and legal order should be measured. And since the 1970s an ever-growing number of institutions have developed to protect human rights from violation and infringement. The power of the human rights paradigm has been growing too, and it is gradually becoming the source of political and legal legitimacy as well as the basis for international criticism of states that continue to violate human rights. The abstract ideal of humanity as a whole is becoming a lived reality.

One of the New Cosmopolitans' most distinctive traits is that they instinctively accept the idea of universal human rights as a core value. They feel that any nation's or religion's claim of intrinsic superiority smacks of racism – and racism is probably the red rag that mobilizes New Cosmopolitans more than anything else. This ethical universalism almost inevitably creates conflict with nations' and religions' demands for unquestioning loyalty. This drama is being played out around the globe, and it is likely to continue for a long time yet. Think of the dreadful conflict experienced in the United States after 9/11 – when the patriotic impulse was stronger than ever – between the impulse to shoot terrorists on sight and the belief that human rights, even those of terror suspects, must be respected at all times.

The conflict between national, religious and tribal loyalties and the defense of universal human rights is ubiquitous. However, for a number of reasons, it has been played out with particular intensity and has commanded worldwide attention in the context of Israel and the Jewish people. Naomi's story helps to explain why. Her parents survived the most heinous genocide in the history of humanity, one that wiped out one-third of the Jewish people. They lost their parents and most of their extended families, and they saw at first hand the unspeakable depths of human evil. Like many Holocaust survivors, they felt that the only justifications for their own survival were to keep the memory of the deceased alive, and to contribute to the continued existence of the Jewish people. For them, as for so many of their generation, the birth of the state of Israel was almost a miracle: from the ashes of the Holocaust, Jews, for the first time in millennia, were no longer the victims of history but its makers. Here was a state that managed to apprehend one of the central perpetrators of the Holocaust, Adolf Eichmann, in Argentina and bring him to justice. It also vanquished the Arab armies that tried to wipe it off the map three times in three decades. After all that the Jewish people had gone through, Naomi's parents were unflinching in their determination to support Israel in every way possible.

But for many Jews of liberal temperament, the moral consequence of the Holocaust was very different: it was not "never again must anything like this happen to us Jews" but "never again must anything like this happen to *anybody*, anywhere, whatever their color, creed or nationality." This sentiment has drawn a large number of Jews into the New Cosmopolitan tribe; it was why Jews in the United States fought alongside blacks in the Civil Rights movement; and it is why many Jews are now engaged in the campaign for human rights around the world.

This conflict between remaining loyal to one's nation and upholding the principle of universal human rights was at the core of Naomi's troubles. In the later stages of her therapy, it emerged that she had not succeeded in overcoming the dichotomy between love for and loyalty to her family and desire, both intellectual and sexual. She had accepted her parents' injunction that she must be loyal to her nation and religion. In her political and academic work, she had returned to the issue of Jewish identity time and again. But she also felt stifled, even suffocated, by such a narrow focus, and believed that she could be free only if she followed her intellectual and sexual desires, wherever they led her. Her intellect told her that ethical universalism was more important and valid than tribal loyalty. This, it transpired later in the therapy, was why her sexual desire was invariably aroused by those outside her tribe, and why all of her affairs were with Gentiles.

Ben: "I have not achieved anything of value"

Ben emailed me from New York, giving me the dates when he would be in Tel Aviv, and asked for an appointment. He was in his mid-fifties, and split his time between Tel Aviv, Paris and New York. You would never have guessed that this wiry, tanned man, with almost translucent skin because of very low body fat, had been quite chubby just four years earlier. His skull was clean shaven, and he dressed in jeans, a T-shirt and sneakers.

The session began with Ben explaining why he had contacted me:

> I need to figure out what really matters to me. I've fulfilled the Israeli dream. I founded a startup company, and I took it all the way to the Nasdaq. I basically no longer need to work; my children and the grandchildren I do not yet have are financially safe for the rest of their lives. I never thought that it also creates a problem when you no longer *have* to do something for a living and when you can ask what you really want. It's quite frightening when you can't find a clear answer to this . . .
>
> Since I retired as active chair of my company four years ago, I've tried a number of things. It all began when my doctor told me that my cholesterol was sky high and that he didn't like the general look of my physical health, and that I should start working out. That soon turned into an obsession: I lost twenty-five kilos, I employed a running coach, and eighteen months after my doctor's injunction I ran my first marathon. Now I run five a year. I'm registered three years ahead for all the major ones.
>
> But running marathons isn't exactly a way to spend one's life. So I've dabbled in philanthropy: I've joined the board of an international human rights NGO; I've even considered entering politics; I invest some money in technology startups; I try to mentor young entrepreneurs. I do all these things that are supposed to be good for humanity . . . and meaningful. My problem is that none of it *feels* meaningful. I feel as if I'm just busy trying to keep my calendar full.
>
> I'm also in a marital crisis. I got married when I was twenty-five, and we celebrated our silver wedding anniversary three years ago. Even then I was very unsure whether I could carry on. I deeply respect my wife; she's been incredibly kind to me and she's raised our three kids wonderfully with a husband who, most of the time, was working sixteen hours a day. But I wonder whether we've reached a dead end. These days I use every pretext to be in a different city than she is. And I've had a number of affairs.

He suddenly looked embarrassed: "My God! I must sound like the classic midlife crisis. So cliché . . ."

I replied: "Ben, even if this question happens to be prevalent in midlife, this is still *your* life, so we need to find *your* way to create new meaning in your life."

Ben's expression changed and he suddenly looked very serious, almost angry. "Do you really believe in this 'meaning' business?" he asked. "To me, it all seems like one big hoax. There is no meaning: either you do something that you find interesting or you don't."

I was a little surprised by the intensity of his tone. Up to that point he had sounded relaxed, almost amused. "I haven't said anything about meaning being objective. But surely you agree that we either experience something as meaningful or we don't? It's not just all about fun, is it?"

Now Ben exuded pain:

> Sorry that I snapped at you. You actually stepped on a sore point. I'm actually *very* preoccupied with the question of whether I do anything of value. To be precise, I often wonder whether I have *ever* done anything of value. True, I've made a lot of money; I have created hundreds of jobs directly and probably thousands indirectly. The product I developed is used in millions of servers. Yet I think: "Some of our competitors' products are not bad. Humanity would live exactly the same if I'd never been on the planet." I don't know whether I ever made a difference; and I'm even more worried that I'll *never* make one.

"How long have you felt this way?" I asked.

Ben rediscovered his humorous tone:

> You certainly want to hear that it's been like this for the last few years, then I'd fit perfectly into the scheme: midlife, increasing awareness of death, then the question of meaning sets in! And it would also fit excellently into my having turned into a marathon runner, trying to prove that age cannot vanquish me.

I wanted to help Ben to stop classifying himself, and instead be more attentive to what he was actually feeling:

> I don't know what I want to hear, Ben, except exactly what has been going on with you, and how you have developed. There certainly are some ubiquitous patterns like the one you have described. But it won't solve the

problem if we just put you into a diagnostic category; we'll still have to understand your very specific life. It certainly seems that you're not making it easy for yourself if you feel that, in order to have lived a significant life, you must have left a mark on humanity.

He looked at me intently. "Well, this might sound grandiose, but I seriously feel that, without leaving a real mark, life is kind of pointless. But doesn't *everybody* feel that way, at least to a certain extent?"

"For most people it's enough to feel that they have mattered to those who are close to them; or even those they've worked with. I think you demand more of yourself than most people do."

He shook his head. "But isn't this logical, actually? Isn't it something like a duty? I have more money than I'll ever need. I have access to anybody I could possibly want to meet. And I have a lot of experience. Doesn't that create some kind of duty?"

Fear of Insignificance

I was well acquainted with Ben's conundrum. I had worked with a number of people who had displayed great ability early in life, and who had both the financial and the personal means to make a difference, and I had come to realize that they frequently suffered from a deep sense of existential guilt about not realizing their full potential (Strenger 2011a). This is becoming a significant problem for many gifted New Cosmopolitans. Never in the history of humankind have so many people generated such wealth in such a short period of time (Reich 2005). And never in the history of humankind have so many relatively young people – including Steve Jobs, Sergei Brin and Larry Page – literally changed the world in profound ways.

This creates a conundrum for gifted New Cosmopolitans: how can they be sure that they have tried hard enough (Conley 2009)? After all, talent and effort are never alone in determining what somebody achieves in the end. There is always the unfathomable factor of luck, timing, coincidence or whatever name we give the circumstantial, elusive element that makes the difference between success and failure. I firmly believe that it is not a desire for fame, recognition or wealth that motivates the New Cosmopolitans' skyrocketing expectations for their lives and achievements. In fact, many of these people, like Ben, are rather self-effacing; they do not seek media attention; and they live relatively modestly, given their bank balances. They genuinely believe that it is their duty to do something special and contribute something that will truly make a difference to humankind (Sloterdijk 2009).

Self-esteem is, by its very nature, comparative, and depends on the range of comparison. Maintaining self-esteem has therefore become much more difficult for the New Cosmopolitans. In the distant evolutionary past, our ancestors' self-esteem was based on their standing within a small horde of a few dozen others. Even in the relatively recent past, most people felt that the relevant scale of comparison that defined whether they were doing well, whether they were valuable human beings, was local. We all need to feel that we are making some sort of a difference in order to feel valuable, but the global scale of comparison is making it progressively more difficult for the New Cosmopolitans to answer the nagging question of whether their lives are significant.

Ben is wealthy by almost anybody's standards, and his life is a well-documented success story. Yet he tortures himself because he feels that he hasn't made a mark. He is haunted by age and wonders whether his best days are behind him. He does not want to live on the laurels of his past; he wants to leave an impact in the decades to come, but he is far from sure that he will be able to do so. The New Cosmopolitans care about contributing something to the world (Appiah 2006). The problem is that their experiential framework embraces the whole globe, and it is much more difficult to make a difference on such a vast scale.

Jeff, the political scientist, felt that his achievement was a sham. His colleagues might have raved about his mathematical models on conflict resolution, but he suspected they were worthless. He is possibly the strongest example of the impostor syndrome among this book's protagonists; he is haunted by dreams in which his high-school teachers prove that his models are invalid.

The New Cosmopolitans have high expectations of life, and the demands they put on themselves are often exorbitant. In contrast to the company men described in the 1950s and 1960s (Riesman 1950), they do not feel at the mercy of their bosses. As Brooks (2000) shows, they have integrated the liberation ethos of the sixties revolution into their way of life. They insist on preserving their freedom, and thus renounce a number of the existential moorings found in more traditional forms of life: they cannot rely on family, community, religion or national identity as a matter of course. Their careers mostly evolve through lateral moves, not only because they want to progress quickly, but because they want to experience a variety of places and contexts. This is the New Cosmopolitans' strength: the better they are at what they do, the more bargaining power they have, because their employers know that they will be in demand almost anywhere. Most of them need to make career decisions every few years, often involving relocation. The price of their freedom is that they need to run their CVs on a tight schedule to count as success stories, and this means that they can rely less on long-standing support networks that have remained stable for many years. Careers have always had timelines and measures of excellence. But today's New Cosmopolitans compete on a global scale, and this is also their weakness: in a globally competitive market, career timelines become an integral part of their market value. How soon have they made it into the higher executive ranks? Have the companies that employ them earmarked them for the fast track, or have they fallen into the category of those who will merely trundle along (Strenger 2011a: ch. 2)?

It is usually when New Cosmopolitans reach their mid-thirties that they start to worry about failing to leave their mark. Jeff's anxiety exemplified this: he was doing well by most standards; he was a respected academic, in high demand at elite institutions. Nevertheless, he labored under the fear of insignificance. He went into academia because he wanted to make a difference, but ended up feeling that the academic network was limited; that his work had some resonance in his discipline, but not in the wider world. Similarly, Ben was hugely successful in his high-tech industry by almost anybody's standards. Nevertheless, he felt that he had not left a lasting mark. Hence, like Jeff, he believed that he had failed to live up to the New Cosmopolitans' categorical imperative of transforming the world.

Mark: Breaking Family Traditions

Mark's first email to me read:

> Dear Dr. Strenger. I'm writing to you even though I assume that you are following the venerable tradition of shrinks to be away for August. I have read a number of your publications, and I wonder whether you would have time to see me. Looking forward to hearing from you. Mark.

Common lore has it that shrinks always take their vacations in August. I've never quite understood why we should do that. In the northern hemisphere you can hardly find a place that's not sweltering with heat and/or flooded with tourists throughout the whole month. Hence, I prefer to lock myself in my air-conditioned study in August, which is fine when I have a book project on the go but a pretty bad idea otherwise, because that is when the questions asked all too often by my New Cosmopolitan patients start to enter my mind, too. Is my life of any value? Am I doing something to justify my existence? Finally, after many years, I am starting to follow the advice I give my patients: don't even ask those questions; life can never be justified; once you ask whether your life has value, you will inevitably go into a tailspin.

I had no book project during that particular summer, so, within a few days, Mark arrived at my office. Typically, the room was quite a mess, but I was more aware of it than usual on account of Mark's phenomenal tidiness. He had dressed quite appropriately for a Tel Aviv summer's day: white linen shirt with the upper three buttons open; three-quarter-length pants; and very light moccasins without socks. You could have called his appearance casual if it hadn't been so pitch perfect in its aesthetic balance. His movement completed the impression: it was fluid, easygoing and almost studiously relaxed.

First meetings are always tricky. Most patients invest a lot of thought into how they will present themselves. They want to be understood, so they want to be precise. But that creates a dilemma: after all, even a psychotherapeutic intake session is a human encounter, and the human desire to make a good impression cannot be eradicated. Incidentally, this holds true for therapists as well: whenever a new patient arrives for the first time, I am painfully aware of my chronic inability to keep my room in order, and the thought invariably crosses my mind at least to put the various papers into a single pile when I hear the doorbell ringing. Of course, by then it's too late. After we sit down, however, I am usually able to focus on getting to know the new patient and forget all about the shortcomings of my consulting room.

Mark made me apprehensive, though. Most patients sit down quickly when I tell them which of my two identical Eames armchairs is theirs, then focus on how to start talking about themselves. Mark took more time; he scanned the room; he seemed to take in all of the details; and only then did he sit down gracefully. He graciously thanked me for seeing him at such short notice, and said he was pleasantly surprised that I was seeing patients in August. He seemed more comfortable in the situation of a first meeting than most people are, and I noticed that his eyes were now roaming my library. I sensed that he was sizing me up, trying to get an impression of who I am, which made me feel vaguely uncomfortable. I made a mental note of this and wondered if he made people uncomfortable in general. This was good professionalism, but it also helped me to establish some distance from the discomfort I was experiencing.

Mark continued to be courteous. He asked if there was any particular order in which I would like this first interview to be conducted. I told him that he should not feel that every word he said carried too much weight; that a first meeting was more about general impressions, and that I would not pigeonhole him on details. Nevertheless, it would help if he could give me some basic information about himself and his life circumstances.

Mark smiled and said:

> There is an obvious dilemma here. On paper, I'm not here to impress or to entertain you. But how exactly can I get over these first few minutes without doing the little pitch of casually mentioning a few facts about myself that will leave you duly impressed?

I laughed, already impressed by his sophisticated self-awareness and the way he communicated it. "Why don't you just do 'the little pitch' then?"

Mark effortlessly moved into a self-presentation that made all the points he needed to make to convince me that he was gifted, worldly and successful without being overly ostentatious. He was in Tel Aviv on a fact-finding mission for a major private equity fund from the US East Coast. He checked whether the name was familiar to me (it was) without making it too obvious that this was what he was doing. They were looking into various possibilities of investing in Israel's thriving high-tech startup market. Mark was unsure how long he would be in town; in part, it depended on the model that he would devise. He paused briefly, then said: "I think I should probably mention that I am homosexual."

I was surprised by his choice of phrase – I would have expected him to say that he was gay – but even more by his pronunciation. It was almost quaint: he said the word in much the same way as a far older American might enunciate it, with long, drawn-out "o"s, almost as if he felt that both the term itself and the phenomenon were difficult to stomach.

After another short hesitation, Mark asked, "I assume that you need to know a bit about my background, don't you?" Again I noted his great courtesy, the way he was trying to accommodate my needs, so to speak.

He told me he came from a well-established East Coast family. They were Irish Catholics but their ancestors had immigrated to the United States long before the great wave of Irish immigration in the nineteenth century. According to Mark's description, they had developed an almost aristocratic self-consciousness and bearing. Mark's great-grandfather had built a law firm and, despite the handicap of being Catholic-owned, it had become a fixture of the city. The wealthiest local families still entrusted their business and family affairs to it, just as they had for the previous one hundred and fifty years.

> My grandfather and my father resisted the temptation to merge with other major firms, even though this had a major downside. Corporate clients prefer huge law firms with nationwide offices, and it was clear that by refusing the merger offers over the last fifty years they made a conscious

choice to forgo some very lucrative clients. They preferred to keep the firm comparatively small and to stick to their traditional clients: wealthy families who wanted counsel they trusted personally.

Mark explained that the family had always been extremely cautious about who they employed:

> My father and my grandfather very consciously differentiated themselves from the new high-powered firms that were expanding at great pace. They were very careful not to take in the super-ambitious graduates who were obviously looking for fast careers and craved shiny status symbols. They were unimpressed by candidates who showed off their brilliance and tried to give the impression that they were willing to work very hard to be successful. This was one reason why they looked deep into the backgrounds of potential candidates, and preferred those who came from privileged backgrounds. They didn't want them to be too hungry. And they also wanted men who had the poise and class that often comes with such a background; they wanted their clients to feel at ease with every lawyer at the firm. This wasn't just snobbery, it was sound business sense; they did not want to expand, and they knew that the firm's cachet was one of its assets.

Despite keeping the firm small, the family had done very well financially. Sound investments over many years had created a sizable family fortune that was managed conservatively and with great care. Mark said: "In our family nobody would say something as ugly as 'We are rich.' We thought of ourselves as 'comfortable' and 'well established.' 'Rich' was a term for social upstarts; not for us."

Then there was religion. Mark described his family as devout but by no means bigoted. For generations, the family had preferred their children to marry other Catholics, but they didn't make it a principle. A number of sons and daughters had indeed married into WASP families, and that was fine.

"Jews were a different matter", Mark said with a fleeting smile.

> Until a few decades ago, the idea of a Jew marrying into the family was utterly anathema. I wouldn't say that my grandfather was anti-Semitic. He just didn't like Jews, if you know what I mean; nor did the circles in which he moved, the clubs he belonged to. I would say the family disliked Jews about as much as America's higher classes did in general at that time. This changed in the 1970s, when a twice-removed cousin of mine married a

> Jewish physician. He was a star surgeon, so that was fine in terms of prestige; and I think the family realized that keeping a distance from Jews was no longer fashionable, so they didn't make a fuss about it.

I asked Mark whether he mentioned this because I was Jewish. "Oh no," he said with another smile. "I just want you to get a sense of the family tradition. I think you will find it important to understand my own mentality."

His father became the family firm's managing partner when Mark was in his teens.

> Physically, you can imagine him as quite similar to me – or, of course, I should say I'm quite similar to him. We are all at least six feet one; we are all athletic; and most of us are reddish blonds, but luckily we all tan well. A good breed, if you don't mind my saying so.

Listening to Mark, I became quite intrigued. He spoke about his family background with pride, and seemingly with great love. Yet there seemed to be a light tinge of irony – as if he was trying to indicate that he didn't take this family honor quite as seriously as others. I wondered whether he was doing this because he assumed, correctly, that my family has no such aristocratic bearing; because I am Jewish; or because his relationship with his background was more complex than he had made explicit so far.

I wanted to know more about why he felt he needed help, so I asked him to explain why he had come to see me. Mark tensed up visibly and fell silent. I said, "Mark, it's completely understandable if it's a bit difficult to talk about this. You are about to talk about the most intimate aspects of your life to somebody whom you have known for barely twenty minutes."

His smile was slightly forced, but then he spoke for several minutes without a break:

> Well, I understand it's time to move on to the next subject matter. Let me first say that I have been overtly homosexual since the age of eighteen. I had become aware of my homosexuality at age twelve or thirteen. Before that I didn't quite differentiate between the friendship I felt towards some boys and my erotic leanings. At first I simply thought that it was natural that I liked to hug my friends, but then I realized that there was more to this. I tried to push it aside, and began dating girls. In our family and our circles homosexuality was not spoken about, and I didn't know any openly homosexual people. I began to read about it; I tried to get my hands on

novels about homosexuality. And by the age of fifteen it was clear to me that I was homosexual.

I was utterly mortified. I knew that homosexuality was an unspeakable sin; and I assumed that my parents would never accept a homosexual son. I didn't know what to do. We had a family doctor who had known me since I was a child, and whom I trusted. I spoke to him. He was very good about this. He said that he understood, and asked me whether I wanted him to speak to my parents about this. But then he said, "There is no choice, my son. You can't go on without talking to your parents."

In the next day or two I was frantic. I tried to read my parents' faces. Did they know already? What did they think? What did they feel? In our family, nobody wears his heart on his sleeve; everybody is emotionally rather restrained.

Anyway, after three days, my father asked me to come to his study. He was very calm and collected. He told me that he had had a long conversation with the family doctor. That he had understood from him that nowadays homosexuality was no longer considered to be pathology; that it had been removed from the diagnostic handbook of psychiatry. He said to me, "I want to make it very clear to you, Mark. You are our son, and you will be our son no matter what. But I don't need to tell you that we take religion very seriously; and you know that the Church considers homosexuality an abomination. I have asked the doctor to make enquiries. I understand that there are psychiatric methods that might conceivably change people's sexual orientation. I assume that there is an element of choice about sexuality; otherwise, our religion would not forbid it. I would suggest that you see a psychiatrist and see what can be done."

I felt two things: first, tremendous relief that my dad was so calm and collected; second, I realized that, even though he said that I would still be their son, they would never truly be able to accept me as a homosexual. So I went to see that psychiatrist. I'll make it short: the therapy failed miserably, and I knew I would be homosexual for the rest of my life.

At age eighteen, I decided to move away. I knew that I couldn't live an openly homosexual life in my parents' vicinity. Even though my family had been alumni of one of the East Coast's most prestigious universities, I opted for a West Coast college. I knew that this also meant that I would never be part of the family firm, even though, since childhood, it had been clear to me, and to everybody else, that I would be.

As I said, I have been openly homosexual for eighteen years now. But I have never succeeded in building a stable relationship, and I am beginning to feel lonely. I see homosexual couples who build families, adopt children. I've never gotten even close to this. Do you think you can help me, Dr. Strenger?

Mark's tone of voice had changed in the last quarter of an hour. He still spoke with restraint, but there was a powerful sense that he was keeping a huge, deep pain locked in his chest. I was moved, and many thoughts crossed my mind.

> Mark, this is just a first session, so it would be reckless for me to suggest that I already know what I can do for you. But I would like to share two thoughts with you before we end this session. The first is that I have been struck from the very beginning by your pronunciation of the word "homosexuality." You sound as if you are from a different age whenever you use it. I wonder whether this means that somewhere, deep down, your relationship with your sexuality is still strongly influenced by your background. I will have to know more about your religious views to gain some more understanding of this.
>
> The second thing is that you are extremely courteous. I felt that you are so concerned with making me feel at ease that you can't allow yourself to express your feelings more openly. Nevertheless, I can sense the huge pain you're carrying inside yourself. I hope that, as we get to know each other better, you will start to feel more at ease.

Mark's eyes seemed to express gratitude. I thought, but did not yet tell him, that he was still powerfully bound to his family, even though he had lived apart from them for a long time.

Excommunication and the Liberal Impulse

Mark exemplifies a slightly different style of New Cosmopolitan existence. When he came to therapy, he was more conservative in his tastes than Jeff. He put great value on style, appreciated some of the trappings of his upper-class lifestyle, and took pride in his exquisite taste in everything from clothes and art to wine.

Yet his story shows another way in which New Cosmopolitans can be forced out into the wider world. Those who do not fit into their environment, for whatever reason, often suffer a cruel fate: they feel excommunicated. Often quite early in life, they realize that the protection their community of origin has given them depends on certain norms and assumptions that they do not meet.

In Mark's case, his sexual orientation – something that he firmly believed he could not choose as it had been imposed on him by nature – pushed him out of his environment. It was simply part of who he was. I say this without venturing into the contentious issue of how sexual orientation evolves. The phenomenological fact is that the vast majority of gay people – particularly males, but also females – do not feel that they have any more choice about their sexual orientation than they have about their hair color. At most, they can merely cover it up.

Excommunication is a harrowing, frightening and deeply painful experience; and more often than not, its impact is negative. The lives of those who feel that their communities no longer accept them can take tragic turns. They can develop negative identities, feeling bad and rejected. Many of them join groups of other social outsiders who unite around their shared experiences. This can lead to detrimental results, ranging from drug abuse to criminality.

New Cosmopolitans are mostly protected from such a fate by their superior intellectual gifts. Like Jeff and Mark, they are likely to find new identities that are positive and constructive. Mark had the background and talent to move effortlessly into another world – international finance. This suited some of the cherished traits his family had given him: style and a certain elitist flair. It is therefore easy to believe that such New Cosmopolitans must feel very good about themselves. But the early experience of not fitting in tends to remain very painful, as both Mark and Jeff show in their different ways. And it is an experience that is sure to stay with them for the rest of their lives.

Ella: Making the Past Right

I knew Ella's striking face from television, as I had seen her reports from a variety of war zones. The thought had crossed my mind a number of times that she did not fit the traditional image of a war correspondent: she was petite; her features were soft; her skin was almost translucent. Yet she succeeded in projecting an air of authority and strength.

She contacted me by phone to ask for a consultation. She was in Israel at the time, covering the growing tension generated by the incessant shelling of the south of the country from the Gaza Strip. When she entered my consulting room I noted, once again, her combination of delicacy and strength. I was also struck by the formality of her appearance: her blond hair was pulled back tightly; and she was dressed in a dark, knee-length skirt and formal buttoned blouse.

She seemed very tense when she sat down, didn't lean back, and her crossed legs gave the impression of coils that were ready to jump. As she had on the phone, she first spoke to me in English, which I found surprising, as I assumed she knew that I am fluent in German. She looked around the consulting room, her gaze skimming a few bookcases, then directly at me with an expression of surprise.

"Strange. I don't know how to begin . . ."

"What do you think is the matter?" I asked.

"Somehow . . . I feel that I don't have a good reason to be here. You probably treat people with severe problems. I'm suddenly afraid that it will seem as if I'm just a spoiled brat."

"Ella, I assume that people who seek help always have a good reason to do so. Why don't you just start telling me about yourself?"

> OK. I'll start with the immediate reason why I am here. I am thirty-six years old, I am not married, and I don't intend to marry. I have no children by choice, and I'm pretty sure that I don't want any. For obvious reasons, I will soon not be able to give birth. I have decided that I owe it to myself at least to make sure that my decision not to have children is well grounded. Is that a good reason for therapy?

"I certainly think so. Would you like to tell me for how long you have thought that you do not want children?"

She hesitated, then said:

> I think there are two answers to this. For a long time I have thought that I made this decision on my thirtieth birthday. I was in London at the time. I had just had one of the major breakthroughs of my career in journalism, when the network decided to formalize my position as foreign correspondent. I hadn't been in a stable relationship for a while, but didn't really miss it.
>
> I didn't have any close friends in London, so I decided just to have some acquaintances and colleagues over for drinks to celebrate my birthday. The evening was enjoyable; people congratulated me on my job. I knew that within a few days I would probably be flying to Afghanistan, and I was thrilled about that. Everything felt light; everything seemed so open-ended. Life seemed full of possibilities. For some reason, the discussion turned to Milan Kundera's novel *The Unbearable Lightness of Being*, which, it turned out, most of the people in the room had read. Somebody suggested that each of us should say which character we identified with and why.
>
> Most of the women chose Tereza, the photographer whose quest is for a man to love her so deeply that she will feel recognized and vindicated as an individual human being and as a woman. The men split quite evenly

> between Tomas, the surgeon who never commits to a relationship and lives according to the principle of non-binding erotic friendship, and Franz, the professor who tries to make unhappy women – his mother and his wife – happy, and who is searching for a larger cause to which he can devote his life. Nobody chose Sabina, the painter whose deepest motivation is that she needs something or somebody to be unfaithful to, because she hates the collectivist, totalitarian environment in which she grew up so deeply.
>
> When my turn came, I said that I had a dilemma. I felt most like Tomas, because of his detachment, his refusal to be tied down and his endless curiosity. But I also identified with Sabina, because of her hatred for totalitarianism. The people at the party insisted that I must decide, that the rule of the game was that you had to commit to just one character. At that point I remembered the paragraph where Kundera condenses Tomas' past. Tomas divorces, then has endless fights with his ex-wife about his son's education. Finally, he can no longer take it, so he severs all ties with his ex-wife and his son. As a result, his parents break off all contact with him. Then there is a sentence that has stuck in my mind ever since I first read it: "Thus, in practically no time he managed to rid himself of wife, son, mother and father."

Ella paused.

> I have always found that sentence truly comforting. The idea that you can rid yourself of all connection to your family was immensely attractive to me. I had only one problem: I thought that it was deeply immoral for Tomas to cut his ties to his son. A wife you can divorce; and if you hate your parents, you can cut your ties with them. But you should never do that to a child.
>
> So, in the end, I chose Sabina, because she was consistent. She made sure she never had ties that she couldn't cut at any time. And then I realized that this meant that I did not want children, because I would never walk away from a child. This, I thought for a long time, was the evening when I decided not to have any children. But in the last year or two, I've started to think that the decision was made much earlier, in my teens.

"Why? What happened then?" I asked.

She looked at me with a stony expression. Her blue eyes expressed cold rage. "I found out that my grandfather had been an SS Obersturmbannführer."

There was a long silence; Ella's expression remained stony.

I tried to take in what I had just heard. I tried to imagine the terrible shock she must have felt. Then the question crossed my mind: "How could anybody live with this knowledge?" I wanted her to tell me more, but didn't want to push. Then, out of nowhere, I found myself saying: "Is this why you speak to me in English rather than in German?"

She seemed puzzled, but then smiled.

> This is really strange. One of the reasons why I sought you out was that I saw an interview with you on a German TV channel. I found your analysis of Israel very interesting and looked you up. When I learned that you're a practicing analyst I thought: "If I ever want to do therapy, this might be the guy. He speaks German; he's Jewish; and he lives in Israel."

"What did my being Jewish and living in Israel have to do with making that decision?" I asked.

> In the year I found out about my grandfather's Nazi background, I joined an organization called Aktion Sühnezeichen, which organizes trips to Israel for young Germans who want to deal with German responsibility for the Holocaust. I spent a summer here, then a few more. So Israel has always played an important role for me.
>
> Your being Jewish matters, because I . . . for some reason I couldn't trust a German Gentile on this matter. I know it's irrational. I can't explain it.

"Have you noticed that you are still speaking in English?" I asked.

She shook her head violently:

> I can't speak in German now. Please don't push me. And don't speak to me in German, unless I tell you to. *Please*. This is important. I can't explain it, but it's important.
>
> You may have noticed that I work for English-speaking channels. It's been tremendously important for me to do that. At age eighteen I decided that I wanted to become an investigative journalist. I wanted to unmask lies; I wanted to tell the world the truth. And I decided that I had to do this in English. English has been a protection for me. The fact that there are global media is a blessing for me. I feel protected by their power, by their reach, by the fact that they broadcast in English. And, for the time being, I need that protection here as well.

The session was nearing its end, so I said:

> Ella, you said at the beginning that you were afraid I would look at you as a spoiled brat. From the little I have heard, I feel that you have every reason to want to find a place to sort out your feelings and thoughts. I hope that I will be able to help, but I don't think this journey will be short.

Global Networks as Home

It was a long time before Ella was able to tell me her whole story. It turned out that she had never forgiven her parents for hiding her grandfather's past from her. And it was a long time before she was able to mend her relationship with Germany. It also turned out that English had indeed become her language of choice, even though it was not her native tongue.

Ella had very specific reasons for putting distance between herself and her family, but she exemplifies a theme that is often found in the lives of other New Cosmopolitans. Almost without exception, they have good command of English, and many of them use it at least in their professional lives, whatever their mother tongues may be.

Ostensibly, this is done for pragmatic reasons. New Cosmopolitans work mostly within global networks: academia, the media, technology, global NGOs and the financial sector all function primarily in English, which has become the world's *lingua franca.* So fluency in it is a prerequisite for succeeding in these networks. However, for a large proportion of New Cosmopolitans, English also becomes something of a second home. Because they are so tightly linked to the global networks in which they work and live, the language plays a deeper role in their identities than it might do otherwise: it allows them to live as they do and, in a profound sense, to be who they are.

The specifics of Ella's story are, of course, atypical of most New Cosmopolitans. But one aspect of her development can be identified in almost all of her peers: as we also saw with Jeff, Mark and Naomi, something in the basic New Cosmopolitan character feels stifled by locality. They always feel that they need open space, and each of them, in their own way, experienced tremendous relief when they realized that they could join networks that spanned countries, continents and cultures.

Cosmopolitanism becomes much more than practical worldliness and a tool for success: it becomes the center of the New Cosmopolitans' identities. They may love the city where they live, be it New York, Paris, London, Tel Aviv or Bangalore. But they also have an instinctive need to know that they can move elsewhere; that their network allows them to make that move; that they will never be trapped in one place if they want to leave. They also feel that their network is not only powerful but represents the best of humanity: rationality, justice and compassion.

The following chapter will show that one of Freud's more interesting, albeit little discussed, speculations can be applied to improve our understanding of and assist an iconic group in today's culture: the global entrepreneurs.

Chapter 4

Global Entrepreneurs

Myths and Realities

The archetypal hero of the New Cosmopolitans is the entrepreneur who has changed the world. As we saw in the previous chapter, such figures as Bill Gates, Steve Jobs, Sergei Brin, Larry Page and Mark Zuckerberg have risen to prominence over recent decades. Their staggering impact on the way we live is undeniable, and they cast a huge shadow over the New Cosmopolitans. But this undeniable reality has also created a pornography of success: the press keeps running totals of all of these icons' personal fortunes, publishes details of how much the companies they founded are worth, produces graphs showing the number of users they have acquired (or lost) and fills pages with the great rivalries between Apple, Google, Microsoft and Facebook.

Another aspect of this pornography is the inevitable question of whether there is a recipe that will enable aspiring New Cosmopolitans to emulate their icons' achievements. The answer, to all intents and purposes, is that there is not. Malcolm Gladwell (2008) has synthesized an impressive array of data to show that, in addition to talent, determination and courage, the goddess Fortuna plays an enormous role in determining who will become a global icon, who will become "only" a successful entrepreneur, and who will fail miserably. Nevertheless, the question remains whether certain psychodynamic factors might predispose some entrepreneurs to success and others to failure.

This chapter presents a psychodynamic hypothesis that formulates some necessary conditions for entrepreneurial success. It may come as a surprise that the inspiration for this model was Freud's short book on Leonardo da Vinci, published in the early twentieth century (Freud 1910). I first read this book as an adolescent, and it generated two contradictory responses in me that have remained consistent to this day: I found – and find – its basic hypothesis both intriguing and counter-intuitive.

Freud tells us that Leonardo da Vinci was the illegitimate son of a Florentine nobleman who did not acknowledge his paternity until Leonardo was five years old. Leonardo therefore spent those first five years alone with his doting mother. Thereafter, his father legitimized him and took him into his home. Freud formulates an intriguing hypothesis from this: until the age of five, Leonardo did not experience the weight of forbidding paternal authority, hence his infantile curiosity about sexual and other matters was uninhibited. Freud's image of the father was primarily that of a (literally and metaphorically) forbidding authority figure (Freud 1905). Hence, he believed that fatherlessness could be liberating.

As a result, Leonardo developed a mind that could roam freely. This would later lead him tirelessly to investigate nature, the laws of painting and perspective, mechanics and any other topic that caught his attention, without relying on external authority. Of course, he is most famous now for his talent as a painter, but he was also a multi-talented entrepreneur, engineer and inventor, not to mention a good salesman: he moved restlessly from one Italian city-state to the next, selling his services to the highest bidder.

If it has some truth value, Freud's hypothesis might explain why entrepreneurs display a disproportionately high frequency of fatherlessness. After all, they need to branch out on their own. They need to feel that they do not need external permission to do their own thing. And they need an extraordinarily high degree of independence to build their own framework. Therefore, I shall call the idea that fatherlessness contributes to the propensity for entrepreneurship the *Leonardo effect.*

As mentioned, Freud's hypothesis also seems counter-intuitive: after all, most research on the matter both in psychology (Lamb 1997) and in sociology and cultural studies (Faludi 2011) shows clearly that fatherlessness is one of the most powerful factors predisposing young men to spiral into crime, drug use and a persistent lack of direction – that is, the precise opposites of the character traits required for successful entrepreneurship. One of the more entrenched assumptions of both common sense and academic psychology is that good fathering is crucial in the development of positive masculine identity. If the father is strong, consistent, caring and provides a positive identification model, his sons are likely to develop similar character traits (Lamb 1997). So, if that is the case, why should weak, absent and inefficient fathers be relatively typical of male entrepreneurs? What role does a failing father or fatherlessness – as I call the experience of growing up with insufficient male parenting – play in shaping the entrepreneurial psyche?

I will attempt to integrate Freud's idea about the Leonardo effect with the cumulative evidence to the contrary – that is, that fatherlessness generally has highly negative results – through the following hypothesis: men who come to terms with their fatherlessness and, in a psychological sense, become their own fathers are capable of creating successful businesses (as long as they have the intellectual and temperamental tendency and tools for business, of course). Others never come to terms with their fatherlessness, so, even if they become entrepreneurs, they continue to suffer from an inner void, rage and difficulty with authority. As a result, they are likely to become *self-destroyers* or *grandiose dreamers*, as I call two typical syndromes of failing entrepreneurs.

Some caveats are in order at this point. This model is not meant to be a primer for the successful entrepreneur, because the necessary psychodynamic conditions are in no way sufficient, in themselves, to guarantee success. Furthermore, this model is limited to *male* entrepreneurs, because it is based on a combination of four sets of data: the first is quantitative research on entrepreneurs that, so far, has focused only on men; the second consists of the intuitions generated by my own therapeutic and consultative work with entrepreneurs, all have whom have been men; the third was generated by invaluable discussions with Jacob Burak, founder and formerly managing partner of Evergreen, one of Israel's earliest and most successful venture capital funds, who developed an interesting methodology that he used to identify which entrepreneurs were likely to succeed; finally, the fourth data set arose from a series of in-depth interviews I conducted with twenty-five entrepreneurs about the biographical sources of their entrepreneurial drive and vision.

First, let us look at the quantitative research on male entrepreneurs (for a review, see Malach-Pines et al. 2002), which consistently reiterates an intriguing finding: entrepreneurs tend to experience their fathers as weak, inefficient and physically and/or emotionally absent (Miner 1997, Malach-Pines et al. 2002, Kets de Vries 1985). My own experience – which, of course, is qualitative only and does not constitute a statistically significant sample – confirms this finding. Most entrepreneurs I have interviewed or worked with describe and remember their fathers as weak, disappointing, failures, or models to be avoided rather than emulated. Some of them talk about their fathers with visible pain, others with hidden anger, and still others with overt disdain or barely concealed rage.

I will exemplify men who become their own fathers, self-destroyers and grandiose dreamers through three extensive case presentations, provide an analysis, and conclude with some practical applications: the selection of entrepreneurs for investment; and the prevention of business failure through early identification of the syndromes. I therefore hope to show that Freud's thinking, if combined with contemporary research and theory, can be useful in uncovering the human reality behind the iconic image of the global entrepreneur, particularly in today's global culture. I have previously argued in detail (Strenger 2004) that our social and cultural reality is increasingly characterized by fatherlessness in a much deeper and wider sense: generations X and Y and the millennials increasingly feel that their parents are incapable of guiding them into the world in which they have to find their place, because their parents are often no longer in tune with the technologies, jobs and organizations in which the generations of the global world now move. Those born from the mid-1960s onwards often rely more on media and their peers to find their way through life than on what they experience as diluted parental authority. In fact, the whole notion of paternal authority on which Freud relied seems to have lost its relevance (Conley 2014). But this does not mean that the paternal role, albeit in a transformed version, is no longer relevant in our globalized culture: fathers continue to be desperately needed.

Psychodynamic Functions of Fatherhood

As a general statement, the Leonardo effect cannot be a correct hypothesis. Fatherlessness does not, in itself, foster independence; nor is it a sufficient condition for entrepreneurship. A large proportion of men who grew up with insufficient fathering end up as disoriented adults who cannot find their way in the world (Erikson 1959). Absent fathers are not blessings; rather, they usually constitute burdens on their sons. The question is why one subgroup of fatherless sons is able to turn this – in and of itself painful – experience into a motivation to develop into entrepreneurs.

Freud's depiction of the father as forbidding authority is lopsided. It does not take into account that fathers have another, very different function for their sons. The psychoanalyst Heinz Kohut (1971, 1977, 1979) provided a fruitful analysis of this highly important function. The father, among other things, provides the son with an ideal of what it could be like to be a man. This idealized image will, in due time, provide the foundation for the adult son's sense that it is worth striving for some goals. The child's experience of his father as admirable and worth emulating constitutes the developmental cornerstone of the adult's sense of orientation.

Kohut provides poignant descriptions of the enormous difficulties little boys face when their fathers fail to provide a model that can be idealized. If the father behaves in a disappointing manner, the son experiences shock, a sense of emptiness and unbearable loss. Ultimately, the result can be a lifelong lack of ideals and an absence of joy of life. A father who fails to provide an ideal image can become the source of overt or covert depression, disorientation and a weak sense of self.

Kohut's description of the father's role would lead us to expect the opposite of the Leonardo effect: fatherlessness is likely to produce men who are weak, prone to depression and lacking in direction. They are also likely to harbor a deep sense of disappointment and rage for having been deprived of a crucial source of support in their development. Therefore, we need to find the answers to two questions. How do some successful entrepreneurs manage to overcome the wounds inflicted by their failing fathers. And under what conditions do they instead exhibit the Leonardo effect?

Freud's Leonardo effect hypothesis certainly points to some truth: the lack of paternal authority generates a space of freedom. Yet, living with this freedom is difficult, and does not necessarily lead to success. Because entrepreneurs have become cultural icons, we tend to forget that at least nine out of ten startups fail. And while fatherlessness may indeed predispose some men towards entrepreneurship, it does not predispose them towards *successful* entrepreneurship. What makes the difference? Under what conditions will the fatherless son feel that there are no rules or boundaries, and hence come into conflict with social rules and regulations? By contrast, what must happen in order for the future adult to be able to use his freedom to create something within the bounds of social acceptability?

Freud (1910) raises this question in his study of Leonardo. He argues that psychoanalytic exploration cannot explain why Leonardo became a genius, while others who grew up in similar circumstances did nothing extraordinary. I do not claim to have the answer that eluded Freud, and I cannot formulate all of the necessary conditions for the development of successful entrepreneurship. However, I would like to explore a hypothesis about a factor that perhaps helps to explain at least some of the differences between successful and failing entrepreneurs. The crucial question concerns the emotional impact that is left by the experience of fatherlessness.

Kohut's theory addresses basic paternal function. Therefore, it generates a hypothesis that is warranted by both common-sense psychology and research: fatherlessness is, first and foremost, a burden on the child; and its effect is likely to be detrimental. So, in order to be conducive to successful entrepreneurship, the experience of fatherlessness must be transformed in significant ways.

Fatherlessness can lead in one of two directions. The more common direction is the rejection of rules and boundaries and a persistent tendency to disregard reality (Omer 2000). Children deprived of guidance are often unable to negotiate the complex developmental task of acquiring a strong sense of reality on their own. The seeming freedom from external authority tends to generate a weakened sense of direction, or even overt conflict with social authority. The result can be a lack of persistence and stamina, or indeed delinquency.

So how might fatherlessness instead become the cornerstone of *positive* character traits? The essence of entrepreneurship is the creation of an independent institution that is run by its founder, and paternal failure provides the future entrepreneur with the incentive to create his own environment. He learns in early childhood that he cannot rely on external sources of comfort, strength and support, so he prefers to create an environment over which he has total control (for an extreme example, see Roman Polanski's (1984) autobiography). Entrepreneurship is often a way for such men to deal with the pain engendered by their fatherless childhood (Kets de Vries 1985, 1996). Future entrepreneurs realize at a very early age that they are on their own, that they cannot rely on any external sources of strength. They need extraordinary inner strength to overcome the pain and loss they feel as a result of being deprived of adequate fathering experiences. However, if that pain engenders the desire to create a more life-sustaining environment than the one in which the entrepreneur grew up, he is more likely to succeed. Fatherlessness obviously cannot in itself constitute the foundation of *successful* entrepreneurship. The Leonardo effect may provide a sense of independence from external authority, and this early realization can become the cornerstone of a powerful sense of inner authority. Entrepreneurs do not wait for external empowerment; they generate the empowerment from within.

But fatherlessness may also generate unrealistic hopes and casual disregard for genuine threats and problems. If it leaves the future entrepreneur with an inner void and/or rage at having been deprived of one of the essentials for healthy growth, he is likely to become a self-destroyer, an unrealistic dreamer, or both. Let us therefore take a closer look at the human drama behind both successful and failing entrepreneurship engendered by the experience of fatherlessness.

Benjamin, Entrepreneur and Social Conscience

Benjamin was the son of two immigrants who moved to the United States from Central Europe after the Second World War. They did so to escape the dire reality that was created by the incorporation of their country of origin into the Eastern Bloc under Soviet hegemony. At the time, they viewed the United States as a land of opportunity in which they would be able to live a more fruitful and open life.

They settled in a small town on the East Coast. Benjamin's father had an enterprising streak: he was an inveterate tinkerer who loved to try out new pieces of machinery and combine older ones into new configurations. He was also something of an entrepreneur, but in that respect he was extremely unsuccessful. "My father had a singular lack of business talent," Benjamin told me, before adding, almost with pride, "He did not have a merchant's soul." Each of his small business ventures went down the drain, one by one.

The family moved to a larger town when Benjamin was six years old. It had some very good schools, and Benjamin enrolled into one of them. His father continued to open a series of businesses, all of which failed. Meanwhile, his mother still had the academic aspirations she had harbored before the war. The closest she came to realizing them was to become an assistant librarian at the local university.

> My parents were very busy with their lives. My father was involved with his failing businesses; my mother with desperate attempts to get closer to the professors. Neither of them had any time for me; nor did they have much interest in what I was doing. So I basically raised myself. I went to school and was a good student. But I also roamed the streets, playing games with the other kids.
>
> Then I started to develop an interest in science. I kept fixing things, conducting experiments, taking machinery apart and putting it together again trying to figure out how it worked. Not far from the school there was a poor neighborhood, primarily black. The kids there didn't go to school, and I began to understand that they were in trouble; that they were heading for criminal careers from early on.

At fifteen, Benjamin started to talk to the heads of his school about bringing the black kids into the mechanical workshops. He felt that some of them might be saved if they were given the opportunity to learn that repairing broken appliances was interesting and fun. Intrigued, the school authorities agreed and let Benjamin use the premises for his projects. "This was basically when I found out that I was an entrepreneur," Benjamin said. "I was an ideas man, then as now. I saw what had to be done, I convinced people around me that it was worth doing, and I set up the structure that would make it happen." He also discovered that he was capable of combining everything he wanted into a life structure.

He continued to roam the streets, and by sixteen he was sleeping more often at his girlfriend's house than at home. This was not because he had to; it was simply to maintain his freedom. A little later, his parents suddenly noticed that they had completely lost control of their son, and they made a brief attempt to discipline him.

> That was the only time when we were in overt conflict. I explained to them that there was no way they could tell me what to do, and it didn't take long for them to understand that they didn't stand a chance. So they left me alone.

After finishing high school Benjamin contacted a philanthropic foundation and convinced its leaders to let him set up a center for homeless kids in the black neighborhood. He convinced some like-minded late adolescents to join him in this venture, and spent a year building and running the center. "When I was convinced that I had a good successor, I quit. It was time to move on."

Along with all of his extracurricular activities, Benjamin was an excellent student: he scored astronomically high on his SATs, which gained him entry into a first-rate college and then into a graduate program in engineering. During vacations he would backpack around Europe, the Far East or South America. "I took those trips without a penny, so I often slept on the streets. My wife, whom I had met in college, became my partner on those trips, as well as in my later ventures."

After completing his studies, he took the first of three jobs, all of which were chosen to help him achieve his ultimate goal.

> The first job, in a large high-tech company, gave me experience in research and development. Then I moved west, to Silicon Valley. The second job, in a smaller, more dynamic company, taught me how to run projects. The third, also in a small company, allowed me to gain experience in strategic planning and marketing. Then I felt ready to do what I knew I wanted to do.

His eyes had long been set on what he considered to be one of the most beautiful landscapes in the southern United States.

> I knew it would not be easy to lure talent away from Silicon Valley, but I wanted to set up a company that would be different. I wanted it to be a place where people could flourish, develop their creativity. I also wanted to create a community where people could combine their careers with family life. The company would provide facilities for children, and we would make them part of the general atmosphere. My wife, who was a social scientist, helped me to turn these ideas into reality.

Benjamin founded his company on another principle, too:

> At heart, I am an inventor. I didn't want to create a company around a single product. I wanted the company to be constantly inventive. I predicted that outsourcing would become a major trend in the semiconductor industry, and I was proved right. We developed several products that were highly successful because they truly met the needs of the industry.

Benjamin was not looking for a quick kill. The company grew rapidly, but conservatively. After four years and several rounds of raising venture capital, it was generating sales of forty-five million dollars with fewer than fifty employees. The largest players in the industry bought Benjamin's products, even though they could scarcely believe what they saw when they visited the company.

> They would talk about "Benjamin's kindergarten." They couldn't understand how a place that looked more like a playground than an R&D facility had come up with all of these incredible technologies. But the whole point was the atmosphere: the people at my company were not brilliant; nor am I. The secret was in the synergy of the teams and the fun people had when working.

Benjamin did not lose the social conscience he had developed as an adolescent by becoming a business entrepreneur. From the very beginning, he set aside twenty-five percent of the equity for the company's employees. If necessary, he contributed his own equity to maintain that percentage.

After four years, he launched a successful IPO based on a market capitalization of four hundred million dollars. However, Benjamin maintained a controlling shareholding, and, while continuing to take care of his employees, did rather well for himself. Because he insisted on selling only fully developed and well-tested technologies, the company continued to grow solidly but relatively slowly, compared to some other businesses in the same sector. After another two years, sales stood at one hundred and twenty-five million dollars and profits at forty million dollars. "At the time the market sought fast growth, not profitability. Hence, the share price did not reflect the company's real value. I understood that in order to solidify the business I needed a strategic partner, because clients wanted integrated solutions." Benjamin found that partner and negotiated a good deal. He stayed on for another year as CEO, ensured that the character of the original company would not be harmed, then gradually retired. "It was a good merger that created a lot of value; I'm happy about that."

Benjamin lives in another part of the country now.

> I really need time to reconnect to myself. Those years as a CEO demanded a lot of hard work. And I'm not sure whether negotiating investment deals is what I'm about. I'm glad I did all this; but now I want to be able to write poetry again. And I'm thrilled about not having the slightest idea what I will do in five years' time.

It would have been easy to miss out on the fact that Benjamin and his wife have set up a philanthropic foundation that is involved in community-building in poverty-stricken neighborhoods. He is still an entrepreneur with a social conscience.

The Human Reality behind the Leonardo Effect: Turning Pain into Motivation for Growth

If you met him, you would never believe that Benjamin is the founder and ex-CEO of a high-tech success story. He is somewhat shy and his presence is low key. However, once he starts to talk, in his quiet, pensive voice, you are enthralled. When answering questions about his emotional life, he is reflective and sometimes puzzled. When discussing his ideals, his business decisions and the company he created, he emanates quiet but powerful enthusiasm.

The simple fact is that Benjamin was a neglected child. His parents were busy dealing with their own existential frustrations, and they had little time or energy for their son. He speaks of them with some resignation, but it is difficult to detect any anger towards them. When he describes his childhood and adolescence, his face often breaks into a mischievous smile. He loves the memories of the freedom he created for himself.

Listening to his story, the first hypothesis that comes to mind is that, as he was a neglected child, he decided very early on that he could not rely on his parents or any other adults. His way of dealing with the pain of neglect was to find ways to help others who were in similar or worse plights to his own. In adolescence he fell in love with the idea of communities that foster growth and creativity, and all of his activities since then, whether in business or in philanthropy, have been guided by that notion.

Benjamin is not psychologically minded. When I suggested that, by taking care of neglected children, he was also trying to heal the wounds inflicted by his own childhood neglect, he was puzzled. As usual, though, he did not dismiss the idea out of hand. Instead, he said: "I should really give this more thought."

His relationship with his father is rather fascinating. On the one hand, he sees him – realistically – as a man who failed both as a father and as an entrepreneur. Yet, there was that hint of pride when he said, "He did not have a merchant's soul." In a way, Benjamin's life is a vindication of the possibility of achieving success without being driven primarily by the desire to make as much money as possible. His considerable financial success is almost a by-product of acting in accordance with his social ideals and his love for invention.

Again, Benjamin's transformative powers come to the fore here: even though he was let down by his father, and even though he could not use him as a role model, he wanted to preserve at least some of the love and pride he felt for him. He did this by turning his father's lack of business acumen into a strength. He showed that it was possible to be successful without being money-minded. Again, when I suggested this, he was puzzled by the hypothesis. He could not confirm any conscious intention to vindicate his father . . . but he liked the idea.

Jim, the Self-Destroying Entrepreneur

Jim was the third and final child of a devout Catholic family. His parents were very active in the church community, and they had a very clear idea of what comprised the good life. They expected respect and devotion – and they had very little time for expressions of emotion.

Jim felt uncomfortable with his surroundings from very early on. He had little time for his parents' disciplinarian attitudes; nor did he care much about the community's demand for submissiveness. The open conflict with his parents began in his early teens. When they found out that he had skipped religious instruction and spent his time playing baseball with kids from the adjoining neighborhood, they tried everything to discipline him: beatings, scolding and trying to bully him into submission were their main means of trying to persuade him to comply. It was all of no avail. Their youngest son could not be beaten into submission. Finally, they resorted to telling him systematically that he was a piece of shit, that he would burn in hell for committing mortal sins, that his disrespect for his parents was reason enough alone for his eternal damnation. He reacted with rage, and his rebellion became even more pronounced.

By his late teens, the tension was unbearable. His parents told him: either you comply or you leave. Jim left and began to roam around the state. Sometimes he slept on the streets; sometimes he found odd jobs that helped him to stay afloat. His pride would not allow him to return home, but there were nights when he would break down crying, utterly dejected. He even contemplated suicide as the only way out.

Then came a lucky break. He happened to be in a town with some major tourist attractions, and many tour groups came to visit. One day, one of the tour guides fell ill and the hotel asked Jim – who had done some odd jobs for the owner – whether he would step in and show the group the sights. He had never done anything of the kind before, and he was scarcely even familiar with the town's attractions, but he needed the money, so he agreed. In the two days he spent with the group, Jim learned that he possessed two great assets. First, he had an incredible ability to connect with and fascinate people. When he lacked the required knowledge, he more than made up for it through sheer *chutzpah.* In addition, it transpired that he was tremendously resourceful and calm under pressure. At one point, the tour bus broke down, so Jim improvised another outing while mobilizing a fleet of taxis to ferry the tourists to the next site.

The story of how Jim saved the day quickly got around, and the tour company hired him as a full-time guide. Within three weeks he paid a visit to the company's owner. He had some ideas about how to make the tours more original. The owner did not know whether to be angry at the youngster's impudence or impressed by his innovative ideas.

By the age of twenty-one, Jim was developing new tour packages. He also turned out to be very good at sales. He quickly understood that selling the packages to institutional and other large groups could multiply the company's turnover very rapidly. But this required a massive investment in marketing, and the owner was a conservative man and would not hear of it. Jim became angry, then abusive: "How could this old idiot not see that I was offering him a gold mine?" Their relationship became ever more strained, and Jim was on the verge of being kicked out of what, in a sense, had become his adoptive home.

Then came the epiphany. Jim's family, while devout, had never felt much connection to high culture. But now, one his tours included a visit to a local church where a choir and orchestra were due to perform Mozart's Mass in C-minor. Jim had never heard the piece; in fact, he had hardly heard of Mozart. However, he thought it would be a good idea to include the performance in the tour package, so he made sure that his group arrived in good time. Thus, he came to hear Mozart's great mass. Of course, given his upbringing, he was familiar with the text – "Kyrie eleison, Christe eleison . . ." – but he had only ever known it as a meaningless recitation. Mozart's music made the words come alive for him for the first time. When the first soprano began to sing above the background of the choir, tears started streaming down Jim's face; and he could not stop crying until the end of the mass. For the first time in his life, he dimly began to realize that Catholicism was not just a pointless set of dogmas, injunctions and prohibitions, but a rich culture that had created tremendous beauty and could generate profound spiritual and emotional experiences.

In the months that followed, Jim integrated ever more music into his tour packages, and he himself was drawn ever more deeply into it. He also started to read about the artworks that he had previously merely pointed out to his tourist clients, and began to appreciate the true genius of these masterpieces for the first time. But his newfound awe did not stop him realizing that organizing tours based on the treasures of the Catholic tradition was also a tremendous business opportunity. He contacted various Catholic organizations with great clout and substantial financial resources and pitched the idea to them. He suggested that the guides should all be Catholics with a deep knowledge of art history, and that their aim should be to establish a link between the tour groups' – often rote-learned – faith and the great art that Catholicism had inspired over the centuries. The Catholic organizations immediately saw the immense financial potential of the idea, but also felt that it would serve their religious goals very well.

The new company was up and running in less than a year and it quickly became a huge success. But three years later Jim fell out with his backers. Even though his epiphany was obviously linked to his Catholic upbringing, he did not consider himself a Catholic any more. And he felt that his business model would work equally well for every other religious tradition. So why not also cater to Buddhists, Protestants, Jews and others? Understandably, his Catholic partners did not welcome these expansion plans, so once again Jim found himself at a crossroads. But now, after three years of running a successful business, he was more confident than ever. He spoke to some banks and arranged to buy out his original backers. They had little choice but to acquiesce, as Jim was the life and soul of the company. At the age of twenty-nine, he was finally his own master. The company was highly leveraged, but it was his, and he did not have to rein in his creativity and ambition.

Jim's mind was bubbling. He devised a series of new concepts that combined tourism and culture. Sometimes an idea would come to him in the morning and by the evening he would have sold out the first five tours, before even considering the practicalities. His endless resourcefulness generally allowed him to resolve any problems on the spot, and he put no effort into developing an organizational structure that would have provided him with the means to plan ahead more systematically. He proudly called his modus operandi "management by chaos." He also had little knowledge of the company's finances: he just knew that he was making operating profits despite the firm's unfettered, chaotic growth.

In his early thirties, he ran the company like a little kingdom: he would dispense favors to potential clients, give them free tours, without ever establishing whether this largesse was actually good for business. His love life was similarly disorganized. He was usually involved with several women at the same time, and he began to use the business as a resource to feed his voracious sexual appetite. He would instruct one of his trusted employees to draw up a list of the most attractive women on a tour, then turn up halfway through to meet them. His charm and charisma, combined with his status as owner of the company, inevitably won them over . . . at first. But many of them reacted furiously when they learned that he was sleeping with several other women on the same tour.

Once again, though, Jim's endless resourcefulness usually allowed him to escape unscathed. So he stepped up the ante and started affairs with several company employees. Some of his most trusted lieutenants warned him that the business climate in the United States had become extremely sensitive to anything that smacked of sexual harassment: "It's only a matter of time until one of your cast-offs sues you," they said, but all to no avail. Jim had several near misses and paid off several female employees who had been hurt by his high-handed and often humiliating behavior. But he continued to pride himself on being impossible to pin down.

At this point, Jim was still riding high – at least to casual observers – but with the benefit of hindsight it seems that he was determined to orchestrate his own downfall. His numerous affairs had not quite led to that, but his next step would. He had been the heart and soul of his company from the outset, and his hands-on approach had prevented the chaos from turning into a disaster. He had always kept a close eye on every tour, every cruise, every event. If there were any operational problems, he would step in, even to the point of playing tour guide again. But now he wanted more time for fun, so he hired a CEO while retaining the company's chairmanship. The CEO was horrified by the mess he discovered on arrival and demanded a more structured management. Jim gave him free rein for about six months, but then the CEO told him that his latest idea could not be implemented until the reorganization had been completed. Jim sacked him the following day, and subsequently had to fight a bitter battle over severance pay. He was furious. He had enjoyed the lack of pressure over the previous six months and loved not being responsible for day-to-day operations. So, after a short period as CEO himself, he promoted one of his most trusted employees – a man who had extricated Jim from many of his amorous entanglements, who was intensely loyal to him, and who wouldn't dream of trying to limit either his financial or his sexual behavior.

Things went downhill fast. The new CEO awarded himself a higher salary and convinced Jim – who had never been particularly concerned about what he earned – to increase his own salary and bonuses exponentially. Company cars became more lavish, while Jim started to hire helicopters to meet up with the tour groups in style in the hope of impressing even more women. He ignored his CFO's warnings, and just two years later the company filed for Chapter 11 amid widely publicized allegations ranging from financial incompetence to fraud. Jim left the United States and now ruefully compares himself to Roman Polanski, who fled the country after accusations that he sexually assaulted a minor.

The Anatomy of Self-Destruction

Jim never truly got over the wounds inflicted upon him by his upbringing. He deeply identified with his parents' view of him as the bad boy. His rebellion against his tyrannical but emotionally distant father took the form of constantly playing at the border of what was acceptable. Throughout his career, he continued to flaunt his disdain for his father's values. He was driven to perpetuate his existential role as the bad son. "I am Ivan Karamazov," he would sometimes say during interviews.

Jim was not a cold cynic. He did not simply play the bad boy. He desperately sought something that would make him feel that there was true value to be found in the world. The epiphany of hearing Mozart's great Mass C-minor involved more than spotting a lucrative business opportunity. It was also a cry from his soul that there was such a thing as true beauty and that religion could be something other than coercive, condemning indoctrination. Jim wanted to create true value; he wanted to give his customers something that he had never received himself.

Yet, he was torn between the constructive, paternal aspect of his personality and the child-like part that continued to rage at the ways in which his father had let him down. In the end, his obsession with transgressing the rules of society proved stronger than his equally genuine desire to create value.

Jim's fixation to his intrusive and oppressive father is palpable during interviews. He has a strong self-dramatizing streak. He enjoys playing out the drama of his life. At the same time, there is a distinct impression that he is uncomfortable with the situation. He often reacts to questions and interpretations as if they are threatening impositions; he has an obsessive need to create something of value himself. He attempts to locate almost every topic of conversation in a context of power struggle. To this day, he experiences himself as locked in a deadly, raging, perpetual struggle with authority.

Arnold, the Man who Wanted to Prove He Was Valuable

Arnold's family was proud of their lineage. Soon after Jews were allowed into German universities, one of Arnold's ancestors became a famous legal scholar. He founded a dynasty of scholars and researchers in law, medicine and philology. In the 1920s Arnold's grandfather moved to Palestine, and he went on to become one of the founders of Israel's first university. Over the next few decades, in their quiet ways, he and other members of his family contributed significantly to Israel's intellectual and academic life.

Arnold's father was a mathematician. Even though he did not produce any outstanding work, he was highly competent, served as chairman of his department, and organized and participated in international conferences. In his late twenties he married a woman who suffered from a deep depressive streak that became more dominant after the birth of their first child, Arnold. The treating psychiatrist advised the couple to refrain from having more children.

Arnold's mother would spend whole days in bed, and Arnold learned very early on that he was not to disturb her. If he asked for something, or simply sought her company, she might burst into a rage, after which she would return to a state of passive helplessness. His father knew about this, but had no idea what to do about it. Being well connected, the couple sought out the best psychiatrists in Israel, but none of the treatment helped. Arnold's father's way of dealing with the emotional deadness of his wife was to invest himself more deeply in academia: he took on several administrative functions, traveled widely, and generally tried to avoid being at home.

Consequently, Arnold grew up in an emotional wasteland. Surrounded by photographs of his father, grandfather and great-grandfather in black robes at various academic events, he knew that the family boasted a proud lineage. His grandfather was still alive until Arnold reached his mid-twenties, and Arnold spent quite a bit of time at his grandparents' house. They were caring but emotionally remote people who would primarily lecture Arnold on the importance of academic achievement. But Arnold could not concentrate on his studies. From an early age he felt an inner void and chaos. He did not feel truly connected to anyone. He disdained his father and felt that all of the family's apparent respectability was a façade. How could the chairman of the department be incapable of taking care of his own son?

The extended family soon gave up on Arnold as he seemed to have none of the qualities that had made the family into a dynasty of great scholars. They knew about his mother's depression, but their tendency to maintain emotional distance did not allow explicit discussion of the problem, so Arnold continued to live in an emotional vacuum. Nevertheless, he managed to finish high school, and thereafter he was exempted from military service because of his asthma. Instead, he attended one of Israel's leading universities, where he studied law. Once again, he could not truly invest himself in his studies, but he graduated and then began an internship.

One of the firm's clients was a wealthy man who had no children. He was fond of Arnold, whose endearing charm, good looks and quick mind managed to conceal a deep insecurity about his true abilities. Eventually the client asked Arnold if he would be interested in managing his investments. Arnold accepted the offer, because the man's warmth and willingness to trust him had finally made him feel appreciated. In this new role, Arnold would soon discover that he was not – in contrast to what his family had always believed – intellectually deficient.

He came to know a world that his family despised. They had always regarded business as an inferior field for primitive, greedy people who were incapable of serious intellectual work. But now Arnold realized that it could be intellectually fascinating, challenging and much more suitable for his restless temperament, which sought action and movement rather than quiet immersion in books, theories and data. He eagerly learned from his mentor, who had a wealth of experience in real estate development, and discovered that he had an inherent knack for business. He could identify valuable assets instinctively, and his mind, which had felt numb during his academic studies, shifted into top gear whenever he assessed business opportunities or set up deals. His charm and mercurial temperament were now valuable assets, helping him to negotiate deals by overcoming deadlocks through wit and personal magnetism.

Eventually, he expressed a desire to venture on to the stock market. His mentor was a little wary of this, but he gave Arnold permission to try his hand at trading some shares. Arnold turned out to have a deft touch here, too, but his mentor demurred when Arnold urged him to take larger positions on the stock market.

Then, unexpectedly, the mentor died from a heart attack. Even more surprisingly, it transpired that he had left Arnold a considerable sum of money in his will. Arnold, by now in his late twenties, was inconsolable at first: the only father figure who had ever cared about him and cherished his talent and personality had been snatched away from him. It took Arnold a year to overcome his paralysis, but then he felt that he had to justify his mentor's faith in him. He decided that he was going to become a big success.

All of this took place in the early 1980s, during Ronald Reagan's first term as US President. Stories of brokers making millions overnight and corporate raiders buying huge companies were beginning to capture the financial world's imagination. Arnold decided that New York was the place to be. He was lucky and without too much effort landed a job at one of the major investment banks, where he became part of a team that handled some spectacular takeovers. Again, he proved adept at his job and was paid a lavish salary, as were most of his colleagues at the time (Lewis 1989). Independently of his job, he also invested his own money and doubled it within two years.

He soon began to live the high-flying life of the New York Yuppie scene. He donned expensive designer suits, wore a gold Swiss watch and moved into a fashionable apartment. He loved the glamor, the adrenaline and the fact that he was a member of the emerging upper class of young financial hotshots. Yet, his inner void remained, his self-esteem had not increased and nagging self-doubt continued to plague him. He realized that the pain he felt deep inside was due to his family never acknowledging that his achievements had true value. So he decided that it was time to show them what he was made of.

This was a time when everyone expected to make huge returns on their investments. Financial stars like Ivan Boesky and Michael Milken were fueling everybody's imagination, and Arnold felt that he had it in him to make it big, too. Of course, in his line of work he met many wealthy business people, and he started to ask them if they would be interested in investing in a new hedge fund. Unsurprisingly, given Arnold's track record, most of them were very interested indeed, so he took the plunge and branched out on his own. His first year was a phenomenal success: he generated more than eighty percent ROI (return on investment) for his original investors, and dozens of others were soon clammoring to join the fund, too.

Arnold was well connected, he got good tips and knew how to evaluate them, and before long his hedge fund had grown to a remarkable size, as had his personal fortune. He invited his frugal family to New York, put them up in the most expensive hotels, and tried to show them a good time. However, although his parents and cousins accepted his invitation, he was certain they were not impressed. "All they saw was a despicable money-maker," he felt. Again, he had failed to convince them that he was a respectable human being who was creating something of value.

He decided that making a personal fortune was not enough: he had to do something truly spectacular. He put together a new group of investors who were willing to back his latest venture – corporate takeovers. He found a suitable target, then asked his old employer, the investment bank where he had learned his trade, to handle the takeover itself. After months of strenuous, exhilarating work, the takeover was finalized.

But there was a twist. Arnold's plan was different from those of the standard corporate raiders of the 1980s who bought failing companies, dismantled them and sold off their assets, often leaving thousands of people out of work. He wanted to salvage the company and prove that he could not just make money for himself and his investors but also create genuine social and economic value for the newly acquired firm's employees. In short, he wanted to demonstrate that he was a good and valuable person. Some of his friends and colleagues expressed their concern: Arnold was a brilliant investor, and he had proved to be a gifted player in orchestrating the takeover, but turning around a failing company demanded corporate skills and experience that he simply did not possess. However, Arnold's mind was made up: he would prove that he was more than a skillful manipulator in an Armani suit. He was so confident in his own ability that he managed to convince his investors that he would make them a lot of money.

The demise came quickly and, with the benefit of hindsight, inevitably. As his friends had warned him, Arnold's lack of experience was a fatal flaw. He picked the wrong CEO for the company; he bet on the wrong restructuring strategy; and in less than a year he was forced to surrender his controlling shares to the financial syndicate that had funded the takeover.

Arnold retreated from business and fell into a rather deep depression. He felt that he had missed his one great chance to leave his mark. Although he was still extremely wealthy, he could not see any value in what he had achieved. It was on his return to Israel that he sought me out for psychoanalytic treatment. After several years he finally came to understand what lay at the root of his poor decisions. His desperate need to fill the void in his soul, and his fierce desire to show his family that he was a valuable individual, had led him to lose touch with his true talents and chase a fantasy that did not suit his capabilities.

After his father's death in the early 1990s, Arnold went through another crisis. He realized that his deepest desire – finally to gain the respect of a man who had always been both physically and emotionally distant – would never be fulfilled. Yet, in his analytic work, he could also mourn his own destitute childhood and begin to understand that he needed to live his life despite never achieving that goal. He remarried and returned to the field that he should never have left. Together with a partner, he built an investment-banking boutique that flourished during the high-tech boom of the nineties, then survived the bursting of the dot.com bubble in the early 2000s and the financial crisis of 2008.

I saw him briefly for a few sessions in these later years. His life was certainly more stable than ever before, and his marriage seemed moderately happy. But I had to conclude that he remained an unhappy man. It seemed as if the gaping void in his soul created by growing up with a depressed mother, an absent father and an extended family who could not find it in their hearts to cherish him had never been truly filled.

Anatomy of a Grandiose Dreamer

As so often happens with children who grow up in an emotional vacuum, Arnold could not see his parents' weaknesses for what they were. He inferred that their emotional distance was a function of his own lack of value as a human being, and embarked on a desperate search to prove that he was capable of creating something of value.

He might never have got as far as he did without the good fortune of experiencing some emotionally significant mentoring. Sometimes future entrepreneurs find a father figure who provides them with the self-confidence they have been lacking. Unfortunately, in Arnold's case, the years he spent with his mentor were cut short and ultimately proved insufficient to fill the void in his soul. They also did not temper his desperate need to prove to his parents that he was a valuable human being. As a result, Arnold could not attain the level of self-knowledge that is crucial for successful entrepreneurship. At the crucial juncture in an otherwise successful career he could not distinguish between his real abilities and the image of what he wanted to be. He had genuine talent, but his achievements never healed the festering wound in his psyche. Consequently, and inevitably, he made a crucial mistake.

Arnold's story is doubly instructive because it shows that self-knowledge can prevent fatal mistakes and help entrepreneurs to make full use of their talents. He needed to come to terms with the fact that he was fatherless in order to understand both his true abilities and his true limitations. After several years of psychotherapeutic work that dealt with his profound pain and the source of his failure, he was able to build a new business in which he could express his considerable gifts more realistically. In turn, that allowed him to live not a fantasy of grandeur, but a genuinely constructive life, even though his existential scars would never quite heal.

The Leonardo Effect Hypothesis Reformulated

Benjamin, Jim and Arnold were all fatherless, gifted men with proven abilities in their respective fields. Benjamin led his company securely through various stages of successful development; both Jim and Arnold took wrong turns that led to the downfall of their creations. Fatherlessness was crucial in all three outcomes. So why did it lead Benjamin to success, and Jim and Arnold to failure? The question is intriguing, because the downfall of both Jim and Arnold was not a function of lack of competence or talent. Both succeeded for several years before making catastrophic moves that led to their failure. So why does the Leonardo effect seem to work well for some entrepreneurs, yet fail for others?

Something about the Leonardo effect hypothesis is compelling: the published evidence and clinical experience combine to make the idea difficult to resist that a surprisingly large proportion of entrepreneurs are fatherless.

Yet, my case studies indicate that Freud missed a large part of the human drama of fatherlessness. His theory had strong autobiographical roots. As various biographers (e.g., Jones 1953–1957, Gay 1989) have shown, he was born into an interesting family constellation. He was the first-born son of his mother, who in turn was his father's second wife. He had half-brothers who were a full generation older than himself. He was his mother's darling and prince, and from early on felt that he was destined for a level of greatness for which his father was by no means a suitable role model. Driven away from Sigmund's place of birth by bankruptcy, Jacob Freud never quite made it as far has he wished, and he cut a less than heroic figure.

Sigmund Freud was very familiar with vaulting ambition (Breger 2009): he dreamed of making his mark from early on in his career, and this restless drive led him up several blind alleys. For a while, he thought that his investigations into the effects of cocaine would make him famous (with disastrous consequences for one of his friends), and in the early 1890s he thought he had solved the puzzle of hysterical neurosis with his theory that it was caused by the trauma of sexual abuse in early childhood. It was only after his father's death in 1896 that he embarked on the course that would turn him into one of the most significant thinkers of the twentieth century – a status that is not denied even by those who think that his theories and the therapy he invented are wrong-headed. During the years after his father's death he experienced a number of crippling hysterical symptoms but simultaneously formulated the theory of the Oedipus complex and the basic outline of his general theory of neurosis. He also completed his masterpiece, *The Interpretation of Dreams* (1900). Soon after, he initiated the psychoanalytic movement that would continue his work into the twenty-first century.

So Freud, one of the great entrepreneurs of Western intellectual history, could not use his father as a role model, but his mother's ardent love instilled a deep conviction that he was destined for greatness. As has been amply documented, he needed a paternal mentor – the respected Viennese physician Josef Breuer (whom Freud abandoned once he had served this purpose) – in order to acquire some self-confidence and build his private practice (Breger 2009). But his actual father had been sufficiently influential to make Freud's road to success rocky: his intense guilt over surpassing his father's achievements led to severe neurotic symptoms that he shared with his friend and confidant Wilhelm Fliess during the crucial years when he formulated the foundations of his later work (Freud 1985a). Only after he had worked through his intense ambivalence towards his father could he fulfill the destiny in which he consciously and unconsciously believed.

Because of his own father's benign and largely unobtrusive presence, Freud never quite understood how much sons need their fathers. Future generations of psychoanalysts and psychologists, including Heinz Kohut (1971), have provided greater insights into the depth of the paternal role. The case studies in this chapter exemplify the need for fathers who can be idealized and provide true guidance. They also show the depth of the despair, rage and sense of loss engendered by paternal failure, and how difficult they are to leave behind.

Freud was one of the great masters of deciphering human drama, yet he did not fully grasp the depth of boys' attachment to and need for their fathers. As Simon (1988) has pointed out, he simply repressed half of the Oedipus myth: after all, the original story begins with Laius' decision to kill Oedipus before his son has an opportunity to do the same to him and fulfill the oracle's dark prediction. The beginning of the drama between father and son therefore resides in the father's ability to deal with the complexity of his own emotions towards his son – an element Freud never integrated into his formulation of the Oedipal conflict. The continuation resides in the son's desperate need to have a father he can admire. Freud, because of his own psychological makeup, could not face this part of the Oedipus complex.

In this chapter I have described three men whose fathers failed to live up to their expected roles. We have seen how difficult it is to overcome the wounds inflicted by paternal failure. Hence, we can now rephrase the Leonardo effect hypothesis with more depth. Men whose fathers have been emotionally absent are faced with a tremendous psychic task. They need to come to terms with disappointment, loss and the lifelong pain of feeling deprived of essential psychic nourishment. A small proportion of them will manage, early in life, to mourn the lack of good fatherhood. They will develop a deep and lasting conviction that it is pointless to rely on external sources of support and empowerment. Consequently, they will make full use of the type of freedom Freud (1910) associated with fatherlessness in his study of Leonardo. There is a good chance that they will become entrepreneurs who are guided by a powerful sense of inner authority, and do not feel that they need anyone's permission to do their own thing. As a result, they will develop the inner strength and resilience to shape their own destiny and create enduring, successful organizations. In other words, they will become their own fathers and will go on to play a paternal mentoring role for the many people who accept their leadership in the organizations they build.

However, more often than not, fatherlessness leaves a psychic scar that expresses itself through a lifelong and fruitless fight with authority. This fight is fueled by rage, disappointment and a constant desire to engage authority in a perpetual struggle. Unsurprisingly, the result is often destructive: if rage, guilt and the perpetual attempt to fill an inner void fuel the entrepreneurial drive, the chances are that the enterprise will falter at some point. The raging entrepreneur lacks the inner guidance to help him decide what is possible and what is not. Instead, he is driven by fantasies of proving to the absent father that he did not recognize his son's true value. Consequently, this sort of entrepreneur often fails to recognize the limitations that may lead to the downfall of his enterprise.

Contemporary global culture amplifies these fantasies through countless messages. I have already mentioned the most iconic of these – Nike's advertising slogan "Just Do It!" – but there are many others, such as Adidas' "Impossible is Nothing." Numerous self-help books, often written by authors with questionable credentials, also bolster the myth that if you probe into your self's deepest resources, there are no limits to what you can achieve. The result, as I have argued elsewhere (Strenger 2011a: ch. 3 and passim), can be disastrous: millions of people whose abilities do not allow for sustained hard work feel that they have lived insignificant lives because they have not made any sort of mark within celebrity culture. Meanwhile, many gifted, hard-working New Cosmopolitans labor under the persistent fear that they have not created anything of significance, as we saw in the previous chapter. All of this proves that it is difficult to live with fatherlessness, whether individual or cultural.

When Does the Leonardo Effect Hypothesis Work?

There seem to be two forms of fatherlessness. Some fatherless men forever search for the caring, supportive father they were denied in childhood, or remain attached to the failing father and forever seek his approval, as we have seen in Arnold's story. They do not achieve full inner authority, and their judgement tends to be clouded at crucial junctures. Others, like Jim, carry the rage and pain of early humiliation in their psyche and continue to be rebellious. As a result, they never give up the fight against authority and, deep inside, remain the raging, hurting children of failing fathers.

By contrast, the fatherless entrepreneurs who succeed have come to terms emotionally with their fathers' failures. For them, entrepreneurship becomes a way to repair the emotional damage of being let down as children. They become the fathers that their own fathers were unable – or refused – to be. Benjamin developed this trait while still a teenager, when he began to help adolescent black children who were growing up without paternal guidance.

Where, then, lies the truth of the Leonardo effect hypothesis and the liberating effect of paternal absence? The answer, I believe, does not reside in a clear-cut set of external circumstances. Rather, it is to be found in the way the experience of fatherlessness is transformed within the entrepreneur's psyche. The successful entrepreneur truly comes to terms with the fact that nobody will ever assume the paternal role that his own father has failed to fulfill.

Entrepreneurs who Become Their Own Fathers

We can see this most clearly in the life and career of Benjamin. After he accepted that he could not expect either guidance or support from his parents, he proceeded to make the best of his situation and turned disadvantage into opportunity.

Benjamin exemplifies one of the most striking features of many successful entrepreneurs. They have become individuals even to the point where their parents cease to be a relevant inner audience. Psychoanalytic theory has shown the extent to which we all carry inner audiences with us – figures who have played significant roles in our lives (almost always including our parents). The plays of our lives are then directed towards these inner audiences. However, from a very early age, Benjamin's father was not a member of his inner audience, so he had no need to prove to him that he was a worthy object of attention and love. Benjamin did not "kill" his father; nor did he rebel against him. He simply understood that he had to become his own father; then he extended that paternal role to help others grow, too.

This profound independence was also reflected in Benjamin's adult life. He succeeded in individuating completely. When asked whether he could think of any role models in his life, he replied:

> I have been enthusiastic about things that I have seen people do. But I have never felt deep admiration towards anyone. I have never felt, "I want to be like him." I was far too lucid to turn anyone into a guru, or even a role model. I looked at every person to see whether there was something I could learn from them. But that was it. I accepted ways of acting and thinking, but I never idealized anyone.

Today, Benjamin's soft-spoken, warm presence is striking. He is the ideal interviewee. He experiences the interviewer as neither intrusive nor threatening. He gives due consideration to every question and potential interpretation and does not infer any hidden meanings or implications. He is willing to play and experiment with trains of thought. All of this indicates that he is not threatened by authority; nor does he feel the need to rebel against it. He simply does not experience anyone as an unquestioned authority. While always willing to listen to and consider other people's points of view, he knows his own mind because he has developed genuine inner authority.

Self-Destroyers out of Unconscious Guilt

Jim exemplifies a very different way of dealing with fatherlessness, a way that is more likely to evolve if the father is not only emotionally unavailable but also abusive. He harbored a deep-seated rage against his father, and transferred this rage to all authority figures. He forever needed to fight both real and imagined authorities, and, deep down, remained a rebellious adolescent who was determined to test the limits of how far he could go.

Jim's tragedy was that, along with the rage, he carried tremendous guilt in his psyche. He never ceased to be the reprimanded son who was told that he was a worthless human being. While overtly confident and impressive, he never truly felt that he deserved success. Even though his business provided aesthetic and even spiritual fulfillment for thousands of customers, he never believed that he had created anything of real value. This deep-seated, unconscious guilt finally drove him to destroy his own achievement, because he was unable to accept that anything he had created had a right to exist. Instead of accepting that he was a talented creator, he believed that he was an impostor who achieved success only by fooling all of the people all of the time.

This was further complicated because Jim's father's abusiveness created an indelible impression in Jim's mind, which led him to see all authority as wanton, willful and unjustified. Deep down, Jim did not accept either the rule of law or ethical precepts: they felt like pompous injunctions imposed by institutions that he did not respect. As a result, he felt that he could – and even should – disregard the law, and that the only valid injunction was not to allow himself to be caught. Unconsciously, he did not even believe that basic economic rules applied to him: his entrepreneurial ability allowed him to create a remarkable company; but his disregard for the financial reality of the balance sheet led him to destroy that creation and run into trouble with the law.

As we will see in the following section, this disregard for limits is often powerfully reinforced by a pervasive tendency in today's financial sector to believe that anything is possible and that every rule can be bent without ultimately having to pay a price.

Grandiose Dreamers in the Global Bubble

Arnold exemplifies a group of men who feel the desperate need to gain their fathers' attention and love. They try to prove to them (even if they are no longer alive) that they failed to recognize their sons' true value. They feel an inner void, and a desperate need for the attention that they did not receive. They can never quite accept that they didn't receive what they needed, and internally remain dependent on the neglectful parent.

Consequently, they develop grandiose fantasies of becoming great successes, and they are driven on by the desire for adulation and recognition of their achievements. This becomes an *idée fixe.* They feel that they need to realize this fantasy, because they expect it to fill their inner void, their painful yearning for paternal love and recognition. The problem is that external success rarely has the power to heal their childhood wounds. Nevertheless, they push themselves to achieve even more, in the hope that they will finally quench their thirst for recognition. Along the way, they are likely to lose the ability to differentiate between their actual (and often considerable) abilities and their fantasized grandeur. They ignore warnings and push the envelope too far, which often leads to their downfall.

This tendency is also strongly reinforced by contemporary global culture. As Lewis (2010) has documented in great detail, the financial meltdown of 2008 was in part generated by the modern financial community's disdain for the careful, conservative banking culture of the past. Numerous complicated financial instruments were created, including, notoriously, collateral debt obligations, which were based on securitized bundles of mortgages that were issued in total disregard for the most elementary rules of financial prudence. Traders who did not understand the complex Black–Scholes theorem (which supposedly made possible the rational pricing of financial derivatives) recklessly sold risks that they could not assess, creating a huge, multi-trillion-dollar bubble of options that were traded around the world and endangered the global financial system. Even more worryingly, this practice has continued since the financial catastrophe that cost millions of families their homes and livelihoods (Lewis 2011).

The Theoretical Puzzle

Of course, it would be wonderful to establish the reason why some fatherless entrepreneurs become their own fathers, while others become self-destroyers or grandiose dreamers. The case examples in this chapter suggest two hypotheses.

Benjamin's father was neglectful, whereas Jim's father was abusive. So perhaps that is the key to explaining the very different paths that they took? In one respect, this seems to be a dead end, as I have worked with two very successful and constructive entrepreneurs whose fathers were highly abusive.

However, looking at the same hypothesis from a different angle, there is something compelling in the idea that neglect might make it easier for a son to go through the mourning process for his absent parent and ultimately become his own father.

The second hypothesis relates to a potentially highly significant biographical factor that I have not previously emphasized in this study: the research literature (Malach-Pines et al. 2002) suggests that the *differentia specifica* might be found in maternal functioning. Many successful entrepreneurs report that their mothers were strong, life-giving women who inspired them with a basic optimism about life. This basic belief in their own life force – and what Erikson (1959) called "basic trust" – might provide these entrepreneurs with the inner strength to move from rage to inner authority, and thus become their own fathers. I offer this second hypothesis with just as much trepidation as I offered the first, as I have met several entrepreneurs who had depressed, withdrawn or weak mothers, as well as abusive fathers, yet succeeded in making the developmental transition that characterizes the Leonardo effect. Nevertheless, as with the first hypothesis, there might be some validity in the second.

These two hypotheses can therefore be considered only as suggestions that demand further investigation. The human desire to find explanations makes it difficult to ignore the intriguing question of why some fatherless men become innovators and leaders while others exhibit identity diffusion or turn to crime. But in trying to find the answer we may encounter limitations that even Freud – whose own desire to find explanations is undeniable – acknowledged. In the last few pages of his Leonardo study (1910: 135ff) Freud writes that, while psychoanalysis may be able to explain a certain amount of Leonardo's development, it cannot explain his creative genius. It may be that constitutional factors and inborn talents are simply not amenable to psychodynamic explanation, and instead need to be explored in the domain of biology and the study of inborn temperamental factors. In this respect, entrepreneurship and leadership may be no different from artistic and intellectual creativity.

The Practical Implications of Psychodynamic Thinking

This elaboration of the Leonardo effect hypothesis has practical implications. For instance, I believe that it is possible to establish the category to which every fatherless entrepreneur belongs. Yet, a word of warning is in order. Deep psychological process will have determined that category – whichever it may be – so substantial time and energy will have to be invested in order to identify it correctly.

The sixty-four-million-dollar (sometimes literally) question is: how do you differentiate between the fatherless entrepreneurs who become their own fathers and exhibit the Leonardo effect and those who self-destruct or become fantasists with grandiose dreams?

Let us consider two possible scenarios. The first involves a potential investor who needs to decide whether an entrepreneur is likely to succeed; the second concerns an entrepreneur who feels that he is heading for trouble.

If offered a business opportunity, potential investors first need to go through a thorough process of due diligence, then they must evaluate the market situation and finally they should assess the business plan. Yet, as every investor knows, even the most thorough evaluation always leaves a lot of uncertainty. One of the crucial factors that will determine the success or failure of any new venture is the entrepreneur's personality. In this chapter, I have described two character types that are almost certain to fail: the self-destroyer and the grandiose dreamer. How might a potential investor identify these types?

Of course, first they should employ the standard tools, such as scouring the entrepreneur's CV for clues. Entrepreneurs who have had a relatively stable and uniformly ascending career trajectory are less likely to belong to either of these two categories than those who have had an erratic career pattern, with many ups and downs. But this can be deceptive. For instance, a graph of Jim's career record until the age of thirty would have shown a consistent, steep upward trajectory and a remarkable learning curve. In fact, it would be another couple of years before he suffered his first setback. Similarly, Arnold's career was remarkably successful until he reached the age of thirty.

So were there any warning signs? In Jim's case, unearthing information about his reckless philandering might have helped. Yet such information is not easy to come by. Meanwhile, in Arnold's case, it would have been difficult to find any clues at all: he was very knowledgeable about his business; he had produced excellent results throughout his twenties; and his career pattern would have given little reason to suspect that he was heading for disaster.

Therefore, we need to look beyond a simple career path to establish whether an entrepreneur is a good investment.

The Family Tree: Did the Entrepreneur Have a Father?

First of all, the entrepreneur's family tree should be assessed. If his family has history of entrepreneurialism, the dynamics will be very different from those within a family that did not foster entrepreneurial activities.

Second, an entrepreneur who has a close relationship with his father is likely to suffer from Freud's own problem: he might feel guilty about overtaking his father, which could result in a ceiling effect. Of course, this is unlikely to be a major issue if he has already overtaken his father financially or in some other way. If he has not, deeper investigation may be in order. Such an investigation should focus on how the entrepreneur deals with competition. Does he feel guilty about winning? Does he have the requisite killer instinct to exploit business opportunities to the full? Or does he tend to avoid competition or persistently fail to win? In other words, entrepreneurs who are too loyal to their fathers, and do not allow themselves to beat them, are likely to get stuck at some point.

Enquire into the Entrepreneur's Relationship with His Father

Potential investors must explore an entrepreneur's relationship with his father. Even without clinical training, it is possible to get a sense of how emotionally charged that relationship is.

There are several features to look out for. First, an entrepreneur who speaks without any affect or brushes the issue aside is likely to fall into one of two categories: he might be consciously hiding something; or he might be completely detached from his own feelings. Neither is a positive indicator.

If he speaks about his father with disdain or rage, it is advisable to enquire respectfully and empathetically into the reasons for his feelings. If he is able to explain those reasons, and reveals that he is in touch with the pain behind the rage or disdain, then there is a good chance that he is not driven unconsciously by these destructive emotions. On the other hand, if he displays a lack of insight into the cause of his pain and rage, there is a strong chance that he will run into trouble in the future.

Enquire into the Entrepreneur's Role Models

Asking about the entrepreneur's role models is extremely important, as it might reveal that he is an unrealistic dreamer. The potential investor should ask not merely *who* his role models are, but *why* they have become guiding influences. It would be a warning sign if the answer pertained to the role models' external trappings of success. This might indicate that the entrepreneur is chasing a fantasy of who he wants to be without understanding what it takes to get there.

By contrast, if the answer touches upon the role models' modus operandi, the character traits and personality characteristics that have enabled them to achieve success, the chances are that the entrepreneur has a realistic understanding of what is required to realize his ambitions, and he will be willing to endure the inevitable hardships along the way.

Take the Time to Get to Know the Entrepreneur Properly

Establishing complete trust with another human being takes time: it will usually be at least ninety minutes before the atmosphere is right and they feel sufficiently comfortable to open up about themselves. Yet many investors have neither the inclination nor the ability to conduct such an in-depth interview. In that case, they have two options: forgo the information that might prove crucial to the success of their investment; or employ a consultant with a background in clinical interviewing techniques who should be able to provide a reasoned assessment of the entrepreneur's personality.

Psychoanalysis and the Entrepreneur

Entrepreneurs often know deep inside when their lives are spiraling out of control. I have seen many who felt that they were heading for trouble, often without being able to identify the precise reason why. Sometimes friends, partners, investors or board members had pointed out potential problems.

The problem is that many entrepreneurs feel that they have to live up to their culturally designated image of super-human icon. But many others understand that they should be attentive to their psychological needs. Entrepreneurs like Jim and Arnold could have avoided their downfalls if they had sought help in time. Sometimes the entrepreneur's instincts issue a warning that something is wrong. In fact, the current climate in the business community often leads entrepreneurs to seek psychological advice even before they encounter trouble, simply because they are aware of the need to counteract the stress and loneliness of their professional activities.

A word of caution is in order, though. As Steven Berglass (2002) has convincingly shown, the currently popular executive coaching methods that are not psychologically informed, far from being helpful, are likely to be damaging. Coaches who work only on entrepreneurs' behavior, self-confidence and communication, without trying to understand and address the psychological dynamics that fuel their self-destructive patterns, often fail to prevent disaster, or even accelerate the downward spiral.

Psychoanalytically informed consultation that has a therapeutic element is not a quick-fix method. However, as I have argued above, and as research confirms (Shedler 2010), psychoanalytically informed consultation need not require four-times-a-week classical psychoanalysis over the course of five years. Intensive work can lead to tangible results in under a year, although it generally takes more time to stabilize the results.

The business community, at this point, is more psychologically minded than it used to be. A growing number of entrepreneurs and high-level executives are aware of the potential benefits of psychoanalytically informed consulting. The negative stereotype of such consultation as psychobabble – good for people who talk a lot and do nothing – and the fear that participating will lead to accusations of craziness are less prevalent than they used to be.

I hope I have shown that entrepreneurship can help people to deal with profound existential and psychological issues. Recognizing this fact does not diminish the cultural and economic importance of entrepreneurial achievement; it merely helps us to appreciate its value. A flexible, interdisciplinary use of psychoanalytic theory and practice can contribute greatly to a deeper understanding of the psychodynamics of entrepreneurship and help entrepreneurs to realize their full potential and contribute to the great value of their achievements for society.

In addition to showing the applicability of the Freudian legacy – in this case, a very particular hypothesis Freud presented in his study of Leonardo – to concrete issues in today's venture capital industry, I have attempted to demonstrate that a complex and often tragic drama lurks behind the iconic images of global entrepreneurship. New Cosmopolitans are not simply the cherry on the global icing: they are human beings who often struggle to find their voice, calling and sense of significance. In most cases, they do not merely want to rise into the ranks of the super-wealthy (although, often, this is certainly one of their motivations). More than anything else, they want to have an impact; they want to justify their existence by making a difference. In doing so, they exemplify one of the most important themes in the lives of almost all New Cosmopolitans, as the next chapter will show.

Chapter 5

The New Cosmopolitans

A Psychodynamic Portrait

In this chapter, I will attempt to present a more general psychodynamic portrait of the New Cosmopolitans, some of whom we have met in the previous two chapters. The New Cosmopolitans are a very influential elite today. They belong to what sociologists and economists call the super-creative core of the knowledge economies that have evolved over the last few decades (Florida 2002). Among their number are researchers in the natural, biological and social sciences; the content producers of the media industries and the arts; the upper echelons of research and development in high-tech, bio-tech and engineering industries; and the non-technical domain of the financial sector (Sassen 2000, Florida 2002). The essence of their work is to apply their intelligence to problem-solving and new developments. They are cosmopolitan because the networks that define and sustain their professional disciplines function independently of geography, and they have found places in all of the developed economies.

This chapter's interpretive theses are that it is particularly difficult for New Cosmopolitans to experience the safety of belonging, and that they find it almost impossible to feel true pride in their (often considerable) professional contributions. As opposed to more traditional forms of life, their frame of reference is global, which means that the context in which they need to contribute significantly in order to feel symbolic immortality is wider than it has been for anyone else in history. As a result, many of the more gifted New Cosmopolitans evolve an ego ideal that acknowledges significance in life only when an exorbitant standard is reached – such as making a permanent mark on global reality (Rothkopf 2008, Strenger 2011a).

While this may sound like a grandiose fantasy of almost delusional proportions, recent history provides several examples of New Cosmopolitans who have achieved exactly that. Steve Jobs – the co-founder, chair and CEO of Apple – introduced the personal computer as we know it today, thereby changing the way that most of us live and work. Next, in his second phase at Apple, he revolutionized the music industry by creating a new, internet-based business model for selling songs. Then he developed the iPhone, revolutionizing our understanding of what a phone should be for and creating our current conception of the smartphone. Finally, in the years before his death, he oversaw the development of the iPad, a new type of computer – the tablet – that once again revolutionized work and leisure for hundreds of millions people. Meanwhile, Larry Page and Sergei Brin, the founders of Google, transformed the way humanity uses the internet and made the vast majority of all human knowledge accessible to everyone with access to a computer. And Mark Zuckerberg, the founder and CEO of Facebook, changed the way in which many of us manage our social relations. Moreover, his company had a major historical impact because of the role it played in facilitating the Arab Spring.

This ego ideal can be understood only against the background of the huge transformations initiated by the recent wave of globalization (Friedman 1999, Sloterdijk 2005). I will therefore integrate data from economics, sociology, cultural criticism and a variety of other disciplines when describing these changes. The subsequent psychoanalytic interpretation will make extensive use of the theoretical model presented in Chapter 2. The human fear of insignificance – as far as we can tell from anthropological data (Becker 1974, 1975, Atran 2002) and current experimental research in existential psychology (Solomon et al. 2004) – does indeed seem to be an anthropological constant. There is also very strong evidence that all humans – in all times and all places – have dealt with the terror of death by viewing themselves as parts of a larger whole: a culture, civilization, nation or religion that is likely to survive the individual (Becker 1974). When individuals feel that they have contributed significantly to this larger whole, they feel that they have attained what Becker terms "symbolic immortality": that is, they believe that they will not simply disappear without a trace. That much seems to be true whether we study African tribes, the ancient Greeks or contemporary soccer fans.

Sociological and Economic Characteristics of the New Cosmopolitans

It is generally assumed that *globalization* began with the integration of the world's financial markets into a seamless, twenty-four-hour-a-day system that was made possible through deregulation and technical advances that allowed billion-dollar transactions to be completed in milliseconds. In turn, this allowed globalization to accelerate because multinational companies could now spread their operations around the globe. It was no longer necessary to keep headquarters, research and development and production in the same city, the same country or even the same continent (Friedman 1999).

However, globalization was not only a business phenomenon; it also had a huge impact in the cultural sphere. This process began with the emergence of global media empires like CNN and MTV in the 1980s but truly came into its own when the internet expanded in a few short years from a tool for high-tech specialists into a global network that was accessed daily by the vast majority of the developed world. The Spanish sociologist Manuel Castells' monumental three-volume work *The Information Age: Economy, Society and Culture* (1996–2000) traces the structural transformation that occurred around this time. The end result was the creation of the network society, which allowed everyone with a computer to plug into and participate within a global network. This became more important than either national or ethnic identity for those who wanted to forge a career in the new economy.

Globalization did not truly decentralize the conglomerates that came to span the globe and control ever-larger chunks of the worldwide economy. Saskia Sassen (2000) early recognized that the global headquarters of multinational companies tended to cluster in a few centers. In 1990 there were only three of these "global cities" – New York, Tokyo and London – but today there are dozens, including Paris, Zurich, Hong Kong, Shanghai, Seattle, Tel Aviv and Toronto. Moreover, because face-to-face contact has remained important for members of the upper echelons of the multinationals, firms that provide them with financial, legal and media services are also concentrated in the global cities.

This has radically changed the economic landscape of these cities. Executive salaries in the multinationals themselves as well as in the financial, legal and media firms that serve them have climbed to new heights and created a new social and economic class that the economist and former US Secretary of Labor Robert Reich (2005) has called the "international symbolic analysts." Service industries in the global cities now focus on catering to the needs of this high-earning group; and they have driven up property prices, forcing out the traditional middle and upper-middle classes.

Within this new class there is a subgroup that is primarily concerned with innovation. The economist Richard Florida (2002) views the members of this subgroup as the super-creative core of the information economies, and they rank highly in a number of globally connected networks: computing and mathematical occupations; architecture and engineering occupations; life, physical and social science occupations; education, training and library occupations; arts, design, entertainment, sports and media occupations; and the executive levels of research and development within high-technology and life-science companies.

The common denominator among all of these professions is that they are organized in global networks that use English as their *lingua franca*, and members of them are all expected to do high-level creative work within their particular domains of expertise. Academia is a prime example: its network is defined by a growing number of disciplines that focus on research; and its prime communication tool is the system of scientific journals that function according to principles shaped around an increasingly standardized mode of evaluation centered on research methodologies and quantitative measures for journal impact. For most academics, a high ranking in the global academic network is central to their identities and a condition for their professional success. Many of them are willing to move around the globe to secure a position at a more prestigious university. In this respect they are quite similar to engineers, mathematicians, computer scientists and financial analysts, the majority of whom are prepared to relocate across oceans to join the leading companies in their respective fields. New Cosmopolitans have therefore developed a new form of identity. Membership of whichever global network defines and enables their particular profession is at least as definitive of their identity as their ethnic, national or religious provenance (Sen 2006).

Nobody is born into the New Cosmopolitan tribe. It is a meritocracy, with entry restricted to those who have achieved considerable success in their field as well as a certain amount of recognition. In other words, the New Cosmopolitans are as exclusionary as any other tribe. Once they have gained entry, members continue to impose high standards on themselves: because their identity is intimately linked to their position in a global meritocratic network, they feel a constant need to justify their membership not only through professional success but through lifestyle. New Cosmopolitans are skilled in any number of rituals, ranging from giving keynote addresses at conferences to running marathons. They have their own festivals – the most iconic of which are probably the TED talks, the string of conferences held around the globe that communicate "ideas worth spreading [in] riveting talks, by remarkable people, free to the world," to use TED's own branding. Physicians, designers, engineers, human rights activists, psychologists, futurists and entrepreneurs give talks of no more than eighteen minutes in which they present ideas that are meant to change the world. These are then uploaded on to the TED website, with the most popular videos seen by millions of people.

The New Cosmopolitan meritocracy extends into the personal domain. As opposed to those who were traditionally labeled "nerds," today's New Cosmopolitans tend to exhibit a considerable sense of fashion and style. They also manage to cram plenty of exercise into their often harrowing schedules. Only those who are cool, stylish and trim attain a place of honor in the New Cosmopolitan crowd (Brooks 2000). They also have high expectations of their relationships. In general, they do not adhere to the traditional conceptions of marriage: while many of them marry and have children, and while they tend to take their parental responsibilities very seriously, they have no qualms about ending a relationship that is no longer gratifying. Each relationship must be self-justifying: it must contribute to both partners' self-actualization; otherwise, one or other will break it up (Giddens 1992). New Cosmopolitans are therefore far from secure in their relationships (Bauman 2002). They can never take them for granted – and nor would they want to, as that would jeopardize their liberty. Yet many of them yearn for more stability and comfort than their liquid lifestyles allow (Bauman 2007). The dilemma between freedom and safety is more pronounced with them than it is with other groups. Hence their potential for loneliness: used to living in their own minds, they easily lose track of intimate relationships (Bauman 2002).

The question "Have I done enough to live a life of significance?" is never far from a New Cosmopolitan's consciousness (Conley 2009). Existential psychology has shown the depth of humans' determination not to disappear from the face of the earth without leaving a trace. This makes the New Cosmopolitans' plight especially difficult: no longer limited to a specific community, they feel that their achievements are measured on a global scale – and this increases the fear of insignificance that is one of humanity's defining traits. But it also pushes them to raise the level of their expectations very high. New Cosmopolitans tend to be impatient with the limitations of traditional ways of doing things (Castells 1996). For instance, they generally have no tolerance for the tortuous machinations of established politics. They want to get things done, and they do not want to have to convince or cajole anyone whom they do not respect into some sort of political compromise. They prefer to exert influence through networks and institutions that are less bogged down by traditions they do not endorse, and by conflict they see as irrational.

Heirs of the Enlightenment

Over the last few decades, it has been fashionable for culturally conservative intellectuals to stigmatize the new elites as self-absorbed, narcissistic and uncommitted to anything but their own lives and careers, and to assert that they do not have any values at all (Lasch 1991, 1995). New Cosmopolitans do indeed invest strongly in their lifestyles and they are highly preoccupied with their careers and personal desirability (Brooks 2000). Nevertheless, it is myopic to suggest that they care for nothing but their own well-being. Most of my New Cosmopolitan patients have clearly defined worldviews and strong values by which they try to live their lives: they do care about the world at large. It would be seductive to characterize them as liberals, but this might be misleading, particularly in a US context. Therefore, let me characterize their worldviews more precisely.

New Cosmopolitans are organized in a number of networks: international journalism and punditry; foreign policy think-tanks and international NGOs that focus on human rights and fostering democracy; academia; and a very strong network of technology developers. They speak a common language that creates almost immediate closeness between people who have never met before, and live in very different circumstances, cultures and climates. Dialogue tends to evolve quickly on the basis of a set of shared assumptions: human rights, social justice, the right to happiness and self-fulfillment are all seen as sacred (Nussbaum 1995, Moyn 2010). There is a common ethos of responsible fact-finding, and consensus on scientific method as the only way to check theories and hypotheses (Castells 1996–2000).

Jeff embarked on his career in political science because he was appalled by prevailing political irrationality and political evil. He hoped that through understanding the evolutionary underpinnings of group processes, bias in decision-making and the workings of prejudice and bigotry he could make a difference in the world at large.

When Ben became a high-tech entrepreneur he also wanted to make a difference for the benefit of humankind, and he continues to believe that technology is the main tool through which humanity will overcome its tribal past. He is currently looking into ways in which international social and political activism might be fostered by improving the functioning of social networks, and he is fired up by phenomena like the Arab Spring and the Israeli social protests in the summer of 2011, both of which were fueled and facilitated by social networks.

The New Cosmopolitans' universalist frame of reference generates an almost inevitable conflict with more traditional forms of life. Their positions in the communities where they live are invariably precarious. Although they are lauded for their talent and economic contribution, they are also envied; and they are resented for not unquestioningly accepting the mores of their town, country or religion (Lasch 1995). They are therefore best understood as the heirs of the European Enlightenment, which, in the seventeenth and eighteenth centuries, unleashed the process of modernization (Gay 1966). The Scientific Revolution destroyed humankind's traditional cosmologies; the political ideas of Hobbes, Spinoza and Locke led to a dismantling of the aristocratic and monarchical orders; and the Industrial Revolution unraveled traditional forms of life. Montaigne, Diderot, Rousseau and Voltaire led a loosely connected network generally known as Les Philosophes in the eighteenth century. They were often hounded by state and Church, even to the point of having to go on the run. But their ideas led to the destruction of the classical European order that was based on a combination of aristocracy and unquestioned acceptance of Christianity (Israel 2001).

While most New Cosmopolitans may not be aware of this intellectual ancestry, they are, most of all, heirs of Kant's moral universalism (Kant 1787). Kant's categorical imperative of the individual – never only to be used, but always to be seen as a goal in itself – guides their politics. They believe in supranational institutions rather than sanctifying sovereignty; they have faith in universal reason rather than in traditionally entrenched forms of life.

The New Cosmopolitans' Precarious Position

Like the eighteenth-century Philosophes, the New Cosmopolitans reject the model of authority on which all traditional religions are based (Gay 1966, Israel 2001). They do not believe that any source of authority is beyond criticism. They are committed to the human pursuit of knowledge and the project of bettering the human condition, and they proudly point to the phenomenal achievements of modernity as proof of the Enlightenment's superiority to every traditional model of authority.

As opposed to the small group of eighteenth-century Philosophes, New Cosmopolitans number in the millions. Like the Philosophes, they rely on their network as a source of strength, but their network spans the globe and their messages travel at the speed of light. They are enamored with soft rather than hard power. If possible, they prefer to exert their influence through words and images rather than warships and bombs (Castells 1996). They are not constrained by the tools of traditional electoral politics, because they make effective use of communication technologies that cut across national borders. Irrespective of whether they are born Jewish or Catholic, they might still adopt Buddhist practices and core values or indeed those of any other intellectual, spiritual or cultural tradition (Florida 2002). And they do not worry whether their original community will accept this, because they do not believe that any group has the right to forbid what, for them, are legitimate life choices.

Because they always belong to networks beyond the confines of where they live, they generate discomfort in those whose identities are more local. Because they do not accept any community's demand for total loyalty, they are experienced as aloof, at best, and arrogant, at worst (Lasch 1995). Hence,

New Cosmopolitans have sparked a reaction that is just as strong as the nineteenth-century reaction to the Industrial Revolution. As the political scientist Benjamin Barber (1995) and the historian of religion Karen Armstrong (2000) have argued convincingly, the fundamentalist backlash that has swept through all major religions since the 1970s is a reaction to the immense power of the global communication networks. Such traditional forms of life are left feeling powerless against the New Cosmopolitans' impact and often respond with rage and resentment (Sloterdijk 2006).

The New Cosmopolitans tend to dislike any form of tribalism, be it religious, ethnic, national or racial (Sen 2006). They often support groups to which they have no natural affiliation, including, in the past few years, Haitians, Congolese, Tibetans and Kosovars. They are viscerally opposed to exclusionary practices, whether on racial or religious grounds, or because of sexual preference. They see bigotry and chauvinism as incongruous remnants of a primitive stratum of human nature that should be abandoned rather than cherished (Appiah 2006).

However, New Cosmopolitans themselves are invariably elitist. Early in their development they discover the mind's power for critical thought, and they value it highly. They have also experienced the enormous power of group pressure – the ways in which irrational – even incoherent – ideas can influence enormous numbers of people. They have little patience for the argument that beliefs have to be respected merely because somebody holds them, and they are often merciless in their criticism of religion (Dennett 2005). They remind traditional Christians that there are different ways to live, and that decrying homosexuality is nothing but archaic prejudice. This has generated a conservative–religious backlash in the United States against the permissive personal lifestyles of the New Cosmopolitans (Armstrong 2000, Harris 2004). They remind Orthodox Jews that following endless commands is a limited way of life, and that it is preposterous for a relatively small group of people to claim that they are God's "chosen people." They enrage traditional Muslims when they argue that limiting women's public role is both inhuman and obsolete.

All of this open criticism has meant that it has become ever more difficult for political and religious authorities to shield their followers from the impact of the New Cosmopolitans. This often generates ferocious hatred, as exemplified by the relentless attempts to delegitimize Barack Obama in the United States. By his origins, upbringing and values, Obama is the quintessential New Cosmopolitan: he grew up in Hawaii and Indonesia; his father's family is Muslim; and his outlook was shaped by attending elite universities (the archetypal Enlightenment institutions) and encountering progressive Judaism in his academic circle. As a result, many conservative Americans have accused him of being "un-American."

Meanwhile, the French sociologist of globalized Islam, Olivier Roy (2009) has argued persuasively that the surge in Islamic fundamentalism is a reaction to the threat posed by the New Cosmopolitans. Parties and organizations with the declared aim of "purifying" Islam of the corrosive effects of what they take to be Western materialism are sweeping through the Middle East and further afield. But the real threat seems to be the anti-tribalism of Enlightenment thinking, which casts doubt on all traditional forms of life.

This is the paradox of the New Cosmopolitans' political role: their universalism is genuine and deeply felt, but their way of life is specific, elitist and highly meritocratic. They forget that they themselves are a tribe, albeit a global one, so find it hard to understand why they are viewed as a powerful elite and why their universalist message is so often rejected. This, in turn, often increases their sense of isolation. They are genuinely concerned with humanity's future, yet their suggestions about how to avoid catastrophe usually generate anger rather than gratitude, because most of humanity's horizons are still defined far more by local custom and traditional upbringing.

Implications for Psychoanalysis

Psychoanalysis tries to contribute to the grand project of formulating the innate hardware and software of the human psyche, and it attempts to understand the historically determined psyches of the patients whose lives and minds we meet in therapeutic work.

Today, no discipline can attempt to pursue the first of these goals in isolation, and in Part II of this book I will present a vision of the place of psychoanalysis in the network of disciplines currently involved in understanding human nature and life under globalization. I believe it has been one of the great mistakes of more traditional psychoanalysis to insist that it can remain epistemically autonomous (Sulloway 1979). Peter Fonagy (in Jurist 2010) has argued convincingly that this is a totally anachronistic position, and together with his colleagues he has shown how psychoanalysis can and must integrate into the vast interdisciplinary landscape of today's human sciences (Fonagy et al. 2005). Similarly, Robert Stolorow has argued convincingly that psychoanalysis needs to widen its philosophical base in order to refine its epistemological self-understanding (Stolorow et al. 2002)

The same, I believe, holds true for our second goal: to increase analytic understanding. In trying to decipher the reality of the new class I have called the New Cosmopolitans, I have been inspired by two decades of clinical work with them. But it is impossible to achieve a full understanding of their existential and psychic reality without placing it within the vast social, cultural, political and economic landscape that shapes their experience. I have attempted to do this by pulling together data from various disciplines to generate my portrait of this new class. We need to integrate an understanding of their new reality into our clinical and theoretical conception of psychoanalysis – a process that has accelerated since the 1990s (Aron 1996). This has led many to claim that the discipline requires – and is in the midst of – a deep paradigm shift (Mitchell 1993) from an intrapsychic to a relational conception.

As yet, I have not touched upon the therapeutic implications of the New Cosmopolitans' psychic and external reality. Along with many of my colleagues, I realized some time ago that the New Cosmopolitans' very high mobility demands the use of contemporary communication technologies, such as Skype, Google Hangout and Apple FaceTime, if we are to preserve therapeutic continuity and provide our clients with the safe haven they desperately need in their fluid, exacting lives. However, it is still too early to say how this ever-widening use of communication technologies will impact therapeutic process and outcome.

To understand more we will need to analyze a vast amount of data and theory from a variety of disciplines. In no way do I see my present formulation as any more than an interpretive hypothesis that will have to stand the test of a variety of empirical investigations, including epidemiological studies, controlled research on the process and outcome of therapy with New Cosmopolitans, and sociological and economic investigations into whether the category itself is indeed credible.

The task is daunting, but the prospective results – I believe and hope to show in Part II of this book – are exciting. If psychoanalysis can regain the exploratory spirit of its early years and transform itself in ways that are appropriate for our present reality, we may soon find the discipline reinvigorated and contributing significantly to our understanding of what it means to live in the twenty-first century.

Part II

Psychoanalysis in the Age of Neuroscience

Chapter 6

Towards an Open Psychoanalytic Culture

Until the 1960s, there was a clear-cut account of the nature and function of psychoanalysis: it was supposed to be a theory of the human mind that included a general theory of development, from which derived an etiological theory of the various psychopathologies and a form of psychotherapeutic treatment. This theory's standing in medicine, academia and society was impressive: psychoanalysts occupied many of the most prestigious chairs in psychiatry at leading universities, and psychoanalysis was a high-status profession, limited in the United States to MDs, who had practices along Park Avenue and commanded high fees that were paid in full by medical insurance.

Half a century later, none of the above is true. Departments of psychiatry no longer employ psychoanalysts; the overwhelming majority of clinical psychology programs worldwide hardly teach psychoanalysis any more; and medical insurance schemes very rarely foot the bill for psychoanalytic treatment. The prestigious academic presses and journals in clinical psychology mostly refuse even to look at psychoanalytic manuscripts, and, as we will see in detail in Chapter 7, psychoanalytic publishing is at an all-time low.

None of this has happened because the general public has lost interest in psychology, mental functioning or mental health. In fact, the opposite is true: books about everything from the psychology of sex to the vicissitudes of self-esteem, midlife transition and various psychopathologies – all topics that were once firmly in the purview of psychoanalysis – continue to fascinate the educated lay public. But today's educated public wants theory, interpretation and advice based on scientific research. They buy books that tell them all about the latest experiments, preferably involving FMRI, EEG and other methodologies of the burgeoning neurosciences. And the theories are generally couched within a framework that has evolved into the paradigm of the evolutionary cognitive neurosciences.

The psychoanalytic mainstream has by and large not dealt with the momentous changes in psychoanalysis's standing. The main tendency has been simply to disregard the boom in the cognitive neurosciences. Psychoanalytic papers and books mostly quote other psychoanalytic papers and books. This has run in parallel with a progressive tendency to introversion in much psychoanalytic writing: ever-fewer papers and books are tackling the great questions of classical psychoanalysis relating to human nature, society and religion; instead, they are focusing on the minute intricacies of the psychoanalytic exchange. Unsurprisingly, this has led the general educated public to lose interest in psychoanalytic writing – a tendency I will discuss in Chapter 8.

Another reaction to these developments has been to decry the scientism of academia and public culture and argue that we are living in an age of progressive shallowness and overestimation of instrumental reason at the price of profound humanistic insight. When I read some of the rather acrimonious reactions to the growing prestige of the natural sciences (e.g., Hoffman 2009) I have a distinct sense of *déjà vu*. In the seventeenth century, Blaise Pascal, one of the founders of probability theory, had a conversion experience that led him, famously, to claim that "Knowledge of physical science will not console me for ignorance of morality in time of affliction, but knowledge of morality will always console me for ignorance of physical science" (Pascal 1670: aphorism 23). This is one of the most famous statements about science and what were then called the moral sciences.

The interrelation between humanistic and scientific knowledge has been a matter of often acrimonious debate in a variety of contexts since the phenomenal rise of the natural sciences in the seventeenth century. Champions of the humanities often accuse science of reductionism and simple-mindedness – an accusation Alfred North Whitehead leveled against his former friend and collaborator Bertrand Russell. Scientists often respond that humanists are invariably muddleheaded, as Russell retorted to Whitehead.

It seems that it is now the turn of psychoanalysis to relive this debate between the sciences and the humanities. Over the last three decades Irwin Z. Hoffman has presented a subtle, rich and illuminating version of psychoanalysis as a humanistic, hermeneutic discipline he calls "dialectical constructivism." In "Doublethinking our Way to 'Scientific Legitimacy'" (Hoffman 2009) he argues passionately that psychoanalysis must in no way cave in to the dominance of instrumental reason, with its emphasis on measurable results and achieving quick symptom relief. Other distinguished analysts, including Philip Cushman and Donnell Stern, have adopted similar positions.

Meanwhile, on the other side of the debate stand Peter Fonagy, Jeremy Safran and myself. For quite some time, Fonagy has argued that the institutional and intellectual isolation of psychoanalysis from the rest of the scientific world, including the social and biological sciences, is self-imposed and must be reversed. In an interview with Elliot Jurist, he went so far as to say that "doing psychoanalysis" will soon no longer be a legitimate job description; that practicing clinicians will have to state what kind of disturbances or problems they deal with, by what technique, and must corroborate that technique's effectiveness through controlled research (Jurist 2010). A few years later, Safran (2013) argued that while the cognitive neurosciences are often overfunded, psychoanalysis should not wall itself off from them and should not eschew standard quantitative methods to ascertain therapeutic results. Finally, I have argued that psychoanalysis's retreat from substantial questions about human nature has contributed greatly to its lack of public standing and that the discipline should explore fruitful ways of interacting with the exciting and burgeoning field of the evolutionary cognitive neurosciences.

The proponents of hermeneutic purism in psychoanalysis often depict quantitative science as the soulless undertaking of reductionist number-crunchers. To my mind, this argument seems to be based on stereotypes rather than on true acquaintance with contemporary scientific work. But there has always been a conciliatory position that has argued that pitching science and the humanities against each other as mutually exclusive views of human reality is both intellectually wrong and politically fruitless. Possibly the most famous embodiment of this conciliatory position in recent history is C. P. Snow's *The Two Cultures*, which attempted to show that both the sciences and the humanities are sure to miss out if they continue to argue that the seemingly competing form of knowledge is inferior (Snow 1958). The evolutionary biologist Stephen Jay Gould followed suit with his witty and deep *The Hedgehog, the Fox, and the Magister's Pox*, whose subtitle proposed "mending the gap between science and the humanities" (Gould 2003).

The present book is written in the spirit of the ecumenical position adopted by Snow and Gould, which in the past has been represented in psychoanalysis by such theorists as John Bowlby (1979) and Daniel Stern (1985) and which is currently defended by Fonagy, Safran and Lewis Aron as well as myself. I therefore make a plea for reintegrating psychoanalysis into the "web of belief," as the philosopher of science Williard Quine (1978) called the human enterprise of understanding the universe. In an age when human knowledge has evolved spectacularly, and in which no discipline can remain autonomous but rather must live in constant interdependence with other disciplines and theories, psychoanalysis's preoccupation with its own purity and autonomy has become deeply unhealthy and counter-productive and has prevented the discipline from addressing some of the burning questions of the present.

I am, of course, far from alone in opposing psychoanalytic purism. Lewis Aron and Karen Starr (2013) have recently published a rich account of a new form of psychoanalysis that is open to both social issues and spiritual modes of thought. Similarly, Robert Wallerstein (2012) has published an impassioned call for psychoanalysis to reconnect with mainstream science and the research universities. He is singularly well placed to issue such a call as he had considerable experience in combining psychoanalysis with controlled research during the famed Menninger study that he summarized in *The Talking Cures* (Wallerstein 1995).

I hope that Part I of this book made a good case for the thesis that if psychoanalysis genuinely embraces close interaction with the grand human enterprise of understanding human nature, it is sure to be tremendously energized by surrounding disciplines, and in turn will contribute to them. The first step must be for many practitioners and theorists to discard the instinctive distrust they harbor towards the evolutionary cognitive neurosciences.

As Nobel Laureate Eric Kandel (2012) has demonstrated in his magisterial study of the intellectual climate in *fin de siècle* Vienna, psychoanalysis began as a precursor of evolutionary psychology as we know it today (see Chapter 9). But it then repressed its roots in evolutionary theory for one simple reason: Freud was a Lamarckian, so many of his core theses – which seemed perfectly rational in his era – are now outdated.

I hope to demonstrate that this repression of evolutionary thinking is both unnecessary and harmful. It is unnecessary because Freud will remain a towering figure in Western intellectual and cultural history – because his integration of nineteenth-century science and romantic thought created a compelling view of human existence – even if we acknowledge that he was not an infallible prophet. It is harmful because there is little doubt that our understanding of human existence has been immeasurably enriched by evolutionary thinking. In particular, I will show that some evolutionary-based psychodynamic models have been used extremely successfully in social psychology, and these are kindred in both spirit and content to psychoanalytic thinking.

A psychoanalysis that is open to the results, methodologies and theories of surrounding disciplines (as discussed in Chapter 8) has the capacity to address many of the concerns of the present, as I hope I have shown in Part I. We live in a world that has changed radically due to the information technologies that have revolutionized both our economies and our private lives, and psychoanalysis needs to deal with these changes clinically and theoretically.

The final chapter addresses the issue of psychoanalysis's virtual disappearance from the public sphere, and argues that the type of open-minded psychoanalytic thinking presented in the preceding chapters could allow it to gain its rightful place in today's global agora. The various sciences, including evolutionary cognitive neurosciences, have found ways to communicate with a wide, educated audience that has a keen interest in their results. The main channels are magazines and websites that address this audience directly as well as significant portions of the high-quality daily press.

I believe that psychoanalysis's absence from today's agora is far from inevitable. True, today's media require communication in modes that are largely foreign to those who have been trained by immersion in complex and often opaque texts. But establishing a presence in these media requires us to reformulate our traditional theses and messages into more concise and punchy forms. I will tell the story of my own gradual entry into the world of global media, through writing op-ed pieces, communicating with business audiences and presenting TED talks. I have decided to tell this story even though it contains some painful and embarrassing failures. At first, I inflexibly insisted on forcing the language and style of my academic and psychoanalytic upbringing on to my audiences, who at best looked at me with incomprehension and at worst walked out. Gradually, though, I started to listen to my friends, who gave me tips on how to reach people, and after some initial resistance I realized that the effort was worthwhile.

Psychoanalysis can reclaim a place of honor in the public sphere if it is prepared to make the transition from a preoccupation with its own uniqueness to the joy of participating in the human race's quest for understanding and knowledge.

Chapter 7

The Marginalization of Psychoanalysis

For more than two decades, conferences and publications have declared that psychoanalysis is in a state of crisis. Yet there has still been no radical reorganization or reorientation of the discipline. As a result, it has become marginal. In the 1960s, psychoanalysts held a large proportion of the developed world's professorships in psychiatry; now they account for practically none. The same is true of professorships in psychology; and hardly any of the graduate programs in clinical psychology are psychoanalytically oriented. Finally, although many psychoanalytic institutes continue to attract candidates, scarcely any patients now sign up for classical psychoanalysis.

The discipline's marginalization is best illustrated by Paul Stepansky's (2009) account of the decline of psychoanalytic publishing. Stepansky was the publisher of the Analytic Press, one of the last houses devoted to psychoanalytic publishing until it closed and its titles came under the umbrella of the publishing giant Taylor and Francis. He claims that psychoanalysis's marginalization came about because it failed to manage the transition towards normal science that characterizes disciplines that can boast a cumulative, progressive trajectory.

Thomas S. Kuhn's *The Structure of Scientific Revolutions* (1962) has become the canonical philosophical and sociological framework for understanding the history of science. Kuhn showed that scientific disciplines become successful when they coalesce around a *scientific paradigm.* Such paradigms include a metaphysics of science – that is, a number of basic assumptions about the basic constituents of the field of enquiry. In physics – the most spectacularly successful modern science – the principal assumption is that the world is composed of a number of basic constituents (particles, fields) that can be described by interlocking differential equations. In biology, the paradigm is organized around Darwinian evolution and the idea that *biological* processes can ultimately be reduced to *biochemical* processes.

Medicine, an applied science, is organized around findings made in the successful basic sciences and statistical research methods that show the diagnostic and therapeutic validity of certain hypotheses.

Stepansky (2009) compares the functioning of psychoanalysis to the pre-paradigmatic stage of medicine in the late nineteenth century, and shows that the former systematically made the wrong choices. He identifies two major reasons for its failure to become a mature science. The first of these is its obsession with maintaining its "purity": Stepansky reports that some major figures in psychoanalysis (for reasons of discretion, he does not name them) threatened to stop working with him if the Analytic Press continued to publish authors whom they considered "insufficiently analytic." The second reason is that psychoanalysis embraced theoretical pluralism, which is inconsistent with the structure of a mature science, in the latter half of the twentieth century.

I think that Stepansky is right to identify the self-encapsulating nature of psychoanalysis as one of the main factors in its marginalization, but feel that he is wrong to cite the discipline's embrace of pluralism as another *cause* of this process; rather, it is the end *result*. I will argue that psychoanalysis, by refusing to go beyond the clinical situation as its main research tool, found it impossible to become a normal science, and that theoretical pluralism was the inevitable result. I will also address Stepansky's suggestion that the discipline needs to learn how to live with its marginal status gracefully – a modest proposal that is unlikely to revive psychoanalysis. Instead, I will suggest strategies that might enable psychoanalysis to escape a future at the margins and become a productive scientific discipline in its own right: first by becoming less concerned with its own purity and instead developing more clinically relevant approaches; and second by integrating into the mainstream of the contemporary evolutionary cognitive neurosciences, which are producing scientifically sound, intellectually fascinating and existentially relevant results.

Theoretical Pluralism: Cause or Effect of the Crisis?

Stepansky supports his argument that psychoanalysis was prevented from becoming a mature science because it embraced theoretical pluralism by describing a number of case studies, ranging from the pluralization of the *Psychoanalytic Quarterly* under the editorship of Owen Renik to the pluralist stances adopted by Mitchell, Wallerstein and many others. He marshals his detailed knowledge of the history of medicine and uses it as a blueprint for comparison. Medicine matured from a craft into a science, and moved from barbers' shops into the halls of academia and the ever more technologically sophisticated environment of the modern hospital. The process that led there was not a decree by fiat that medicine had to become a mature science. Rather, medicine became a mature discipline because it was fed by an ever-growing set of theories and tools employed by a variety of disciplines, primarily biology, chemistry and physics. The discovery of micro-organisms and the roles played by bacteria and viruses in the late nineteenth and early twentieth centuries finally created a framework that allowed for a concrete understanding of many illnesses that no longer moved between different, incompatible models. Medicine's development was also fed by such breakthroughs as the discovery of X-rays and their diagnostic and therapeutic applications, and especially by the discovery of the chemical structure of DNA and its phenomenal implications that are now catapulting the discipline into new domains and possibilities.

Nothing comparable happened in psychoanalysis. Instead, a growing number of psychoanalytic theorists embraced theoretical pluralism. Stepansky (2009: 248) points out, correctly, that maturing sciences never allow such pluralism: no astrophysicist would ever dream of moving playfully between Ptolemaic and Copernican cosmologies, or between Aristotelian and Newtonian physics. Hence, he claims that the psychoanalysts' embrace of pluralism was one of the reasons why their discipline did not evolve into a mature science. This is where I disagree with him, because I feel that his attempt to understand the illness of psychoanalysis confuses cause and effect. Psychoanalysis's problem was not that Renik, Schafer, Spence, Mitchell et al. embraced pluralism. Rather, these protagonists of pluralism *reacted* to a deepening crisis in psychoanalysis. Theoretical pluralism was the historical condition of psychoanalysis at the time, not something these theorists strove to create. In fact, they attempted to salvage the discipline by turning the *de facto* pluralism of a variety of approaches that were incapable of proving their superiority into a virtue.

Throughout the discipline's history, psychoanalytic theorists had hailed what were seen as major breakthroughs: for example, Klein's "discovery" of the developmental positions and projective identification; Lacan's formulation of the symbolic, imaginary and real registers; and Kohut's formulation of the selfobject functions. But if psychoanalysis kept changing its theories without any dramatic advance in therapeutic outcome, maybe the truth value of psychoanalytic theory was really irrelevant to practice (Strenger 1991)?

To use one of Wittgenstein's (1953) most famous metaphors, one might say that psychoanalysis kept pushing buttons without realizing that they were not connected to anything inside the machine. The reason why psychoanalysis splintered into ever more schools and approaches was that the "discoveries" simply did not matter because they had no impact on therapeutic effect.

Emotionally charged wars were fought on questions that seemed to be matters of life and death. Are humans born in a state of primary narcissism, or are we object-related from the outset? How important are the drives? What is the nature of internal objects? But then it transpired that psychoanalysis did not have the tools to differentiate between these issues for the simple reason that therapeutic impact did not depend on them.

The main reason why psychoanalysis never made the journey from pre-paradigmatic to mature science was its refusal to investigate the structure and function of the unconscious mind, human development, the etiology of psychopathology, by the various methods of empirical science. Instead, it relied exclusively on the clinical observation of single cases. In his influential critique of psychoanalysis, the philosopher of science Adolf Grünbaum (1984) put the problem in a nutshell: it was impossible to test psychoanalytic etiological or developmental hypotheses through clinical data alone, but the psychoanalytic mainstream refused to use any other methods. Grünbaum did not claim that psychoanalysis was wrong, or that it was untestable. He simply declared that it was untested.

The reason for the discipline's theoretical fragmentation can be found in the essence of psychotherapy. Claude Lévi-Strauss, in his classic paper "The Effectiveness of Symbols" (1949), argued that the modern psychotherapist and the traditional shaman both rely on the same anthropological mechanisms – later described in detail in Jerome Frank's *Persuasion and Healing* (Frank and Frank 1993). Almost every society has healers who are characterized by three anthropological constants: an institutionalized status acquired by a process of initiation; a myth that explains the origins of the patient's suffering and the ways to overcome it; and a ritual through which that myth is enacted.

Both Lévi-Strauss and Frank (a psychoanalytically oriented psychiatrist) argued that the effectiveness of psychotherapy in general and psychoanalysis in particular is based on these anthropological constants, rather than on the truth value of the theories ("myths") and techniques ("rituals") that are applied. This position was dramatically corroborated in a series of meta-analytic studies that began in the 1970s: most psychotherapeutic effect depended on non-specific factors that had nothing to do with the specific theories and techniques that were applied. The nature of the therapeutic alliance, not the method employed, was the best predictor of success. Hence, psychoanalysis was simply unable to test its theories on the couch.

Schafer (1976), Spence (1982), Mitchell (1993), Renik and other constructivists tried to salvage something of the splendid edifice of psychoanalytic literature by suggesting a new conceptualization of the essence of psychoanalysis: it was not a science, but a hermeneutic undertaking in which patient and analyst co-created an understanding. Psychoanalysis, as Schafer said, was about the "retelling of lives." Hence, it was pointless to fight bloody wars about undecidable questions: psychoanalysis might as well live in a playful universe of co-existing narratives and metaphors. What mattered was that patient and analyst co-created joyfully and fruitfully. Adam Phillips, one of the few psychoanalytic authors who still managed to sell books in the tens of thousands in the 1990s and early 2000s, pushed this conclusion one step further: psychoanalysis, he argued, was about refusing to adopt the position of an expert who could tell the patient anything authoritatively; it was a form of conversation, not a technique. He and the philosopher Richard Rorty (1989) discarded the Enlightenment Freud who had hoped for a theoretical edifice that would progress for ever. Instead, they favored a post-Enlightenment Freud who had basically discovered that there are multiple ways of telling our lives, and suggested that we should find interesting ways to do so, as living rich lives is better than living uninteresting ones.

The pluralist, hermeneuticist, constructivist version of psychoanalysis was therefore not the illness that prevented psychoanalysis from moving towards maturity and respectability; it was a reaction to its failure to reach the status of mature science. It was the line of last defense of a discipline that, by its very nature, was not cut out to join the prestigious club of scientific disciplines that move from one discovery to the next, from one breakthrough to the next that yields even more spectacular results, be they technological or therapeutic. In this respect, it is closer to literary criticism than it is to physics, or even medicine. This proximity is reflected in the fact that most of those who still buy into the idea of psychoanalysis (mostly of Lacanian provenance) are students and teachers in the humanities. Like literary criticism, psychoanalytic interpretation had ceased to make a difference in the wider world; hence it was liberated – and reduced – to playing with signifiers that did not have a major impact outside the discipline itself. Many of the constructivist, hermeneutically oriented psychoanalytic authors do not feel that this status should be mourned; indeed, they believe it should be celebrated. They see the reclassification of psychoanalysis as a humanistic discipline as a process of liberation rather than a loss.

For Adam Phillips (2002), psychoanalysis in the present should be akin to literature more than to medicine, and the global bourgeoisie's anxious search for experts on every topic from child-rearing to sex needs to be resisted. His essays completely eschew the format of the scientific paper, and for inspiration he looks to a tradition that stretches from Montaigne through Oscar Wilde to T. S. Eliot. He argues that psychoanalytic expertise should entail the dismantling of individual and cultural conceptions of expertise and authority.

Like Rorty (1989), he celebrates Freud not for his grand theorizing, but for opening the fascinating option that we can tell our lives as quirky, overdetermined, ever-shifting versions of ourselves. He stands against the psychoanalytic desire to explain everything: psychoanalysis should not try to explain and normalize, and for Phillips there is no such thing as psychoanalytic technique. Psychoanalysis is – and should be – simply a disciplined form of conversation.

One might argue that psychoanalysis, at its best, has never been a science; rather, it is a type of writing located between the subjective and the objective in Winnicott's transitional space of culture. The great authors of the psychoanalytic tradition should be read as generating a style of writing *sui generis*: Winnicott should not be read as a scientist, but as an evocative writer about clinical experience; Bion not as a clinical theorist, but as a philosopher trying to build a mystical Kantianism; Lacan not as a muddled scientist, but as a metaphysical clown (as the German philosopher Peter Sloterdijk has argued). We should look at the writings of mavericks like Michael Eigen rather than at the research generated by Fonagy and Sydney Blatt for inspiration for the future of psychoanalysis.

I am in two minds about this playful version of psychoanalysis, which is willing to trade the status of scientific respectability for the lightness of open-ended writing. There is indeed something unsettling in contemporary culture's anxious quest for experts and authorities on everything, a quest that is fed by the endless stream of self-help books that propose quick, seven-step routes to everything from effectiveness to happiness. Correspondingly, there is something deeply attractive about the idea that psychoanalysis should constitute an alternative counter-culture to this anxious search for normality. But even this playful version does not live well in organized psychoanalysis: the same aspects of psychoanalytic organization that inhibit the evolution into normal science also inhibit the type of free-ranging, playfully explorative writing celebrated by Phillips and practiced by Eigen, Christopher Bollas, Nina Coltart and Robert Stoller, at their best. Searching for orthodoxy and hanging on to authority are not conducive to either writing or a therapeutic style that focuses on liberation.

This playful version of psychoanalysis, which I have described in depth elsewhere (Strenger 2002), is not likely to become the mainstream because its proponents avoid the politics of psychoanalysis and its institutions and recoil from the idea of building schools and attracting followers; and it is intrinsically opposed to the idea of psychoanalysis as a mature science. The merit of the hermeneuticist approach is to keep alive one impulse of psychoanalysis that has been among its most attractive features from early on: a celebration of the mind's unruliness and penchant for madness, of the complex, multilayered expressions of human nature.

Like Freud's vision of psychoanalysis as an ambitious science of the mind, the playful version of psychoanalysis is the project of undermining cultural pressures of normalization. Both are rooted in the Enlightenment vision of human life as potentially free – although the first is more embodied in Kant and the second more in Diderot. For the realization of either vision, psychoanalysis will have to liberate itself from its own self-imposed tutelage.

But the price of the hermeneutic conception of psychoanalysis is enormous: it means that the discipline renounces the ambition of producing knowledge about human nature – an ambition that was crucial to its early success.

The Loss of Explanatory Power and Cultural Relevance

The failure of psychoanalysis to generate actual knowledge – as opposed to interesting narratives – about human nature had dramatic consequences. Stepansky's (2009) most rivetingly depressing (if the oxymoron be allowed) account charts the decline of psychoanalytic publishing in his book's first few chapters. His vantage point as editor in chief of one of the last psychoanalytic publishing houses gives him unique insight into this topic. The figures alone tell a very clear story. In the 1950s and 1960s, psychoanalysis had a wide public. The all-time bestselling analytic author was Erich Fromm, whose books sold millions of copies. Erik Erikson didn't come anywhere close to that, but some of his titles still racked up sales in the hundreds of thousands. Heinz Kohut managed to sell 49,000 copies of *The Analysis of the Self* (1971), but from then onwards the decline was dramatic. Of contemporary authors, Jessica Benjamin probably leads the pack, selling approximately 30,000 copies of *The Bonds of Love* (1988). Other "popular" titles, such as Mitchell's *Hope and Dread in Psychoanalysis* (1993), have hardly broken through the 10,000 copies barrier. As Stepansky (2009: 30) points out, most psychoanalytic books now sell no more than a few hundred copies. This led to some heated exchanges between the editor in chief of the Analytic Press and a number of psychoanalytic authors who simply refused to accept that they were addressing a minuscule niche market.

One of the most important developments since the 1990s has been that esteemed academic publishers like the university presses of Harvard and Yale, who previously accepted psychoanalytic titles, now turn down all but a tiny number of them. International Universities Press, the house that hosted such psychoanalytic luminaries as Winnicott and Kohut, is now defunct to all intents and purposes, while the Analytic Press, which Stepansky led heroically for many years, closed and moved its back catalogue and some of its active series to Taylor and Francis. This leaves hardly any publishers that specialize in psychoanalysis, and ever fewer academic presses that are willing to publish books on the subject.

Here, again, Stepansky's explanation for the demise of psychoanalytic publishing is its fragmentation and endorsement of theoretical pluralism. And, again, I think that he is confusing cause and effect. The pluralism did not cause the lack of unity; it was a reflection of it. Pluralism did not begin when a number of authors embraced it in the 1980s; it had been part and parcel of psychoanalysis since the very outset.

Behind the failure of becoming paradigmatic science stood organized psychoanalysis's systematic refusal to become part of mainstream science. The sociologist Ernest Gellner (2003) has argued forcefully that the institutional dynamics of psychoanalysis should be described primarily in terms of the sociology of religion. From the outset, the history of depth psychology was schismatic: Freud and Jung fell out on issues of dogma, not because of a disagreement that could properly be called scientific. The dynamics were similar in the exclusion of "heretics" like Adler, Rank, Horney and many others who were unwilling to subscribe to this or that dogma or ritual of the "psychoanalytic main church," as Fonagy (in Jurist 2010) wittily calls some of the mainstream schools of the movement.

Psychoanalysis isolated itself from mainstream science from the very beginning, as Frank Sulloway (1979) showed in his groundbreaking intellectual biography of Freud. Sulloway stressed that one of psychoanalysis's principal goals was always to achieve epistemic autonomy. It supposedly did not need any scientific procedures outside of psychoanalytic clinical observation to develop and corroborate its theories. All criticism of this goal of epistemic autonomy was dismissed as resistance against psychoanalytic discoveries, and critics were denigrated as being incapable of judging psychoanalysis.

This introversion was reflected in the sociology of psychoanalytic publishing. In order to publish in the mainstream journals, authors were well advised to keep their references within the club. I will never forget the perennial advice offered by Joseph Sandler, long-time editor in chief of the *International Journal of Psychoanalysis*: "Open your paper with a quotation from Freud; show that Freud didn't deal with your problem because he lived too early; say what you have to say; and end the paper by showing why Freud would agree with you if he were alive today." Of course, Sandler's tongue was firmly in his cheek whenever he said this, but he still felt that all psychoanalytic papers needed to establish their allegiance to the tradition if they were to be considered for publication.

Unfortunately, to this day, most psychoanalytic conferences exhibit a similar attitude: psychoanalysts quote other psychoanalysts and retell their favorite stories of how psychoanalysis evolved. Such stories generally involve an ever-deepening understanding of clinical processes, and there is hardly any mention of results generated by scientific research in other fields. Judging from the speakers at these conferences, the surrounding disciplines have nothing to contribute to psychoanalysis.

If anything, psychoanalytic papers mostly quote research that vaguely seems to support some aspect of existing psychoanalytic theory. Stepansky (2009: ch. 6) mentions several attempts to link psychoanalysis with the neurosciences. The strategy has usually been to point to some neuroscience findings and show that these might be consistent with psychoanalysis. However, as Stepansky points out, these attempts have failed for two reasons. The first is that the central theoretical tenets of psychoanalysis are now anything but clear, so it is impossible to establish which hypotheses should be linked to the neurosciences. The second is that psychoanalysis does not itself fertilize the neurosciences, so it is disregarded by them.

Admittedly, there have been some exceptions. The towering example is John Bowlby's exploration of attachment, which eventually became the basis of an important research paradigm that is generating fascinating results (Bowlby 1990). But Bowlby's work was kept at the margins, whereas, for instance, Melanie Klein's was considered "truly psychoanalytic." Other examples include Emde's (1973) attempt to introduce the basic emotions paradigm into psychoanalytically informed infant research, and Daniel Stern's (1985) interdisciplinary research that attempted to connect self-psychology to empirical infant research. But the psychoanalytic mainstream did not change its character: it continued to argue about questions of ritual (is "real" psychoanalysis four times a week on the couch?) and institutional power structures (do you need to do a training analysis with a member of the institute where you train?), rather than focus on questions of substance.

Quo Vadis, Psychoanalysis – Clinical Considerations

To cure the illness of a fragmented, marginalized psychoanalysis, Stepansky (2009) suggests that the discipline should simply accept its fate and learn to live at the margins. Once again, he turns to the history of medicine for an analogy. He shows that chiropractors and osteopaths practiced at the margins of organized medicine for the better part of a century, that they gradually came to accept that marginal position, but that they now have their place in hospitals and clinics alongside mainstream medicine.

However, Stepansky's proposal suffers from one major drawback: while it describes the status quo of psychoanalysis quite accurately, by no means does it guarantee that the discipline will flourish again. Living on the sidelines means that psychoanalysis completely renounces the possibility of making a substantial contribution to our knowledge of human nature or to generating clinical knowledge that is valued in other fields.

An interesting alternative is sketched in Elliot Jurist's interview with Peter Fonagy (Jurist 2010), one of the most productive researchers and theorists in psychoanalysis over the last few decades. Fonagy's argument is that modern science has made an impact by no longer thinking in terms of churches, while psychoanalysis has made no such transition. Institutions like the IPA and the APSA simply have no creative energy left. Too many of their gatherings are exercises in restating the credo of what psychoanalysis is, and retelling the last stages of its development as they understand it. As Fonagy points out, the so-called "scientific meetings" at psychoanalytic conferences have little, if anything, to do with science. But above all, he argues that "psychoanalysis" – as a job description – is anachronistic. He claims that we are already at the point when it is problematic to tell patients, "I do psychoanalytic therapy"; and that saying anything of the sort will be completely illegitimate in another two decades. As Fonagy sees it, psychotherapists' only legitimate answer to the question "What do you do?" is something like "I treat this or that type of disturbance using this or that technique which has been shown to be effective for this disturbance by research." Moreover, Fonagy has attempted to collate as much of that psychotherapy research as possible in a monumental project with Anthony Roth (Roth and Fonagy 2005).

In other words, Fonagy thinks that psychotherapy is going down the path of medical specialties, where the practitioner is defined by what he cures rather than by his style of work. Hence, organizations like the IPA and APSA will cease to exist for the simple reason that teaching psychoanalytic practice will no longer be a legitimate concept, any more than it is legitimate to have schools for this or that medical style of work. In fact, the abolition of such styles and the parallel organization of a discipline along a central paradigm is the definition of a mature science.

Fonagy's argument could be countered as follows: a large percentage of the people who look for therapeutic help cannot be simply pigeonholed by the DSM-like categorization of pathologies. They may not suffer from any identifiable Axis I or Axis II disorder; hence, techniques developed along the lines of evidence-based psychotherapy may not exist for them. Given that, something like psychoanalytic therapy could be viewed as the treatment of choice for them.

I feel that there needs to be some form of training in some of the baseline skills of psychodynamic work, such as the structuring of a helping relation, the following of affective process and the formulation of empathic understanding. This could indeed be seen as a form of basic psychotherapeutic training. But it is far from enough. Most people who seek help for something other than an identifiable pathology have a specific goal: for instance, they want to find love; or they want to feel satisfied in their work (or merely find a way to survive in the chaotic new world of fluid work). Here we come to one of the glaring omissions in both Stepansky's and Fonagy's analyses: neither of them even mentions the emergence of coaching as a mass phenomenon that has become a multi-billion-dollar industry that may soon surpass psychotherapy in both size and impact (Berglass 2002).

There are good reasons to be wary of coaching as it is currently practiced: the title is unregulated, and people without any legitimate training in either how to handle a consultative relationship or the basics of psychopathology are practicing it. But it would be a huge mistake not to wonder why this phenomenon has reached such immense proportions and what genuine need it is attempting to address.

I believe that the answer lies in the dramatic changes that the world has undergone over the last two decades as a result of the revolution in information technologies. We are living through a social upheaval comparable to that caused by the Industrial Revolution in the nineteenth century, which buried old forms of life and created new ones (Castells 1996). But the current revolution is proceeding at an incomparably faster speed than the Industrial Revolution: entrenched notions such as job security, linear careers and national identity have been all but destroyed in the space of just twenty years.

The spread of the global infotainment network has changed the cultural frame of reference of everybody in the developed world by providing them with instant access to more information and culture than they could ever digest (Strenger 2004). The enormous flexibility of multinational corporations in terms of moving workers, production and management around the globe has made it virtually impossible for the majority of employees to feel safe in their jobs even in the medium, let alone the long, term.

Many of those who seek help for a general existential malaise need more than empathy and understanding. Because of the instability of the contemporary world of employment and social relations, the tools that they received in their primary and secondary socializations simply no longer work. They need help in formulating their life strategies, and sometimes they need the specific tools to implement them.

It may well be that some psychoanalysts will simply say, "Well, let them go to coaches. This is not my business." But such an answer would mean that psychoanalysis is practiced merely as art for art's sake, rather than to meet the needs of its patients. The result is painfully felt: most psychoanalytic institutes have trouble recruiting patients for classical analysis; and most classical analysands are psychoanalytic candidates. Thus, organized psychoanalysis is in serious danger of becoming an introspective universe that is isolated from the rest of the world.

This has been one of psychoanalysis's crucial weaknesses throughout its history. Freud's notion of the "pure gold of analysis" has been taken far too seriously within the psychoanalytic tradition. Maintaining the purity of technique was an obsession that led to such absurdities as Hanna Segal's (1988) pride in treating a schizophrenic patient with pure psychoanalytic technique. I agree completely with Fonagy's argument that psychoanalysis should no longer be preoccupied with its own purity (an essentially religious, rather than scientific, notion). Instead, we should focus on helping people; Fonagy's development of techniques for working with patients with borderline personality disorders is exemplary in this respect (Fonagy et al. 2005).

As Stolorow (2009) and Shahar and Davidson (2009) have argued, we need to be much more concerned with the patient's being-in-the-world. We need to address the full concreteness of human existence in its entirety, ranging from our patients' life goals to their attempts to find their way in the world. Hence, if there is to be a place for more general psychotherapy (as opposed to evidenced-based, specific techniques), it *must* address these existential questions with some urgency, and explore how some form of mentoring or coaching might be integrated into psychoanalytic work (Strenger 2004: ch. 4). In other words, if Fonagy's idea of psychotherapy as specialized treatments for identifiable disorders is to be complemented by something like training for general psychotherapy, psychoanalysis, as it is currently practiced and taught, does not provide enough of the core concepts of such a general psychotherapy. Nevertheless, there could be an interesting development if researchers like Fonagy with truly catholic breadths of interest and knowledge continue to try to find the points of convergence between advances in the brain sciences, attachment theory, mentalization and the first inklings of actual knowledge about coaching processes. Ultimately, though, all of this will have to be grounded in sound knowledge about human nature.

Psychoanalysts Have Merely Interpreted Psychoanalysis in Various Ways; We Need to Change It

This leaves us with one final, great question: are the times of psychoanalysis as a discipline that has something of value to say about human nature, culture, life and meaning gone for ever? It might be easy to conclude that this is indeed the case. After all, psychoanalysis became such an introverted undertaking, no longer venturing out of the consulting room and instead focusing on the minutiae of the intersubjective process between patient and therapist, for a reason.

What allowed psychoanalysts of the past – beginning, of course, with Freud himself – to offer the world sweeping diagnoses of everything from the conflict between human nature and civilization to the nature of religion and the place of sexuality in human affairs were grand theoretical edifices, primarily Freud's own theory of mind and personality. Psychoanalysis, as a discipline, no longer has a vantage point from where it can present grand interpretations of culture of the types proposed by authors like Freud, Jung, Fromm and Erikson. The fragmentation of psychoanalysis – so well described by Stepansky (2009) – is the result of the crumbling of these edifices. Their demise is partially due to psychoanalysis's isolation from cutting-edge science, but it is also a function of historical and social changes. As Eli Zaretsky (2004) has shown, Freud wrote within a very specific cultural context, and the contemporary world is very different from his *fin de siècle* Vienna or even the United States of the mid-twentieth century (Strenger 2004).

Along the way, psychoanalysis has also retreated from its grander goals. It has systematically forgotten (or should we say repressed?) that Freud thought in terms of a program of vaulting ambition: he wanted to uncover the evolutionary roots of the unconscious mind. *Totem and Taboo* (Freud 1913/1930), for example, was not primarily a foray into anthropology; rather, it was Freud's attempt to ground the Oedipus complex in evolutionary biology by arguing that the historical event of killing the primal father was passed on in our phylogenetic inheritance.

As I will show in detail in Chapter 9, psychoanalysis "forgot" Freud's evolutionary program because Freud himself, to the end of his days, continued to think in Lamarckian terms (Sulloway 1979). This seemed quite rational until the 1920s, when Darwinism turned out to be biology's winning strategy. However, some of Freud's early followers felt awkward about their master's continuing adherence to Lamarck, so much of what he wrote was simply skimmed over to spare psychoanalysis the discomfort of having to face a simple fact of intellectual history: Freud, like every major thinker, was a child of his time, and thought in terms of the science in which he had been trained.

The paradox is that Freud's intuition was basically correct: it turns out that the strategy of uncovering the mind's evolutionary strata is very powerful. The evolutionary cognitive neurosciences are now doing exactly that, but on a Darwinian basis. Topics that used to be at the center of psychoanalytic interest, such as the choice of love objects, are now investigated in large-scale research projects that are yielding rather interesting results. This is due to two interrelated factors. The first is that the groundbreaking research by Tversky and Kahneman (Arieli 2008) on systematic biases in decision-making turned into a paradigm that proved enormously constructive to the point of gaining Kahneman (Tversky passed away at a young age) a Nobel prize in economics. The paradigm is basically to study the unconscious means by which we process information and make decisions – a program that has been very fruitfully linked to evolutionary thought. The assumption is that the evolutionary pressures that formed our brains and minds were very different from the conditions of hyper-complex civilization, and they are likely to be counter-productive in the present.

The second factor is that advances in neuroscience and fMRI (Damasio 2003) are finally making it possible to study the brain in action. This has already led to the development of a variety of research programs that have evolved into the paradigm of the evolutionary cognitive neurosciences, which are on the way to producing the integrated science of the mind that Freud hoped to foster. This is why departments of psychology around the world are gradually shifting in this direction, and why major foundations offer lavish funding to the cognitive neurosciences. Both are responding to strong indications that this interdisciplinary program is well on the way to evolving into a paradigm that is fully integrated with evolutionary biology.

This purely scientific success has been accompanied by an increased presence in the general culture – which, of course, was similarly enthralled by psychoanalysis up to the 1970s. Evolutionary cognitive neuroscience is now capturing the imagination of millions of educated lay readers. Authors like the psychologists Steven Pinker (1997) and Dan Arieli (2008) and the neurologist Antonio Damasio (2003) feature regularly in the non-fiction bestseller lists because the cognitive neurosciences are producing fascinating results in topics that are of great human relevance.

Hence, both the academic community and the wider educated public have reached the conclusion that the evolutionary cognitive neurosciences are the true heirs of Freud's evolutionary program. Their discoveries are intellectually stimulating and shed light on questions for which the world at large demands answers. Why do we systematically ignore statistical evidence in decision-making? Why do we fall in love with some people but not with others? Why do we adhere to worldviews that are not based on evidence, and sometimes defend them to the death?

Again, in the past, psychoanalysis sometimes attempted to tackle these topics. Now it does not, partly because it is limited to clinical observation in the analytic situation and so doesn't have the tools to investigate them fruitfully. Mostly, though, its seeming lack of interest is due to its isolation within its own organizational shell, outside the network of interlinked disciplines of contemporary science that continue to generate interesting hypotheses and then research them with the help of generous funding.

Psychoanalysis *could* revive itself if it were to realize that some modes of psychodynamic thinking are currently producing fascinating and highly relevant research. For instance, experimental existential psychology (Greenberg et al. 2004) has become a thriving discipline that addresses large-scale questions, ranging from the psychodynamics of religious radicalization to the motivations of suicidal terrorists and the fueling of religious and racial prejudice. And integrations of evolutionary psychology, anthropology and the history of religion have generated riveting, grand explanatory theories of the evolutionary basis of religion (Atran 2002) that are no less ambitious than those presented in Freud's work.

Therefore, grand theorizing about the human condition based on sound science is not only possible but happening right now; psychoanalysis has just lost track of these developments. I dare not predict that psychoanalysis will eventually overcome its self-induced isolation and avoidance of contact with the mainstream. Fonagy (in Jurist 2010) is right to say that it will take great institutional changes for this to happen. But I am certain of one thing: if psychoanalysis hopes to regain some of its former cultural prestige, and if it wishes to escape from the margins – where Stepansky (2009), for one, predicts it is destined to stay – this will only happen if it manages to reconnect with the fascinating world of contemporary science in the same way as Freud connected to the mainstream of science in his day.

In Chapter 9 we will see that Freud's original intention was for psychoanalysis to become an evolutionary theory of the mind – and that psychoanalysis would gain enormously if it were to reconnect to that ideal by interacting with and allowing itself to be enriched by today's evolutionary cognitive neurosciences. First, though, we must explore the work of certain authors who argue fervently that psychoanalysis must remain in isolation and not succumb to the pressure generated by the natural sciences' prestige.

Chapter 8

Psychoanalysis's Humanistic–Scientific Mission

Psychoanalysis is not the only discipline that has been on the defensive for some time. Humanities departments have been scaled down throughout the world (Nussbaum 2010), and the question of the value of humanistic knowledge has become quite pressing. Meanwhile, the natural sciences have gobbled up all the prestige. As a result, many authors in psychoanalysis in particular (e.g., Phillips 1996) and the humanities in general have tended to frame the debate as a zero-sum game: either the humanities are in some way superior to the natural sciences, which are then often caricatured as soulless enterprises, or the humanities are doomed to extinction.

My argument is that psychoanalysis should not present its case for the value of humanistic understanding by arguing that quantitative scientific methodology is soulless: first, because this claim is empirically problematic; and, second, because it does not serve the case of psychoanalysis. Instead, psychoanalysis should occupy a new place in the web of knowledge. Instead of isolating itself from the exciting developments in the natural and psychological sciences, it should participate in the quest to increase our understanding of human nature.

The Debate about the Epistemological Structure of Psychoanalysis

Freud, as has been pointed out quite often (Ricoeur 1965, Habermas 1968), envisaged psychoanalysis as part of the natural sciences. He believed that clinical data were enough to support psychoanalytic developmental, etiological and psychological theories. But it is important to point out that, steeped in the biological sciences of his day, he also believed that his theories were entirely consistent with them.

In any case, the status of psychoanalysis as a science was not much of an issue within psychoanalysis until well into the 1970s (although it *was* attacked as unscientific from the outside; see Popper 1963). This was partially due to the fact that psychoanalysis was thriving, particularly in the United States. Psychoanalysts held many of the most prestigious chairs of psychiatry; psychoanalytic psychiatrists edited the most important handbooks of psychiatry; and psychoanalytic authors like Fromm and Erikson commanded the public's attention and their books were bestsellers. There seemed to be little reason to doubt the discipline's scientific and institutional viability (Hale 1995).

However, this changed dramatically with the emergence of several competing therapeutic paradigms: first, behavior therapy, which evolved into the cognitive-behavioral paradigm in the 1970s; then the humanistic paradigm, which became very powerful from the 1950s onwards; and, finally, biological psychiatry, which continues to gain both strength and prestige. In the face of these rivals, psychoanalysis rapidly lost its public and academic standing. Splendid institutions like the clinical psychology program at New York University, which had trained generations of psychoanalytically oriented therapists, and the Menninger Institute's Topeka Campus, which had also trained countless clinicians and, like the New York program, had generated important research based on psychoanalytic theory in the 1950s and 1960s, shrank rapidly and ultimately closed. Most programs in psychiatry and clinical psychology turned away from psychoanalysis, and by the final years of the century psychoanalysts held almost no important chairs in either field (Hale 1995). Meanwhile, as we saw in Chapter 7, the psychoanalytic publishing industry shrank to a fraction of what it had been in its heyday (Stepansky 2009).

Psychoanalysis started to feel besieged from all sides. In light of the academic world's rejection of psychoanalytic claims to knowledge, several influential theorists (Klein 1976, Schafer 1976, 1983, Spence 1982) began to ask how psychoanalytic theorizing could be defended. They found an intellectual tradition in continental Europe that, since the end of the nineteenth century, had argued that the humanities' epistemological structure was essentially different from that of the natural sciences.

In the 1960s, two major philosophers applied this conception to psychoanalysis. Paul Ricoeur (1965) and Jürgen Habermas (1968) independently argued that Freud had misconceived his own project by casting it as a natural science. Almost simultaneously, they wrote substantial books arguing that psychoanalysis was a humanistic, interpretive discipline from the outset, and that it should have viewed itself as such explicitly. The model they used was basically that patients seek treatment because they have ceased to understand aspects of their own lives because they have excommunicated certain meanings from their conscious discourse. The analytic encounter is the process in which these unintelligible aspects are recontextualized and reintegrated into conscious discourse.

In the 1970s, three major psychoanalytic theorists followed Ricoeur and Habermas's lead. Heinz Kohut (1971, 1979) argued that psychoanalysis worked on an epistemology based on introspection and empathy. Meanwhile, Roy Schafer (1976, 1983) embarked on his major reconceptualization of psychoanalysis as the art of renarrating lives, squarely placing the discipline within the humanities rather than the natural sciences. His claim was radical: psychoanalysis, as Habermas and Ricoeur had claimed, had misunderstood itself: it was not concerned with causal claims about the etiology of psychopathologies; nor was it developmental psychology in the academic sense. If anything, it was the existential endeavor of renarrating the patient's life in terms of responsible agency. Finally, Donald Spence (1982) presented an integrative attempt to depict psychoanalysis in terms of contemporary literary theory, closer literary criticism than to experimental psychology (a discipline that, incidentally, he knew very well from his own work).

This trend gained a much wider following in the United States with the emergence of the intersubjective and relational paradigms. Robert Stolorow and his associates (Stolorow et al. 1987) widened Kohut's conception of introspection and empathy to integrate phenomenological thought into psychoanalytic epistemology. Stephen Mitchell (1993), within the context of the emerging relational paradigm, reconceptualized psychoanalysis as an activity in which patient and analyst co-constructed a new interpersonal narrative and experiential reality.

It is safe to say that, by the end of the century, most psychoanalytic circles had accepted some version of the hermeneutic construal of psychoanalysis. This model had certainly done a lot to elucidate the actual nature of psychoanalytic clinical work. Much of it was written in densely evocative language, trying to capture the rich, multilayered structure of what happens in the psychoanalytic consulting room. One of the most detailed and sophisticated elaborations of the hermeneutic construal of psychoanalysis, dialectical constructivism (Hoffman 1998), has been particularly useful in showing that the analytic process has an inevitable creative component in which analyst and patient co-create new meanings, narratives and possibilities. More recently, Hoffman (2009) has made the powerful claim that dialectic constructivism cannot and should not be diluted with scientific research. In his incisive and passionately argued paper he argues that psychoanalysis should not try to join the race for scientific respectability. He suggests that the current attempts to turn psychotherapy into an evidence-based discipline akin to medicine are fundamentally misguided, and argues that psychoanalysis is one of the few remaining strongholds for such notions as autonomy, creativity and subjectivity. Therefore, it should stick to its guns and remain committed to dialectical constructivism.

Hoffman (2009) presents several specific criticisms of current psychotherapy research. These have been addressed with great precision and competence by Jeremy Safran (2013) and Peter Fonagy (2013) from their privileged vantage points: they are both psychoanalysts and leading psychotherapy researchers. On the one hand, both agree with Hoffman that there is great value in the in-depth case study, which has been central to psychoanalysis, along with randomized outcome trials and other modes of investigation. The problem, as Fonagy points out, is that Hoffman misrepresents science as some form of mechanized outgrowth of technical rationality. As I will argue later, this misrepresentation carries a high price.

Because I largely agree with Safran's and Fonagy's position on the details, I want to address Hoffman's claims on the level of intellectual history and from the point of view of the sociocultural function and standing of psychoanalysis.

Psychoanalysis's hermeneutic retreat (Strenger 1991) was supposed to safeguard it against dependence on organized science, which is both expensive and requires fighting for a place in the prestigious scientific disciplines. Hoffman argues that this retreat from science should be safeguarded because psychoanalysis is one of the last vestiges in our culture that represents the value of open-ended enquiry into the goals of individual human lives – a bulwark against an ever-narrowing technological reason that takes goals for granted and merely seeks the most efficient means to achieve them. Psychoanalysis is also about living in the here and now rather than ossified conceptions of the so-called "good life."

Some of these are worthy claims, but I feel that Hoffman's basic thesis is problematic because it assumes that there is a chasm between what he calls dialectical constructivism and scientism, or an overemphasis on technical rationality. Hoffman is, of course, not solely responsible for this dichotomy between the natural sciences and the humanities, which was first advanced in the late nineteenth century. My critique of his thesis is based on the assumption of the unity of knowledge that I will spell out in this chapter, and I will argue that the dichotomy between dialectical constructivism and scientific epistemology is wrongheaded (Strenger 1991). Hoffman's claim is a variation on an old theme: that psychoanalysis is epistemologically autonomous and does not require the results and theories of other disciplines.

The hermeneutic construal of psychoanalysis certainly succeeded in capturing crucial elements of psychoanalytic theory and practice. But presenting it as fundamentally opposed to the natural and quantitative social sciences is fundamentally misguided for a number of reasons:

- First, because psychoanalytic hermeneutics is inextricably intertwined with, and even defined by the relationship between psychoanalysis and science.
- Second, because contemporary cognitive neurosciences are by no means enemies of the psychoanalytic project; in fact, they are, in many ways, a continuation of Freud's original project.
- And, third, if psychoanalysis is to recapture the public's attention and imagination, it should do what it has always done best: understand and explain the new culture rather than condemn it.

Psychoanalysis, Science and Psychotherapy Research

Psychoanalytic hermeneutics is inextricably linked to the sciences, as can be shown by slightly adapting an argument made by the philosopher of science Adolf Grünbaum in his path-breaking *The Foundations of Psychoanalysis* (1984), a book that combines in-depth knowledge of the psychoanalytic literature with precise philosophical analysis. Grünbaum proposes the following scenario: a shaman interprets a patient's discourse as the expression of satanic possession; and that shaman is capable of developing this interpretive hypothesis in great detail, skillfully showing how every aspect of the often *prima facie* unintelligible productions can be traced back to satanic influence. I would then add a further element to Grünbaum's scenario: after an exorcist ritual, the patient regains his sanity and happiness. (I add this element because the clinical psychologist and anthropologist Yoram Bilu (1980) has documented a large number of such cures in traditional Jewish and Arab communities.) Now, would any psychoanalyst, clinical psychologist or psychiatrist accept this scenario as evidence for the truth of the traditional healer's theory about what we call dissociation? The answer, obviously, is that we would not, even if the healer's success rate was very impressive.

In *Between Hermeneutics and Science* (Strenger 1991: 6) I proposed a detailed model to explain why we reject theological or demonological explanations of psychopathology out of hand without any second thought. Psychoanalysis has always been built on the assumption that its metaphysic is purely naturalistic. This is one of the central tenets of Freud's thought: he was steeped in the natural sciences of his day and as a matter of course insisted that all psychoanalytic explanations must be consistent with and even cohere with prevailing scientific theory. I called this Freud's demand of *external coherence*, and argued as follows. The shaman's explanation may indeed provide a narrative that has powerful internal coherence. It is internally consistent; it makes narrative sense; and it sounds profoundly convincing to members of the traditional healer's culture. However, this, in itself, does not constitute any argument for the interpretation's truth. We reject demonological explanations because we demand that psychoanalytic interpretation is *consistent* with accepted scientific background knowledge (i.e., it does not contradict it) and that it is at least partially *derived* from such knowledge. This knowledge includes that we know that all entities influencing a patient's behavior are physical and mostly biological in nature, and that they influence the patient by physical, chemical and biological means (e.g., by speaking, hitting, sexual abuse and so on). In other words, we all accept that external coherence with other well-established scientific knowledge is a necessary precondition before any psychoanalytic hypothesis may even be considered. In this respect, psychoanalysis is no different from any other discipline in the natural and social sciences, nor indeed from the humanities.

Another of Hoffman's (2009) claims is that the spirit of psychoanalysis is profoundly opposed to the language and methodology of psychotherapy research. In part this distrust of the scientific research paradigm dates back to early psychotherapy research, which tended to dismiss psychoanalysis as ineffective, particularly in the 1970s, when it argued that anything that can be achieved in long-term therapy can also be achieved in short-term therapy. But recent research – published in one of the most influential journals of academic psychology, *American Psychologist* (Shedler 2010) – shows that psychoanalytic therapy is as effective as other forms of therapy in treating a wide variety of disturbances (Shahar et al. 2010).

Jeremy Safran (2013) has shown that psychoanalysis can be presented and explained perfectly well within the framework of contemporary psychological discourse, including psychotherapy research. Meanwhile, Golan Shahar (2010) has argued that psychiatric nosology, physiological knowledge and clinical pragmatism employing a variety of techniques can be integrated within a psychoanalytic framework. His model is too complex to be presented in full here, but I would like to highlight a particular point of great importance to the current discussion. While Shahar is steeped in the literature of psychotherapy research – some of which has been published in the psychoanalytic literature (Shahar et al. 2010) – he is keenly aware of the importance of the poetic dimension in psychoanalysis. He defines this as follows:

> Patients need an overarching conceptualization of their particular place within the human situation, their stance in the face of thrownness, their submission to, or rebellion against, the vicissitudes of life, which are often traumatic, and are – more often than not – implicated in their plight. Talking to patients about such enormity requires – not only a broad-based, philosophically-minded understanding – but also a soul. It necessitates a language that, in addition to being wise, is also evocative and emotive. It requires poetics.
>
> I use (Winnicottianly) the term poetics to denote a language spoken by patient, therapist, and the therapeutic dyad, in an attempt to capture, emotively and evocatively, the enormity of the human situation and its particular uniqueness for the patient. Poetics, in both literature and psychotherapy, is based on music and metaphors, sound and song. It not only tells. It does. More than lecturing about life, it creates a life of its own, which then has the capacity to transform experience.
>
> (Shahar 2010: 319)

I have quoted Shahar – a leading psychotherapy researcher who is also a creative psychoanalytic clinician – at some length to give a sense of his prose style and the way he thinks about human existence and clinical process, and to illustrate that not all psychotherapy researchers are soulless number-crunchers who are oblivious to the richness of human experience.

Given this, why do analysts like Hoffman (2009) feel that closer contact between psychoanalysis and the sciences might ruin the essence of what they take psychoanalysis to be? After all, as Robert Wallerstein (2012) has argued in an incisive recent essay that, for much of the history of psychoanalysis, there was a much closer connection between psychoanalysis and the sciences than there is today. I think that the deep opposition of some dialectical constructivists to a dialogue with science expresses genuine concern but misidentifies the enemy: it is neither the paradigm of the cognitive neurosciences nor psychotherapy research; rather, it is a much more profound trend in contemporary global culture. They seem to be afraid of a deep contradiction between what Hoffman (2009) – following Horkheimer and Adorno's influential *Dialectics of Enlightenment* (1947) – calls the preponderance of instrumental reason (i.e., the view of reason that limits rationality to achieving preconceived goals as quickly and efficiently as possible) and the following conception:

> In a nonobjectivist hermeneutic paradigm best suited to psychoanalysis, the analyst embraces the existential uncertainty that accompanies the realization that there are multiple good ways to be, in the moment and more generally in life, and that the choices he or she makes are always influenced by culture, by sociopolitical mind-set, by personal values, by countertransference, and by other factors in ways that are never fully known.
>
> (Hoffman 2009: 1043)

Hoffman argues that the current cultural climate exerts enormous pressure on all forms of psychotherapy to focus on symptom removal and on optimizing the patient's functioning as quickly as possible. This, he argues, creates the great danger of flattening psychotherapy in general and killing the spirit of psychoanalysis in particular.

Hermeneutics and Science: A Misguided Dichotomy

One of psychoanalysis's most important tenets is its refusal to succumb to the current cultural craze, where the demand for expertise on everything from sex and child-rearing to career planning has risen to absurd levels. The popular press is constantly searching for new "findings" that will tell us how to get our lives "right." There is also insatiable public demand for expert advice on how to improve one's memory, how to raise one's children, how to have a more satisfactory sex life and how to be more assertive in the workplace (Phillips 1996).

This craving for structured advice is governed by the ideology of instrumental reason. Human beings have goals, and they want to achieve them as efficiently as possible. The theory is that there must be effective ways to reach these goals, and the task of science is to establish what they are. The expert on living is the scientist–practitioner who knows how to apply extant scientific knowledge to life issues. Effective help is given when the scientist–practitioner makes use of this knowledge in imparting it to his or her clients, and trains them to implement it in their lives.

Psychoanalysis opposes this with a conception of life and the therapeutic process that rejects the dictates of instrumental reason and the idea that the patient's life goals should be taken as a given. Hoffman (2009) is certainly right when he claims that the process of negotiating and co-creating an image of the good life is an important value; that much of the current craze for expert advice is, ultimately, a renunciation of autonomy; and that the psychoanalytic conception of an open-ended dialogue is of profound ethical importance. For the time being, many patients still accept that psychoanalysis or psychodynamic therapy is an open-ended process in which goals are rethought and transformed; a dialogue that is conducted with openness to the surprising twist and not from the point of view of omniscience. However, this raises a powerful ethical issue: what if the patient has no interest in exploratory dialogue about life? Many patients want nothing more than to *avoid* existential uncertainty, and the last thing they want is to embrace it. They are simply not interested in celebrating life's open-ended complexity. Rather, they want guidance on how to create more satisfying relationships; how to juggle their numerous roles and tasks more effectively; how to manage their careers; how to rise in the corporate world or make it as entrepreneurs; or how to convince their kids to accept parental authority. This is why so many people now turn to coaching (be it executive, life or parental) and why TV programs that offer simple advice on how to deal with life's problems are so popular (Strenger 2011a: ch. 3).

Engaging the patient in a dialogue that is explicitly designed to achieve the opposite of what that patient consciously wants is by no means an ethically neutral decision. In fact, in doing so, the analyst assumes that his or her worldview – which embraces complexity and seeks openness to the fluidity of experience – is superior to that of the patient, which emphasizes adherence to clearly defined values, stability in life goals and efficiency in attaining those goals.

If we flatly refuse to be part of the scientific game, we must be aware that abandoning the language and method of science comes at a heavy price. If, along with Hoffman, we renounce the legitimacy of science, only two questions remain. What vision of the good life do I find compelling? And which cultural tradition provides me with durable meaning and a structure for my life?

There are many alternatives to psychoanalysis for those who want to escape the global domination of technical reason, and they are gaining ground. In addition to the ever-growing field of alternative therapies, there are spiritualities of various provenance and many forms of pastoral care. While some practitioners are shallow, ill-informed and not even highly trained in the type of spirituality they claim to represent, many do have deep knowledge of and training in their particular spiritual tradition, and so can act as reliable guides on spiritual journeys (Ricard 2007).

The central implication of Hoffman's dialectical constructivism is that psychoanalysis cannot claim intrinsic superiority to any of these forms of spirituality. It is an ethos – an aesthetic of existence, as Foucault (1983) would say – with both merit and intrinsic beauty, and it amply reflects Western late-modern liberal sensibilities, but it is by no means unique in its critique of the technical rationality that Hoffman decries. The ever-growing popularity of Buddhism shows that many Westerners are finding solace from the pressures of lives governed by Blackberries and Excel spreadsheets in disciplines of the self that are very different from psychoanalysis.

It is indeed possible to conceptualize the world of competing disciplines of the self in terms of the art world rather than science. We do not expect art to converge towards one, dominant style. If anything, we abhor this idea. In a liberal society, we do not want to impose one style of painting or filmmaking, as the USSR did by insisting upon socialist realism. And we might argue that the same holds true for ways of living a life. Surely the beauty of a liberal society is that, like the art world, it allows – and even encourages – competition between a variety of ways of life and worldviews? Hence, all that's left is to characterize the psychoanalytic aesthetic of existence in the same way as we characterize a style of art.

The core of the psychoanalytic vision of human life puts the value of facing existential uncertainty and the acceptance of life's fluidity at the center of the psychoanalyst's worldview. Engaging in such a dialogue without informing patients that we intend to change their worldview is ethically problematic, and I am sure that Hoffman would not wish to impose his worldview on patients by fiat. Relational psychoanalysis and the hermeneutic–constructivist ethos is ultimately the result of infusing the language of human rights and the democratic redefinition of positions of authority into our conception of psychoanalytic theory and practice (Strenger 2004: ch. 6). But this democratization also means that today's patients see themselves as clients who have the right to know on what evidence we believe that we will be of help, and how long it will be before they achieve their goals (such as find a partner, jumpstart a career, feel less lonely and so on). They may not want to negotiate these goals, or see any intrinsic value in dialogue about the basic assumption of their lives.

Along with Hoffman, I may not like this: I have argued at length that this technical vision of life and the almost exclusive emphasis on measurable achievement are emptying the liberal ideal of individual freedom of content (Strenger 2011a). Nevertheless, we should not use our professional authority to tell our patients that it is wrong, even if we firmly believe that this is not a good life to live. We may have arguments for the position of dialectical constructivism, but they are by no means conclusive: different Gestalts of the good life can be weighed against each other, and they compete in the marketplace of ideas and political, religious and social worldviews.

Dialectic constructivism is a choice, and psychoanalysis as a vocation requires a particular temperamental structure. You have to love prolonged periods of intense listening, and you must prefer reflection to action; you need to love complexity for its own sake, and celebrate it. For most analysts, their profession has become a means to turn their own temperamental and cultural preferences into a way of life and a way to make a living. The problem is that this cultural preference is out of tune with the spirit of our time. As yet, the dramatic rise of coaching as a cultural force has not been sufficiently addressed by clinical psychology as a whole and psychoanalysis in particular. While the coaching industry has so far been largely unregulated, it is gradually entering a phase of normalization. Journals like the *Journal of Evidence Based Coaching and Mentoring* are publishing research on coaching processes and outcomes, and a growing number of prestigious universities are offering coaching programs. Before long, the discipline will be regulated and will attain both scientific and academic respectability.

That, though, still lies in the future. At present, coaching is a mix of humanistic and positive psychology and a number of techniques that help clients to define and achieve their goals. Many of the experienced and well-trained coaches I have spoken to and worked with are by no means charlatans or technocrats. They are humanistic in outlook, and in certain cases produce impressive results, often in remarkably short periods of time: clients who have procrastinated for years finally get their websites up and running and their businesses progressing; others finally manage to lose the extra kilos they have been carrying for years with remarkable benefits for their self-image and self-esteem. I am not saying this because I think that coaching is the miracle cure that humanity has been waiting for, but because I think it is wrong to stereotype the whole industry as an example of technical rationality run wild (even though, in some cases, it can be). I also believe that psychoanalysts have no choice but to give serious thought to when and how we should integrate coaching techniques into our work with patients. Many of my colleagues have told me that they are already integrating coaching techniques into their analytic therapies; but as yet, as far as I am aware, this topic has not been debated at any conference. It also rarely appears in the literature (Strenger 2004: ch. 4), primarily because psychoanalytic "official" culture still tries to maintain the ideal of "pure psychoanalysis," even though this ideal has little to commend it intellectually, scientifically or clinically (Roth and Fonagy 2005; Jurist 2010).

Hoffman's insistence that we must choose either dialectical constructivism or technical rationality is, I believe, another reincarnation of one of psychoanalysis's most questionable tendencies: its preoccupation with its own purity. However, it is to Hoffman's credit that he does indulge in this pursuit in its most problematic version, under the guise of the claim that pure psychoanalysis is guided by pure truth (Blass 2010) – a thesis that is not backed by any existing epistemological model, and that has been forcefully criticized by Lewis Aron (2009, 2010). Freud's "pure gold of analysis" aphorism may have been one of his least fortunate expressions, as he probably never meant it to be applied as rigidly as many of his followers subsequently did. At worst, this led to the imposition of several highly questionable and detrimental theories and techniques that had no scientific evidence to back them up, including Hanna Segal's indoctrination of obsessive–compulsive patients with interpretations about their repressed aggression (Segal 1994), and attempts to persuade paranoid patients to acknowledge their repressed homosexuality. Both of these techniques were applied to millions of patients over many decades. Thankfully, contemporary psychoanalysis has rejected them completely.

The dichotomy between dialectical constructivism and technical rationality is too rigid to capture the richness of human reality. In fact, Hoffman himself has written some seminal articles (e.g., Hoffman 1998: ch. 1) in which he argues that living in the shadow of mortality obliges us to help patients to make decisions and move ahead in their lives. To my mind, this means that analysts should employ whichever techniques are most effective in helping the patient to move on, without feeling in any way that they are contaminating the "pure gold of analysis" with questionable parameters that need to be analyzed away as soon as possible. Pragmatism, for the clinician, is a virtue, not a vice.

This leads to another ethical issue: patients have the right to ask whether there is any empirical proof that an offered treatment method is effective. As Fonagy (2013) has argued, single case studies are of great importance, both in medicine and in psychotherapy, but they can establish neither effectiveness nor theoretical truth. Hence the juxtaposition of dialectical constructivism and controlled research is not only intellectually but ethically problematic because it places psychoanalysis above a demand that is not merely a reflection of technical rationality but morally justified: patients have the right to know whether there is a strong chance that they will be helped by whichever course of treatment they enter. Psychoanalysis should not stand above this simple requirement, which, as Shedler (2010) has shown, it can meet easily; nor should it forgo the opportunity to expand the application of psychoanalytic ideas to a variety of conditions by proving systematically that such application is fruitful (Shahar et al. 2010).

However, Fonagy's point goes one step further: the web of science cannot be reduced to either randomized clinical trials or any other single method of scientific investigation. Human knowledge is much more complex than that.

I hope that Part I of this book illustrated that psychoanalysis can be integrated within the complex web of knowledge about human nature. In the next chapter, we will see not only that it is misleading and fruitless to pitch psychoanalysis against the evolutionary cognitive neurosciences, but that Freud's original project of psychoanalysis as an evolutionary psychology of the human mind is now more relevant than ever.

Chapter 9

Reviving Freud's Repressed Evolutionary Project

Let us imagine an intellectual historian at the beginning of the twenty-second century. They might offer the following thoughts about Sigmund Freud:

> He is now considered one of the great forerunners of what has turned out to be the most successful paradigm in the understanding of the human mind. In retrospect, it is remarkable that, at the beginning of the twentieth century, when the understanding of human physiology was, to say the least, rudimentary, and the knowledge of human genetics pretty much non-existent, Freud saw that the future of psychology and psychiatry would reside in tracing the functioning of the human mind and its disorders back to earlier evolutionary strata.
>
> Of course, he got the details completely wrong, as his view of human evolution was based on Lamarckian principles. His mythological reconstructions of the origins of the Oedipus complex – in a quaint piece titled *Totem and Taboo* (1913/1930) – are interesting in that they illustrate the distance between nineteenth-century biology and what we know today. Concepts like the Oedipus complex have now disappeared completely. Yet experimental manipulations of the relevant gene have shown that there is indeed something akin to what Freud called the super-ego. We also know that paranoid symptoms arise when this gene is not regulated. Of course, this psychiatric phenomenon is now a thing of the past, because we balance faulty regulation through injection of the regulatory gene.
>
> Yet, Freud should be credited for his speculative genius: on the basis of flawed biology, he dared to assume that there must be an evolutionary basis for psychiatric illnesses. Moreover, towards the end of his life, he acknowledged that the therapeutic value of the method he initiated was very limited, and instead hoped that breakthroughs in biology would soon corroborate his theoretical speculations.

> It is one of those interesting quirks of intellectual history that the movement that carried his name throughout the twentieth century completely abandoned what is now hailed as his greatest discovery. Psychoanalysis survives today only as a sectarian movement of anthropological interest because in the late 1990s its practitioners continued to insist that the future lay in what used to be called psychotherapy (a shamanistic practice based on mythological narratives), rather than in deciphering the genetic and neurological structure of the brain.

Given that evolutionary psychology is fast becoming one of the most promising paradigms in the human sciences, Freud may well soon be acclaimed as one of the great predictors and precursors of the future of psychology and psychiatry. In this chapter, I will provide a brief account of how and why this aspect of his thought has been largely forgotten (or repressed) in psychoanalysis. I will then argue that the current tendency to recast Freud as a major writer and humanist while ignoring the part of his work in which he formulates grand theories about human nature is historically misleading and diminishes his stature in intellectual history. Instead of seeing Freud as a courageous speculative scientist, his explanatory system is being recast as a set of narratives, metaphors and tropes. This process may lead us to forget that Freud was – as every thinker is – a child of his time, and may result in him losing his rightful place in intellectual history.

Freud's Evolutionary Program

Intellectual history, as our (fictitious) intellectual historian pointed out above, tends to progress along the strangest and quirkiest paths. To cite just one example: mathematical physics evolved on the basis of Platonist and neo-Platonist philosophy (Randall 1962), yet today it is difficult to connect quantum physics to the Platonic flights of fancy that guided the founders of what was called "geometrical philosophy" in the seventeenth century. Copernicus' deepest conviction was that God could not have created the universe other than on the basis of the most perfect of forms (according to Platonism) – the circle. It was this conviction, rather than any empirical evidence, that led him to formulate the heliocentric system. A century later, Kepler's conviction was that God produced the world according to the most beautiful mathematical harmonies. After several failed attempts, he finally succeeding in formulating what are now known as Kepler's laws. These, in turn, provided Newton with the basis for his mechanics.

Today, only intellectual historians are aware of the intricate connections between Platonist philosophy and the emergence of the most successful science of the present day. Nevertheless, there is no doubt about the essential role played by Platonism in the early days of mathematical physics. Plato's idea that the essence of reality consisted in mathematical forms was crucial for early physicists and astronomers such as Copernicus, Kepler, Galileo and Descartes.

I would like to look at one of Freud's favorite notions, which, in the course of psychoanalysis's history, has been almost completely forgotten or even actively rejected. He believed ardently in two ideas: first, that all mental illnesses could be traced to relics of our phylogenetic past; and, second, that science would one day uncover the material (i.e., the chemical and neurophysiological) basis of all human behavior.

Frank Sulloway's magisterial *Freud, Biologist of the Mind* (1979) explores the biological foundations of Freud's theorizing in the late 1890s, which ultimately led to him developing the cornerstones of psychoanalytic theory. Sulloway's first thesis is that neither Freud's self-analysis nor some neurotic predilections guided his major theoretical turnaround of 1897. (This theory contradicts the "internalist" reconstruction of Freud's thinking of this period.) In painstaking detail, Sulloway shows that some major theoretical difficulties prevented Freud from finishing his *Project for a Scientific Psychology* (Freud 1895). For Freud, establishing a biological foundation of psychoanalysis was a *conditio sine qua non* for the viability of his theory, and Sulloway argues that evolutionary thinking became the solution for what had seemed an intractable problem. In the *Project for a Scientific Psychology*, Freud had tried to provide a neurological model for repression. He never finished it because every one of his possible models ended in a logical conundrum: if the brain put a repression barrier ("counter-cathexis") in the right spot, how could the brain know in advance that the content located on the neurons "later" in the system was unpleasurable? Sartre (1943) saw the self-same problem in the very notion of the unconscious: in order to realize that a certain thought, feeling or desire creates guilt or shame, it seems that it first needs to become conscious; but then repression itself would not be an unconscious mechanism that saves consciousness from psychological distress.

Sulloway's second thesis is that Freud's switch from the seduction theory of hysteria to the theory of internal conflict was guided by one central idea. Freud hit upon a fascinating solution for the question of how the brain "knows" where to erect repression barriers: individual contents that need to be repressed are incidental; repression needs to occur *biologically*, because humans complete their sexual development after birth. We go through the oral, anal and phallic stages outside the womb; hence, psychosexual development is peculiarly vulnerable to developmental fixations. There are many other instances in which early phylogenetic structures are "repressed" during embryogenesis: think of our diminished tailbone, of whose existence we are painfully reminded whenever we fall on to our backsides.

When discussing this, Sulloway solves one of the riddles of Freud's intellectual development – why he never gave empirical arguments for the particularities of his psychosexual theory. Sulloway argues that Freud did not believe that any such empirical argument was necessary, as he could ground his theory in some of the prevalent biological theories of his time. He had no doubt that evolutionary biology supported his theory and assumed that early forms of sexuality are phylogenetic structures that need to be biologically repressed: organisms had evolved from one opening, to two, then three, and he believed that oral, anal and phallic sexuality were the ontogenetic sediment of this phylogenetic series. Hence, he developed the idea of primary repression: the brain is genetically programmed to repress early forms of sexuality in the same way as the body is programmed to "repress" our ancestors' tails. Freud assumed that human embryogenesis ends only after birth (he often refers to the "premature birth of humans"); and, because sexuality is the main function that fails to mature inside the uterus, it is particularly prone to getting stuck or deviating in its development.

Later, Freud began to trace every major form of psychopathology to presumed evolutionary periods. As we have seen, though, his thinking was Lamarckian, so his timetables were far shorter (measured in tens of thousands of years) than those accepted in Darwinist thought. For example, he believed that obsessional neuroses reflected inhibitory mechanisms that humans developed during the last ice age because they needed to refrain from sexual reproduction during a time of limited food supply.

Freud's major collaborator in this project was Ferenczi, who contributed many ideas to it. In return, Freud endorsed Ferenczi's speculations enthusiastically, and elaborated on them throughout his writings. In particular, it is interesting to see *Totem and Taboo* (Freud 1913/1930) in a new light – as a phylogenetic speculation of the basis of the Oedipus complex. This book is generally seen as Freud's attempt to prove that psychoanalysis could compete with Jung in explaining religious and anthropological phenomena, but Sulloway shows that it actually served a theoretical purpose of the first order: Freud wanted to show that the Oedipus complex was phylogenetically ingrained in the biological basis of our minds. The story of the patricide by the primal horde was used to explain both Oedipal rivalry and the foundation of neurotic guilt.

Interestingly, Sulloway's book was published before the discovery of Freud's unpublished 1915 manuscript – *A Phylogenetic Fantasy: Overview of the Transference Neuroses* (Freud 1985b). In this fascinating work, Freud attempts to provide a systematic outline of all the transference neuroses by correlating each of them with a particular phylogenetic period of human development. This text, which is still little known, is fascinating in its own right, and helps to explain many otherwise obscure passages in the rest of Freud's work. We must not forget that, until the end of his life, Freud continued to think in Lamarckian terms. The whole argument of one of his last works, *Moses and Monotheism* (Freud 1939), rests on the notion that Jewish psychology is based on genetically transmitted guilt about slaying the Egyptian-born founder of monotheism. This, Freud argues, has been essential in transmitting the Jewish propensity for abstract thought and the Jewish people's high valuation of the spiritual domain (in the German sense of *Geistig*, not in the sense of mysticism or obscurantism).

Today, it is difficult to imagine that the final victory of Darwinism occurred only in the late 1920s, when Freud was already in his seventies. When Ernest Jones asked him to avoid Lamarckian speculations in his *Civilization and its Discontents*, Freud curtly answered that he could not understand how biology was possible without Lamarck. These were the years when he no longer kept up to date with ongoing scientific developments and was no longer willing to discard long-held views that had been essential to his thinking. In any case, he never gave up on his program of psychoanalysis as evolutionary psychiatry, even though in the 1920s the decisive victory of Darwinism over Lamarckism had made his particular version of it obsolete.

It needs to be emphasized that Sulloway's aim is not to discredit Freud by showing the depth of his Lamarckian roots; rather, he argues that Freud was much more rational than he seems when read out of historical context. Some of Freud's stranger ideas (from today's perspective) are actually quite compelling when set against the background of the accepted science of his day. But for many decades mainstream psychoanalysis had trouble accepting that the founder of the discipline was not a prophet who had discovered the unconscious and described its structure correctly. This claim, in any case, was historically incorrect: nineteenth-century philosophy and psychology were replete with writings about the unconscious, and some of Freud's more specific theses were foreshadowed by other thinkers, particularly Arthur Schopenhauer (Gay 1989). However, a much more important factor in the psychoanalytic literature's failure to read Freud correctly was its determination to ignore the Lamarckian dimension of his thinking once Darwinism emerged as the victorious theory of evolution. It seemed that the only way to rescue the master from obsolescence was to look away respectfully whenever a Lamarckian passage occurred in his work. Meanwhile, some of his (seemingly) problematic concepts were reinterpreted as metaphors, rather than viewed as concepts that should be given serious consideration.

Sulloway shows that this led to a systematic misreading of Freud's ideas. More importantly, Sulloway's Freud is a great, deep, fascinating thinker who makes full use of his command of the scientific theories of his day. Some of his ideas – which have long been interpreted as irrational, idiosyncratically determined or of neurotic origin – make complete sense when set against the background of the prevailing biology of the late nineteenth and early twentieth centuries. Hence, Sulloway offers a convincing response to those who have argued that Freud misconceived his own project by formulating it as science, when he should have realized that he was developing a humanistic discipline. Freud certainly was a great interpreter of the human condition, but his vision of human life was based on a specific understanding of the biological underpinnings of human nature – as every such interpretation since *On the Origin of Species*, of necessity, has had to be.

Freud as a Precursor of Evolutionary Psychology

A new paradigm for an encompassing theory of human nature is emerging. It is evolutionary psychology. Research by a new generation of thinkers – including the evolutionary biologist Richard Dawkins (1976), the anthropologist Jared Diamond (1991), the neurologist and neuroscientist Antonio Damasio (2003), the neurobiologist Gerald Edelman (1992), the philosopher Daniel Dennett (2005) and the psychologist Steven Pinker (1997) – is generating a compelling new picture of human nature and of how the human mind works.

This brings us back to Freud's evolutionary project. Evolutionary psychology and the neurosciences are doing exactly what Freud believed would be the psychology of the future: they are deciphering the phylogenetic strata of the mind and the behavioral programs that are genetically ingrained in our hardware.

Eric Kandel (2005, 2012) has shown, time and again, that Freud's evolutionary program was on the right track: he sought to formulate a psychology that was consistent with what was known about brain structure at the time. And the fact that he got the biology wrong does not detract from his achievement. Freud's case is no different from those of many other major figures of intellectual and scientific theory, including, as we have seen, Copernicus and Kepler. We do not denigrate their achievements because they were based on long-discarded metaphysical assumptions. Human knowledge does not evolve in a linear fashion, but, as Thomas Kuhn (1962) showed half a century ago, through a series of paradigmatic revolutions. Freud, like the founders of mathematical physics, based his program on assumptions that have since been discarded. But his basic vision of an evolutionary theory of the mind has turned out to be one of the most fruitful ideas of modern intellectual history. It is currently being realized in Darwinian terms, taking into account the unprecedented advances of molecular biology, the decoding of the genetic basis of evolutionary processes and the exploding domain of the cognitive sciences – an area to which Kandel (2007), who was inspired by psychoanalysis in the early part of his career, has contributed decisively.

Today, evolutionary psychologists and psychiatrists are tracing mental illnesses to genetically hardwired patterns that have adaptive value. Even Freud's seemingly strange idea that mental illnesses are reflections of early evolutionary mechanisms is gaining some support: good theoretical approaches show the evolutionary value of mechanisms like depression and anxiety, and it seems that even Freud's idea that there is a biological disposition towards certain illnesses (his problem of the "choice of neuroses") is rapidly gaining ground. And it is even more fascinating to watch highly "Freudian" ideas reemerging in mainstream science.

Freud always believed that the "conditions of loving" are determined at a very early age, and he explained this by the idea of libidinal fixation to our first objects. One rather successful research program in evolutionary psychology is trying to prove a rather similar hypothesis, albeit along a very different track. There is growing evidence that men's criteria for falling in love are determined at a very early age by the facial proportions of their mothers and sisters. It is assumed that early childhood constitutes a critical period in establishing with whom we will subsequently fall in love. Darwinian thought attempts to show that this genetically hardwired pattern makes evolutionary sense: by linking our "conditions of love" to similarities in the basic features of close family members, evolution ensures that we do not stray too far in diversifying the human gene pool.

But the methodology by which these models are developed and potentially tested is very different from the psychoanalytic database of listening to individual patients. Huge amounts of data from anthropology, biology, social psychology and the neurosciences are being used and integrated in these novel approaches. Interdisciplinary integration is all the rage. Hence, psychoanalysis, which mostly limits its database to clinical interactions, has largely lost touch with today's most promising explorations of human nature.

Science and Human Nature

The cultural impact and importance of psychoanalysis in the twentieth century were not due primarily to its ability to help people in distress. Psychoanalysis provided a theory of human nature and a language that explained to the educated classes who they were and why life was complex (Zaretsky 2004). From the point of view of cultural history, Freud's great achievement was that he created a language that combined two of the major languages of European modernity: the romantic fascination with the irrational and the Enlightenment belief that science was a progressive enterprise that would gradually unlock all of the secrets of nature, including human nature. Freud's enduring legacy was a synthesis of the fascination with the irrational mind in German romanticism and the biological science of his day: he was a combination of Schopenhauer and Lamarck, with a tinge of Dostoevsky.

But psychoanalysis would never have gained the place it came to occupy in modern culture if it hadn't been couched in the language of science, because by the twentieth science was the authority that had replaced religion in the West. Had Freud said that he was merely offering a language for narrating the self that applied Enlightenment concepts to the romantic understanding of the self as deep, conflicted but creative, he never would have gained a hearing. Of course, this is not to say that he used scientific language as a cynical ploy to establish a form of respectability that would otherwise have eluded psychoanalysis. Rather, he deeply and seriously believed that science was the only legitimate way to make a claim for truth.

A century later, the situation is somewhat similar, in that science is the one great undertaking that can make a powerful claim to legitimate truth on two grounds: first, the staggering growth of scientific knowledge throughout the twentieth century and the ensuing technological explosion that has changed the face of the planet; and, second, the intellectually compelling, interlocking edifice of the natural sciences, which is generating an ever-widening and -deepening understanding of the universe, from the subatomic level to the cosmos.

The reason why psychiatrists, clinical psychologists and clinical social workers (the basic disciplines that compose the majority of psychoanalysts) have a status that is different from those of spiritual healers, certified coaches and simple motivational speakers is that our doctorates and MAs give our profession a reputation of belonging to the scientific world. Hoffman's exasperation with "playing the science game" does not take into account that there are several good reasons why patients want the reassurance of science when they seek help. This is not just due to the craze for instrumental reason, and I think that it would be myopic to attribute it to brainwashing by a culture that worships science.

The mysteries of human nature that preoccupied Freud are investigated today in an evolving paradigm that connects evolutionary biology, cognitive psychology, the neurosciences and anthropology. Truly great questions – such as "Why do most humans believe in religion?", "Why is there little correlation between sexual attraction and personal respect?" and "Why do humans systematically disregard empirical evidence in their decision-making?' – are starting to receive ever more convincing answers (Pinker 1997, Atran 2002).

Evolutionary biology and the neurosciences have provided a framework that has allowed psychology to become truly interesting again. Studying biases in decision-making started as a research paradigm developed by Amos Tversky and Daniel Kahneman (Arieli 2008), but since then this has connected with evolutionary psychology to create a powerful explanatory framework in which sound empirical evidence amassed through decades of research has merged with knowledge derived from the neurosciences (Pinker 1997). This framework is now being applied to economics, and this seems to be leading to a paradigm shift in economic theory through the emerging discipline of behavioral economics (Arieli 2008).

Closer to the immediate concerns of psychoanalysis is experimental existential psychology, inspired by the work of Otto Rank and the anthropologist Ernest Becker (1974), which I presented in Chapter 2. The result has been a psychodynamic paradigm of great explanatory power and intellectual beauty. Hundreds of experiments conducted in dozens of countries have created a sound evidential foundation for an ambitious, fascinating theory that has applications in a number of fields: for instance, it has been applied to politics, to the study of terrorism and to research into prejudice (Greenberg et al. 2004).

I am aware that notions like "human nature" do not enthrall many thinkers in contemporary psychoanalysis. During the heyday of postmodernism, such concepts were seen as instruments of domination masquerading as science. Meanwhile, the indeterminacy of interpretation, the multiplicity of perspectives and the free play of signifiers were viewed as instruments of liberation from social pressures (Deleuze and Guattari 1972).

Much of contemporary psychoanalysis is still in the throes of these postmodern conceptions. However, while such an insistence on a space of freedom remains of great importance (Foucault 1984), I do not believe that the desire to understand human nature is a function of a cultural fad or just an attempt to pressurize people into conformity. Why humans fall in love and why they hate, why they go to war and why they adhere to irrational belief systems – these questions have preoccupied thinkers since the dawn of intellectual history, and it is quite desirable to lift the search for answers from the domain of untestable competing interpretations to the domain of systematic empirical research, which, of necessity, involves a large number of disciplines.

Hence, the evolutionary cognitive neurosciences are important not just because they use high-tech tools like fMRI and sophisticated statistical methods of analysis. Rather, their importance resides in the fact that they are plumbing into a growing body of knowledge with extraordinary explanatory power and coherence. Science, as its students like Kuhn (1962) and Quine (1978) have shown, does not work through isolated pieces of knowledge but through integrative paradigms. It always works in what Quine (1978) has called "the web of belief." It is the ever-increasing density of the network of scientific theory and research that constitutes science's great strength.

The evolutionary cognitive neurosciences have indeed evolved into such an integrated paradigm. As a result, they are now addressing large-scale questions that used to preoccupy psychoanalysis in the days when the discipline was full of theoretical conquistadors. For example, since the turn of the century, the anthropologist Scott Atran (2002) has formulated an integrated theory of the evolutionary background of religion as well as a compelling theory about why the human mind is so susceptible to religious narratives and ways of life. He has also made use of his sophisticated theoretical tools to research the genesis of suicide terrorism and has presented research results that are not only intellectually compelling but have practical applications in addressing the threat of global terror (Atran 2010).

Another example is the work of the neurologist Antonio Damasio (2003), who has made use of recent neuroscience research to explore the relationships between mind and body, and between reason and emotion. In a remarkable integration of hard-core science and humanistic imagination, he has made a strong case for the thesis that the Cartesian image of conflict between reason and emotion is highly misleading (Edelman 1992). Instead, Damasio is working towards a sophisticated reformulation of Spinoza's more complex picture of the interrelation between these two aspects of the human psyche.

While, as Jeremy Safran (2013) points out, it may be true that the current prestige enjoyed by the cognitive neurosciences attracts more funding than may be warranted, any accusation that the field is a soulless, technical enterprise is misleading, to say the least. At its best, it deepens our understanding of the human condition, and allows us to address some of the great questions of the philosophical tradition in an intellectually compelling manner. But Safran makes another point that must be taken very seriously: he argues against Hoffman's opinion that the scientific community must be avoided by psychoanalysis because they share no common ground for dialogue. Safran (2013) warns that the tendency towards insularity among psychoanalysts has not served us well in the past, and it certainly will not serve us well in the future.

This is the principal weakness of psychoanalysis nowadays: most psychoanalytic writing and theorizing has very little connection with the exponentially growing body of theory and research that is modern science. Instead, it sticks to the language of literary theory and cultural criticism, as if these disciplines were in some way superior to those of the sciences. It has largely forgone the option to say something about human nature, with most psychoanalytic writing focusing on the minutiae of clinical interaction. As a result, it has lost the interest of both the scientific community and the educated lay readership, as Paul Stepansky (2009) has documented. It has also lost its cultural function. In the mid-twentieth century, the Western educated classes felt that psychoanalysis gave them the tools to understand their lives. Now most of them believe no such thing.

Psychoanalysis and Science: A New Vision

What are the implications of the picture that has emerged so far? For me, the main problem with Hoffman's perspective is that it perpetuates, albeit in a new form, one of the principal flaws of psychoanalysis throughout its history, one which Frank Sulloway (1979) diagnosed many years ago: the assumption of epistemic autonomy; the idea that psychoanalysis has some sort of unique access to a truth that cannot be attained elsewhere, and so does not need and should not use knowledge that is generated by other scientific and academic disciplines (Gellner 2003).

Psychoanalysis's preoccupation with itself is not healthy. In particular, the endless quest to establish what makes psychoanalysis different and special is probably more of an occupational hazard than an intellectually valid or worthwhile mission. It is the type of task that is pursued by religions, spiritual traditions and artistic styles. This does not make it illegitimate, but its true nature should be realized: it is a preoccupation with identity and an insistence on specialness. As Adam Phillips (1996) has quipped succinctly, the preoccupation with its own importance is unlikely to make psychoanalysis interesting to anyone other than psychoanalysts.

One practical implication of abandoning this preoccupation would be to allow psychoanalysis to become more clinically pragmatic – a point made time and again by several important authors (e.g., Jurist 2010). It should ask how it might be most useful to its patients, rather than busy itself with the narcissism of little differences. In the modern market place, psychoanalysis no longer has the prestige of being a profession with strong legitimacy (Jurist 2010). However, to my mind, the most important implication of the picture presented above is that psychoanalysis should open its gates and discourse to the enterprise of generating an evolutionary understanding of human nature – an enterprise in which Freud sincerely believed and one that was dropped by his followers principally because he remained a Lamarckian throughout his life; although we should not forget that in the 1920s Lamarckism was still a legitimate scientific position. But psychoanalysis's discomfort with its master's blunder, and its retreat from the dialogue with other disciplines, has been a significant factor in its subsequent intellectual isolation (Sulloway 1979, Gellner 2003).

The hermeneutic retreat has reached a point where most psychoanalytic thinking and writing has all but abandoned any attempt to tackle this issue, in the same way as it has given up on theories about human nature in general. The hermeneutic construal of psychoanalysis often presents this as progress, but I think that such a view idealizes the hermeneutic retreat, which, it should be remembered, was primarily a reaction to the fact that psychoanalysis no longer had a good epistemological basis on which to ground large-scale claims about human nature (Spence 1982).

Psychoanalysis has always been part of the naturalistic worldview that underlies modern science: the hypothesis that nature is a coherent whole governed by a unitary set of laws. Hence the assumption of the unity of knowledge: in the end, our theories about various aspects of reality need to cohere with one another (Quine 1978). This does not mean that all sciences ultimately must be formulated in the language of physics. It means that the theories about various levels of reality (subatomic, chemical, biological, psychological, sociological, political and economic) need to be consistent with each other (Strenger 1991: chs. 5, 6).

While the truth of the assumption of the unity of knowledge cannot be proven, it has been the metaphysics that has guided the enterprise of science, and so far very successfully. This is why most psychologists and most psychoanalysts assume that the explanation for human behavior will not be found in dybbuks, ghosts or punitive measures by God, but in varieties of interpersonal relatedness, biochemical variations in brain functioning and genetic factors. In turn, this is why the split between hermeneutics and science, when taken as total, is wrongly conceived: every hermeneutic act is guided by assumptions about the structure of reality, as can be seen clearly in the following example. An interpreter of the Bible who assumes that the text is of divine origin assumes that every word must be totally true. Furthermore, this theological interpreter assumes that if the text contains seeming contradictions, the divine author must be trying to get something across through these contradictions. This is indeed how the Talmud approaches biblical texts. By contrast, an interpreter who assumes that the Bible is an earthly creation does not assume that every word is totally true; instead, he believes that we can learn something about the worldview of the authors, their limitations, aims, intended public and effect. Furthermore, the earthly interpreter assumes that repetitions, contradictions and stylistic discrepancies within the text indicate that a variety of earlier texts were integrated by an editor or editorial team. He will use information from all domains of knowledge, ranging from archeology and history through philology to, where relevant, physical methods of establishing the age of artifacts to date texts.

In other words, hermeneutics is always guided by a metaphysic, and psychoanalysis has always been committed to the metaphysic of science: all of its great theorists, from Freud to Erikson, from Ferenczi to Kohut, have worked within this metaphysic, and they were all conversant with the science of their day. This is why psychoanalytic interpretation and theory cannot possibly be detached from surrounding disciplines: at the very least, psychoanalytic interpretation must be consistent with science; and, ideally, it should be in a relationship of mutual enrichment with science.

In claiming that psychoanalysis must be part of the edifice of modern science, I do not mean that psychoanalysts should don white coats and relocate to laboratories: many other disciplines are already doing lab research quite successfully. Instead, psychoanalysis should ask itself what it could gain from the great and increasing body of knowledge generated by the evolutionary cognitive neurosciences and social sciences ranging from sociology to political science, and, in turn, what it could contribute to them.

Psychoanalysts have a privileged perspective that other social scientists often lack as a result of their protracted and almost uniquely open-ended immersion in other people's subjective worlds. The discipline that is closest to psychoanalysis in this respect is anthropology, with its emphasis on prolonged participant observation. In both fields, participant observation is, of course, strongly influenced by theory. And the only way to choose between rival theories – about the nature of the family, of totemism, of sadomasochism, of borderline personality disorders or of identity diffusion – is through systematic validation across disciplines. Neither anthropologists nor psychoanalysts are able to decide which theory is most likely to describe the nature of human reality on the basis of their data alone.

I also believe that cognitive neuroscientists would benefit greatly from learning how psychoanalysts formulate their cases, and how they describe their patients' inner worlds and interpersonal relatedness. Let me give a hypothetical example of how this might work. There has been a plethora of hypotheses about what causes borderline personality disorder. Is it a high level of oral rage and a weakness in ego organization (Kernberg 1975)? Is it due to a genetically based temperamental propensity (Kagan 1989) or to insufficient mentalization (Fonagy et al. 2005)? Is narcissistic vulnerability a function of insufficient parental mirroring in critical developmental stages (Kohut 1971), or of a cyclothymic temperament to be located on the spectrum between normality and bipolar affective disorder (Kramer 1993)? Has the tendency towards narcissistic vulnerability increased in recent decades (Lasch 1979); and if it has, could this be related to the impact of the global infotainment network, with its tendency to focus on extraordinary success stories (Strenger 2011a)?

To address these questions, close clinical description would need to be combined with epidemiological data, molecular genetics, neurophysiologic research and longitudinal developmental studies. The day may come when neuroscientists who sit in on case discussions might generate hypotheses about how to measure brain functioning under conditions of increased affective volatility and search for differences in brain structure and function between various personality types. But psychoanalysis should not only interact with the evolutionary cognitive neurosciences; it should also forge closer relationships with disciplines like sociology and political science. Psychoanalysts are as well placed as anyone to explore correlations between the changing nature of the clinical pictures they encounter and macro-social and macro-cultural developments that are often driven by technology. For instance, I think that it would be extremely interesting to write the history of changing favorite diagnostic categories in psychoanalysis and clinical psychology, and the social structures in which they emerged and were useful. There are already several indications of the potential of this approach (Lasch 1979, Strenger 2004, Zaretsky 2004).

But we can go a step further. Phillips's (1996) claim that excessive reliance on social authorities is deleterious – which I endorse – is amenable to scientific enquiry. It is definitely feasible to investigate whether the search for comparative data to establish that one is "doing well" and "living a normal life" contributes to well-being or, conversely, generates a constant sense of insufficiency and lowers autonomy.

As Harris (2010) has argued convincingly, many questions about moral life are amenable to scientific investigation, and scientific knowledge is definitely relevant to them. Hume's suggestion that there is a total disconnect between questions of fact and questions of value is misleading; as is the idea that we must decide between humanistic and natural science methodologies when trying to understand the human condition. C. P. Snow's (1958) call to bridge the gap between the sciences and the humanities, rather than cast them as competing cultures, remains valid.

All this is not meant to discard the core of the hermeneutic understanding of psychoanalysis, which at its best is one of the heirs of the philosophical conception of the examined life and the search for freedom and autonomy. But this worthy ideal in no way requires the maintenance of a spurious distinction between the humanistic disciplines and the natural sciences. And it requires even less the exaltation of the humanities and the disparagement of the natural science model: they do not compete with but complement each other.

I think that the vision of a psychoanalysis that is open to the vast field of expanding knowledge is exciting. Abandoning the notion of psychoanalysis's epistemic autonomy is no great loss: on the contrary, it will allow us to get rid of an illusion that had no intellectual justification in the first place. While the loss of illusions can sometimes be painful, we should, along with Freud (1927), see it as a way to open a space for autonomy and innovation.

Chapter 10

A Personal Journey into the Global Media

When approaching the shores of the United States, Freud famously told Jung and Ferenczi: "They don't know that we're bringing them the plague." It is a truism to say that psychoanalysis was a transformative cultural force in the twentieth century. After initial resistance, the United States came to embrace psychoanalysis as the *lingua franca* through which the educated middle classes might understand their lives. Psychoanalytic language pervaded everything from courtrooms to psychiatric hospitals. At mid-century, psychoanalysis still held most of the power positions in American psychiatry.

The decline of psychoanalysis's public standing has been described time and again. I discussed it in Chapter 7, but it is worth restating the highlights here. Eli Zaretsky (2004), in his valuable study of the cultural background of psychoanalysis, claims that its influence started to wane as early as the 1960s. Philip Rieff (1955), one of Freud's great sociological interpreters, similarly describes a triumphant therapeutic culture that replaced Freud's austere analytic attitude in the 1960s. And Nathan Hale (1995) has written an integrative history of the rise and subsequent crisis of psychoanalysis in the United States.

In Chapter 7 we also saw how psychoanalysis's standing plummeted in the world of publishing. Until the 1970s, authors like Fromm and Erikson enjoyed bestseller status. But Stepansky (2009) has highlighted that the number of publishers willing to publish psychoanalytic titles has declined dramatically over the last few decades, while the major university presses are no longer willing even to consider psychoanalytic titles. The same holds true for high-quality trade presses that once published very successful psychoanalytic books, such as Erikson's *Childhood and Society* (1959).

What are the reasons for psychoanalysis's decline in public status? One is certainly that the discipline has largely lost its foothold in the universities, as Robert Wallerstein (2012) has shown recently. Major institutions in the history of US psychoanalysis shrunk and ultimately closed. Most programs in psychiatry and clinical psychology turned away from the discipline, and by the turn of the century psychoanalysts held almost no important chairs in either field (Hale 1995). This was largely due to the biological turn in psychiatry and the emergence of the cognitive neurosciences as the dominant paradigm in psychology departments and journals around the world. Wallerstein (2012) has trenchantly argued for a renewal of psychoanalysis's institutional ties to academia on intellectual, scientific and institutional grounds. This argument is laudable, but it fails to consider that the current climate in academic psychology and psychiatry makes such a renewal unlikely: it is hard to see an imminent academic surge of interest in psychoanalysis, given the current power of the paradigm of the cognitive neurosciences.

In this chapter, I would like to address an additional sphere that is of great importance today. Over the last few years, a new agora – a marketplace of ideas – has arisen. John Brockman (1995) coined the term "Third Culture" for the sphere that bridges the gap between the community of scientific specialists and the wider educated lay audience. He has been doing much to promote this Third Culture on his Edge website, where leading scientists present important developments in their respective fields in accessible language. He has also been very successful in promoting books written by leading scientists and published by major trade presses that address a wider educated audience.

The Third Culture has spread remarkably over the last decade. The science sections of major newspapers and magazines such as the *New York Times*, *Time*, the *Washington Post*, the *Guardian* and others have discussed it at length. Academics often contribute to the op-ed sections of these papers, too, sometimes in their domain of research, sometimes going beyond these spheres, assuming the role of public intellectual. A number of websites are also highly active in disseminating ideas to a wider public. One of the most influential sites is TED.com, which was originally devoted to technology, entertainment and design. Today, it encompasses most scientific disciplines and many topics that are of interest to a wider public, ranging from environmental protection to new education technologies. It is built on a series of talks, each of which may be no more than eighteen minutes in length. The videos of these talks then appear on the TED website. At the time of writing they had accumulated more than seven hundred and fifty million views, making TED the most viewed website in the Third Culture. Similar sites, such as bigthink.com and Sciencemag.org, have emerged more recently, and today's social media, including Facebook and Twitter, have increased their reach.

Psychoanalysis has been all but absent from the Third Culture (Prince et al. 2012). This is unfortunate, because participating in this space is not just important for the promotion of the discipline. I believe that psychoanalysts have a great contribution to make to the general public, and that our reticence about entering the new agora of thinking deprives the public of ideas that could be helpful not only to individuals but to globalized culture at large. Consequently, I shall present a strategy for psychoanalysis's entry into the Third Culture based on a psychodynamic understanding of the fetishization of ratings and rankings presented in Chapter 1 and my interpretation of the plight of the New Cosmopolitans in the rest of Part I. I will argue that psychoanalytic models can be presented in ways that help educated lay audiences to understand their own persistent discontent generated by the deification of numbers.

Psychoanalysis shares a problem with all other cultural traditions in the era of global capitalism: all are threatened by the craze of quantification. One of the best examples of this is the fate of the humanities in academia. They are engaged in a fight for survival, with student enrollment falling because young people do not see how studying literature, history or philosophy will improve their competitiveness in the labor market. The humanities are also finding it hard to prove their relevance because they cannot point to any technological discoveries that have an immediate impact on the economy, public safety or public health (Nussbaum 2010). They have tried to decry the shallowness of global capitalist culture, but this has proved no more helpful for the humanities than it has been for psychoanalysis (Barber 2008).

I will argue that, unlikely as it may seem, psychoanalysis has the capacity to adapt to many of the new forums without betraying its essence or its message, as opposed to what Irwin Hoffman (2009) argued in his influential paper (see Chapter 8). At the deepest level, psychoanalysis's most important message has always been that the self's complexity, far from being an impediment to leading a good life, is one of the most important sources of meaning. In the past, psychoanalysis has been singularly good at communicating the gripping drama of the psyche's emergence, and I hope to show that it can regain its function of helping our culture to embrace and celebrate complexity rather than shun it. Of course, this will require some work on our individual and collective anxieties and resistance to losing our identity.

I have learned that maintaining a distance between oneself and an audience is one of the strongest impediments to getting a message across, and that personal stories are usually the most powerful and effective means to communicate complex ideas. Many other psychoanalysts have realized this and put into practice over the last decade, too. Our literature no longer preserves the fiction of the opaque and objective analyst, and many of us have written much more openly about our own processes. With this in mind, I will relate the story of my own personal journey into the Third Culture. It was replete with failures, frustrations and resistance to learning from experience, but it also taught me that I needed help from others in order to venture into a world that initially seemed alien, given my psychoanalytic and academic background. On the basis of many conversations with colleagues, I now believe that my fears, resistances and apprehensions were by no means unique, and I hope that this chapter will engender further discussion about the rightful place of psychoanalysis in the public sphere.

To participate fully in the Third Culture, psychoanalysis needs to be able to communicate some of its central intuitions clearly. One of D. W. Winnicott's (1965, 1971) enduring contributions has been to show that humans can maintain psychic health only in an intermediary space, located between the subjective and objective. Winnicott specifically placed the whole domain of culture – art, religion and ideology – within this space, and his work showed in detail how the space of culture evolves developmentally from the infant's bridging of the subjective and objective worlds through transitional space. Throughout his life, Winnicott investigated the complex balance between the space of illusion necessary to stay alive and the psyche's ability to accept the external world as independent of the subject. Time and again, he argued that psychic survival from childhood to death requires that the individual's and the group's intermediary spaces be respected (Winnicott 1971: passim). In the same way as the good enough mother does not question whether the infant has created its transitional objects or whether they were there from the outset, cultures can survive only if the ontological status of its objects of belief and the source of its values are not questioned, whether these be prophets, saints, canonical works of art or the rituals that hold a culture together. But this is becoming progressively more difficult when the reach of the global infotainment system intrudes everywhere, and even traditional forms of life realize that they are but specks within a global system that is immensely more powerful than any particular cultural form of life.

Global capitalism (Sloterdijk 2005) has developed a way of dealing with the relativizing of all cultural frames: the deification of numbers. If no cultural tradition can claim absolute validity, is there a way to define value that is, so to speak, unassailable? As I showed in Chapter 1, contemporary global culture's response has been to search for "absolute" answers in the scales and rankings of humans along variables that can be quantified. I emphasized that these scales enjoy high levels of prominence and visibility because they are publicized in numerous media outlets, which in turn has meant that the craze for rankings has seeped into the strata of those who do not stand any chance of making it into them. Today, children and adolescents invest great effort in collecting "friends" and "likes" on Facebook. The self is not only quantified but shaped from within by the new realities, and psychoanalysis is starting to probe the depth to which the internet is shaping intrapsychic and interpersonal processes, such as the development of our sense of reality (Žižek 2004, Gibbs 2007) and of sexual identity, often shortcutting these in dangerous ways, as Alessandra Lemma (2010) has shown convincingly.

A Difficult Personal Journey into the Third Culture

The psychoanalytic tradition has a lot to offer the members of global culture. It has always resisted simplistic myths of the "Just Do It!" type. Well into the 1960s it was successful in communicating compelling theories about what it means to live a human life that celebrates complexity rather than shuns it. The retreat from the twenty-first century's public sphere therefore comes at a heavy price: the psychoanalytic message that the self's depth and complexity are a source of meaning, and that there is more to identity than the self's marketable properties, is today more important than ever. This is why psychoanalysis should make a serious attempt to communicate its view to the Third Culture – today's marketplace for ideas.

Participating in the Third Culture certainly does not come easy to psychoanalysts. In contrast to the dominant academic culture in the natural and social sciences, psychoanalysis has never been infatuated with novelty. It has insisted on the relevance of its own canon, and on integrating its own history into its writing and self-understanding, thus preserving the transitional space of its own culture and history. If modern scientific research mostly puts a premium on the novelty of results and the technology by which they are generated, psychoanalysis continues to place its thinking within the context of more than a century of psychoanalytic writing and theorizing, thus creating a richly textured, multilayered cultural tradition with a poetic dimension that is irreducibly intertwined with theory and practice (Shahar 2010). Psychoanalysts experience the long, complex history of their discipline as a holding environment that creates historical depth. This makes it ever more difficult for psychoanalysis to capture the Third Culture's attention, as historical depth is not one of its features (Strenger 2004). In addition to being out of reach for most of the educated lay public, the psychoanalytic canon has become inaccessible for the overwhelming majority of mental health professionals, because most of the training programs in disciplines like psychiatry and clinical psychology no longer teach it.

So, how might psychoanalysis join the Third Culture? The clinical pursuit of psychoanalysis is a very private matter, and it takes years to acquire the skill to communicate about these intimate processes. Then again, the history of psychoanalysis is replete with gifted communicators, ranging from Freud himself through Reik and Erikson to Fromm and Winnicott (who made a point of regularly addressing lay audiences). All of these men succeeded in making aspects of psychoanalytic thought and practice intelligible to wider circles.

I expect a simple objection:

> In the days of Reik, Erikson, Fromm and Winnicott you could still expect audiences to listen to long lectures and to read complex books. They did not expect intellectually and emotionally demanding material to be pared down to the size of a TED talk, a Big Think interview or an op-ed piece in the *New York Times*!

This argument is weighty, yet I still believe that psychoanalysts must find a way to enter the Third Culture, and not only to make psychoanalysis popular. The quantification of value and the "Just Do It!" myth that everything is possible are generating enormous suffering. Psychoanalysis must do what it can to show the ways in which individuals can validate their subjectivity over and above quantifiable achievements in a globalized culture.

In order to communicate with the Third Culture, we must participate in its rituals and speak its language. Most psychoanalysts are used to reading papers, whereas the Third Culture requires speakers to engage with audiences more immediately. We have all been socialized to build our lectures by connecting our questions to the psychoanalytic tradition. To join the Third Culture, we must find ways to reach the audience without presupposing a common theoretical background. We must try to reach them through stories and experiences to which they can relate in a more direct manner.

Over the past few decades I have ventured into the Third Culture, but the journey has been far from easy. My intellectual development was defined by immersion in the classical texts of the European philosophical tradition and psychoanalysis. For a long time, I felt that there was no way of transmitting what I had learned to audiences that did not share this background and were either unwilling or unable to follow the complex theoretical reasoning. Moreover, I was suspicious of attempts to simplify ideas to make them more accessible.

The process of change was gradual. It began in the 1990s, when I delivered several courses on Freud and psychoanalysis for popular audiences that forced me to make this tradition accessible for people who had no preparation for it. These courses – each comprising about ten lectures – worked quite well. The problem came when I was asked to speak at conferences for the business community, and was allocated no more than half an hour. To give a simple example, the world of high tech has been thriving on the myth that it has squared the circle because its employees never feel as if they are working hard (Illouz 2008). They can work endlessly without feeling cheated of their lives because their work is really just the playful self-realization of their deep selves, so they are able to combine financial success with an authentic life. In some lectures I tried to debunk this myth by presenting Winnicott's (1971) idea that in healthy development we do not simply adapt to the external world's demands but require a complex negotiation that allows us to maintain contact with the true self. I wanted to point out to the audience that this cultural myth could rob those who believed it of an authentic life, and that they needed to be attentive to their feelings to avoid such a fate.

I tried to explain some of Winnicott's core concepts without sacrificing too much of his idea's richness but, with only half an hour at my disposal, I failed miserably. I lost the audience after just ten minutes, and it was quite painful to remain on the podium for another twenty minutes and look out at a sea of blank stares, at best, or the backs of people's heads as they left the hall, at worst. Friends who were listening pointed out that I had not adapted my vocabulary or my mode of presentation to the audience's needs, but at first I rejected their well-meant suggestions. I thought that I could not go beyond a certain level of simplification without betraying the psychoanalytic tradition I was trying to represent.

However, my attitude to one friend's admonitions changed when I realized that, by insisting on a more classical style of presentation, I was effectively renouncing the opportunity to speak to the professional groups that most needed to understand the cultural pressures under which they were living, especially members of the high-tech sector, who function under enormous pressure and are in far more need of self-understanding than my "natural" audience, who probably have a background in humanistic disciplines. The rapprochement between my "native" psychodynamic language and that of non-psychoanalytic audience took some time and involved several rather painful failures and embarrassments, but I was fortunate to receive help from a number of friends and colleagues. As a result, my encounters with wider audiences have become more fruitful and gratifying for both sides as the years have gone by.

Against my earlier principles, I began to use PowerPoint presentations during lectures. At first, I filled them with far too many words, with the result that they were quite useless. Gradually, though, I accepted my friends' advice to think in stories rather than abstractions, and began to realize the phenomenal power of images to illustrate and amplify those stories and reach audiences' minds and hearts. This process required some self-analysis. I needed to work through my fear that I would have nothing to say if I dispensed with a complex vocabulary and wide cultural associations. It was not easy to accept that I often hid behind a professional vocabulary in order to maintain distance from my audience and establish a sense of authority. In fact, all I was doing was failing to make emotional contact with the audience, which made it impossible to reach their minds and hearts.

After further adjustments, I started to reach audiences, including those from the high-tech and financial sectors, and the reactions were encouraging. Members of the audience would approach me after a lecture and say: "I now know what has been driving me crazy for years!" or "I finally understand the source of my discontent and the fear that I'm living a useless life!" My long journey – with all its mistakes and blind alleys – had finally brought me to the point of being able to communicate in a way that allowed audiences to understand my message. Much more importantly, though, those audiences now understood a message that was derived from the psychoanalytic tradition and they were encouraged to think more deeply about the cultural myths that were making them miserable.

Another learning process began in 2005 when I teamed up with a friend, Arie Ruttenberg, formerly a successful advertising executive, to work on a new concept of midlife transition. My own ideas were strongly influenced by Elliot Jacques's seminal paper "Death and the Midlife Crisis" (1965), which introduced the world to the notion of the midlife crisis. Jacques investigated the creative trajectories of many artists and concluded that their creativity underwent a transformation from exuberance to what he called "sculpted creativity" – the ability to see life's tragic dimension and integrate it into their work. He interpreted this as a deep working through of the depressive position, in Melanie Klein's sense.

Of course, I ran into a number of problems: Klein's notion of the depressive position is not easy to explain to readers unfamiliar with psychoanalytic thinking – and Ogden's (1993) splendid elaboration of this notion even less so. Fortunately, Arie was adamant that we must make our ideas accessible to a wide audience, so we decided to try to write an article for the *Harvard Business Review.* Because it is one of the world's most influential business publications, we hoped that this would help business executives to take our ideas seriously and implement them in their lives and their organizations. Here my own resistance to change found a most suitable object for projection. Arie, after all, had been an advertising executive for most of his adult life. So whenever he pushed for more accessible formulations, I would reply: "This is exactly how you guys ruin culture. You have no interest in complexity; you just look for the punchline. You're turning this into an exercise in copywriting instead of a contribution that generates genuine insight!" This was an easy way to externalize my conflict about reaching out to wider audiences: I simply projected the part of my self that wanted to do so on to Arie.

We were lucky to work with a *Harvard Business Review* editor – Diane Coutu – who had a profound understanding of and interest in psychoanalysis. She helped us to find formulations that made psychoanalytic ideas like Klein's depressive position and Winnicott's differentiation between dreaming and fantasizing accessible to a community that is far removed from psychoanalytic thinking. The resulting article, "The Existential Necessity of Midlife Change" (Strenger and Ruttenberg 2008), generated wide interest and was discussed in, among others, *Time* and the *Washington Post.*

In the same period I became progressively more concerned about political developments in Israel that I felt were profoundly dangerous for the country's future (Bar-Tal and Schnell 2012) and conflicted with some of my most deeply held values and beliefs. I approached *Haaretz*, Israel's leading liberal newspaper with a strong tradition of dissent (Remnik 2011), because I hoped to be of some use in formulating many Israelis' deepest fears, which were pushing them ever more towards right-wing nationalism. Once again, I was fortunate, because two of *Haaretz*'s editors, including its current editor in chief Aluf Benn, worked patiently with me on my style of presentation. They pointed out that I often used the names of scientific or psychoanalytic authorities in ways that neither contributed to my argument nor were of any real value for a readership that had no idea about these names or their theories. I had to learn the difference between academic writing and the op-ed format, and accept that what I took to be good academic etiquette came across as pompous in the latter format.

Here, again, there was a psychodynamic aspect to my problems. Not only was this medium new for me, but I had to learn to deal with my own fears. Israel's political scene is emotionally very heated, and from early on I was faced with some aggressive reactions to my ideas. These could go as far as to wish that my family had perished in the Holocaust so the Jewish people would be spared self-hating specimens such as myself. Of course, it is not easy simply to brush aside such comments, and my desire to seek protection behind the mantle of external authorities increased. My writing communicated to readers: "Please don't attack me personally. I represent a class of specialists, so my political views are buttressed by superior knowledge!" It took me a while to realize that this was inauthentic. While much of my political writing was indeed based on and inspired by psychodynamic thought and other social science theories and data, the bottom line was that I was defending a liberal political position that was not particularly popular in Israel. No amount of name-dropping would change that. If I wanted to venture into the emotionally charged area of Israel's identity, morality and survival strategy, I had to accept that I would no longer be able to shelter under the umbrella of specialist knowledge. Moreover, my strategy did not even serve the purpose, because readers often felt that I was pontificating. I finally understood that I had to accept the medium on its own terms and renounce the safety of academic discussion.

The true risk of participating in this discourse became dramatically concrete when, in September 2008, a right-wing zealot put a bomb at the doorstep of a fellow *Haaretz* commentator, professor of political science and historian of French fascism Zeev Sternhell. Fortunately, he was only slightly hurt, and he has continued to voice his trenchant criticism of Israel's policies ever since. I found his courage inspiring and expressed my outrage about the terror attack in an op-ed piece entitled "I Accuse!" (Strenger 2008). I also decided that I could no longer let my fears influence my public writing. I am grateful to *Haaretz* for hosting my blog (Strenger 2009), which integrates psychodynamic thinking and political analysis, over the last few years.

Early in 2012, I was invited to present a paper at a TEDX event – a sub-brand of TED, one of the Third Culture's most influential venues. I decided to use this opportunity to explain the complex developmental process through which today's New Cosmopolitans (described in Part I of this book) develop their complex non-tribal identities. But how would I compress psychodynamic formulations that I had developed over a decade – and which had filled two books – into eighteen minutes? I think I sweated over this short talk more than I had ever sweated over an academic paper. There were moments of despair – at one point I was on the verge of telling the organizers that I would have to cancel – and I dithered between self-denigration and rants about the shallowness of the TED format. The TED coaches, Michael Weitz and Abigail Tenembaum, rejected my early drafts because they were too abstract and uncommunicative. At first, I thought Michael and Abigail were just trying to cheapen my lecture, and I resisted a simple realization: even though I had been lecturing in a variety of contexts since my early twenties, they knew considerably more about effective delivery – certainly within the context of a TED talk – than I did, so I had a lot to learn from them. Gradually, though, they managed to soften my resistance against the rather simple strategy that they know works supremely well in TED talks: telling personal stories. I finally realized that my theme of how New Cosmopolitans develop by working through early attachments, conflicts with family and tribe and the resulting process of individuation is a story – even if it is codified in psychoanalytic theories. With some reluctance, I accepted the coaches' advice to use my own life story as the entry point and spoke about my difficult process of individuation in adolescence and early adulthood. From there I moved to stories about Freud and other inspiring figures who upheld universalist values in their lives and work. In this way the idea of cosmopolitan identity and world citizenship became much more accessible.

The talk has not become a smash hit on YouTube (Strenger 2012), but I learned a great deal from drafting and delivering it. After watching it, I realized that I still have much to learn if I want to continue to work in this medium. I also have no illusions that I could ever communicate the full complexity of the individuating processes of New Cosmopolitans in the TED format. But that is not the goal of such a talk. Rather, it should simply make the audience realize that psychodynamic thinking has something to offer them – self-understanding and the possibility of self-liberation from shackles they have always felt but could never define.

The Psychoanalytic Message in the Third Culture

I have related my own learning process in some detail precisely because I think that it is not unique. After many conversations with colleagues, I have come to the conclusion that my own fears and resistances on the journey of venturing from the safety of the consulting room and academia and into the wider world reflect the difficulties of many others in the psychoanalytic community who long for a place and a voice in the contemporary public spheres.

Moreover, these fears are shared by those from all cultural traditions that currently feel overwhelmed by the bulldozing power of the global capitalist system that deifies quantification. We all feel protected by the transitional space Winnicott (1971) has shown to be essential for our psychic survival, and we are all profoundly afraid of the possibility that this cultural space might be punctured and flattened by the craze for quantification.

My own journey exemplifies this dynamic. Time and again, I was afraid of losing my professional and personal identity if I abandoned the vocabulary of the psychodynamic tradition. I was also afraid of emerging from the protection of the cultural space that psychoanalysis provided: the rituals of analytic work, the psychoanalytic seminar and the intimacy generated by dialogue with colleagues who share the same rich, associative frame.

The journey of finding my place and voice in the Third Culture took the better part of a decade. Of course, I still feel more comfortable in the institutions and environments that have shaped my professional identity, and I continue to feel safer with colleagues and students with whom I share many cultural and intellectual associations than with wider audiences whose cultural backgrounds

I generally do not know. But I have learned to feel less threatened in my identity in these voyages into the Third Culture. I am no longer afraid that I betray my cultural roots and psychoanalytic values; and, after all, I know that I can always return to my natural cultural context of colleagues and students to refuel and reconnect with my cultural and professional roots.

Today I feel that the process – even though it was difficult, frightening and replete with some humiliating failures – was well worth the time and effort. This journey has strengthened and deepened my conviction that the psychoanalytic tradition still has a lot to offer the wider public. It has also taught me much about the enormous value of seeking and accepting help from specialists in other disciplines.

At this point, I expect an objection:

> In urging psychoanalysts to join the Third Culture, surely you are asking us to cave in to precisely the craze of quantification that you have diagnosed as a major source of suffering? Surely your proposal is the exact analogue of what Irwin Hoffman (2009) has decried as "doublethinking our way to 'scientific legitimacy'"? If we accept your proposal, won't we empty psychoanalysis of all it has been trying to protect by participating in the trend for packaging complex messages in short formats?

My answer is that I do not think so; and I believe that it has been to psychoanalysis's great benefit to find ways to communicate with the scientific mainstream (Shahar et al. 2010, Shedler 2010). Similarly, my personal experience has taught me that, when we are willing to make the effort to communicate with the Third Culture, our messages are often heard and sometimes gratefully accepted.

Forays into the Third Culture can transmit the core messages of the psychoanalytic tradition to wider audiences: that the self has depth; that the complexities of the psyche and of human existence are not impediments to living a good life but the sources of our identity; that flattening the self into a marketable commodity described by numbers achieves the opposite of its aim – it empties our lives of meaning instead of imbuing them with significance.

Disseminating these messages is a supremely worthy purpose, in today's culture more than ever, and psychoanalysis has the tools to pursue this goal. Indeed, it has a forte that is rarely used when we try to communicate with wider audiences: Roy Schafer (1983) argued many years ago that psychoanalysis is about retelling human lives. We are, in more ways than one, storytellers; and, as cognitive and anthropological research shows (Atran 2002), the human mind is hardwired to remember stories rather than theories. We must get used to reformulating our stories without relying on the theoretical vocabulary that we take for granted when communicating with colleagues. And we must accept that in the new media we need to engage our audiences within minutes: we must wean ourselves off the habit of making long introductions in which we connect what we are about to say with theoretical traditions.

I think it would be a grave mistake to see attempts to establish a place in the Third Culture as caving in to demands that are bound to kill the spirit of psychoanalysis. We should instead see reaching out to the wider culture as our duty; as an integral part of our professional ethos and mission of deciphering human experience and alleviating suffering through understanding. Finding a language through which to disseminate this message in the public space of the Third Culture could become as crucial to the undertaking of psychoanalysis as finding the words to help individual patients understand their lives.

Acknowledgements

The author wishes to thank:

- the editor of *Psychoanalytic Psychology* for permission to use material previously published by the author in that journal in Chapters 2, 5, 7 and 9;
- the editor of the *International Journal of Applied Psychoanalytic Studies* for permission to use material previously published by the author in that journal in Chapter 5;
- the editor of *Psychoanalytic Dialogues* for permission to use material previously published by the author in that journal in Chapter 7;
- and the publisher and editor of *Psychoanalysis and Theism: Critical Reflections on the Grünbaum Debate* (edited by B. Beit-Hallahmi, New York: Jason Aronson, 2010) for permission to use material previously published by the author in that volume.

References

Altman, N. (2009). *The Analyst in the Inner City: Race, Class and Culture through a Psychoanalytic Lens.* 2nd edition. Relational Book Series. London: Routledge.

Appiah, K. A. (2006). *Cosmopolitanism: Ethics in a World of Strangers.* New York: Norton.

Arendt, H. (1951). *The Origins of Totalitarianism.* New York: Meridian.

Arendt, H. (2006). *The Jewish Writings.* New York: Schocken.

Arieli, D. (2008). *Predictably Irrational: The Hidden Forces that Shape our Decisions.* New York: HarperCollins.

Armstrong, K. (2000). *The Battle for God: Fundamentalism in Judaism, Christianity and Islam.* New York: Knopf.

Aron, L. (1996). *A Meeting of Minds: Mutuality in Psychoanalysis.* Relational Book Series. Hillsdale, NJ: The Analytic Press.

Aron, L. (2009). Day, Night or Dawn: Commentary on Paper by Steven Stern. *Psychoanalytic Dialogues*, 19: 656–668.

Aron, L. (2010). Responding to Rachel Blass' Article "Affirming 'That's Not Psychoanalysis!' On the Value of the Politically Incorrect Act of Attempting to Define the Limits of our Field." *International Journal of Psychoanalysis*, 91: 1279–1280.

Aron, L. and Henik, L. (2013). *Answering a Question with a Question: Contemporary Psychoanalysis and Jewish Thought.* New York: Academic Press.

Aron, L. and Starr, K. (2013). *A Psychotherapy for the People: Toward a Progressive Psychoanalysis.* Relational Book Series. London: Routledge.

Atran, S. (2002). *In Gods We Trust: The Evolutionary Landscape of Religion.* Oxford: Oxford University Press.

Atran, S. (2010). *Talking to the Enemy: Faith, Brotherhood and the (Un-)making of Terrorists.* London: Ecco.

Auden, W. H. (1939). In Memory of Sigmund Freud. In E. Mendelssohn (ed.) *Selected Poems*. New York: Vintage, 1979.

Bar-Tal, D. and Schnell, I. (eds.) (2012). *The Impact of Lasting Occupation: Enduring Challenges and Emerging Answers*. Series in Political Psychology. Oxford: Oxford University Press.

Barber, B. (1995). *Jihad vs. Macworld: Terrorism's Challenge to Democracy.* New York: Random.

Barber, B. (2008). *Consumed: How Markets Corrupt Children, Infantilize Adults and Swallow Citizens Whole.* New York: Norton.

Bauman, Z. (2002). *Liquid Love.* London: Polity.

Bauman, Z. (2007) *Liquid Times: Living in an Age of Uncertainty.* London: Polity.

Becker, E. (1971). *The Birth and Death of Meaning.* New York: Free Press.

Becker, E. (1974). *The Denial of Death.* New York: Free Press.

Becker, E. (1975). *Escape from Evil.* New York: Free Press.

Benda, J. (1926). *The Treason of the Intellectuals.* New York: Morrow.

Benjamin, J. (1988). *The Bonds of Love: Psychoanalysis, Feminism and the Problem of Domination.* New York: Pantheon.

Benjamin, J. (1995). *Like Subjects, Love Objects: Essays on Recognition and Sexual Difference.* New Haven, CT: Yale University Press.

Berglass, S. (2002). The Very Real Dangers of Executive Coaching. *Harvard Business Review*, 80(6): 86–92.

Biale, D. (2011). *Not in the Heavens: The Tradition of Jewish Secular Thought.* Princeton, NJ: Princeton University Press.

Bilu, Y. (1980). The Moroccan Demon in Israel: The Case of an "Evil Spirit Disease". *Ethos*, 8(1): 24–39.

Blass, R. (2010). Affirming "That's Not Psycho-Analysis!" On the Value of the Politically Incorrect Act of Attempting to Define the Limits of our Field. *International Journal of Psychoanalysis*, 91: 81–99.

Bowlby, J. (1990). *A Secure Base: Parent–Child Attachment and Healthy Human Development.* New York: Basic Books.

Breger, L. (2009). *A Dream of Undying Fame: How Freud Betrayed his Mentor and Invented Psychoanalysis.* New York: Basic Books.

Brockman, J. (1995). *The Third Culture: Beyond the Scientific Revolution.* New York: Simon & Schuster.

Brooks, D. (2000). *Bobos in Paradise.* New York: Simon & Schuster.

Bunzl, J. and Beit-Hallahmi B. (eds.) (2002). *Psychoanalysis, Identity and Ideology: Critical Essays on the Israel/Palestine Case.* New York: Springer.

Buss, D. (2004). *Evolutionary Psychology.* New York: Allyn & Bacon.

Castells, M. (1996). *The Rise of the Network Society.* Oxford: Oxford University Press.

Castells, M. (1996–2000). *The Information Age: Economy, Society and Culture.* Three volumes. Oxford: Oxford University Press.

Chodorow, N. (1989) *Feminism and Psychoanalytic Theory.* New Haven, CT: Yale University Press.

Chodorow, N. (1994). *Femininities, Masculinities, Sexualities.* London: Free Associations.

Conley, D. (2009). *Elsewhere, USA: How We Got from the Company Man, Family Dinners, and the Affluent Society to the Home Office, Blackberry Moms, and Economic Anxiety.* New York: Pantheon.

Conley, D. (2014). *Parentology: Everything You Wanted to Know about the Science of Raising Children, but were too Exhausted to Ask.* New York: Simon & Schuster.

Damasio, A. (2003). *Looking for Spinoza: Joy, Sorrow, and the Feeling Brain*. New York: Harcourt.

Dawkins, R. (1976). *The Selfish Gene*. Oxford: Oxford University Press.

Deleuze, G. and Guattari, F. (1972). *Anti Oedipus: Capitalism and Schizophrenia*. English translation by R. Hurley, M. Seem and H. Lane. New York: Viking, 1977.

Dennett, D. C. (2005). *Breaking the Spell: Religion as a Natural Phenomenon*. New York: Viking.

Diamond, J. (1991). *The Rise and Fall of the Third Chimpanzee*. New York: Norton.

Diamond, J. (1997). *Guns, Germs and Steel: The Fates of Human Societies*. New York: Norton.

Dimen, M. and Goldner, V. (eds.) (2010). *Gender in Psychoanalytic Space: Between Clinic and Culture*. New York: Other Press.

Edelman, G. M. (1992). *Bright Air, Brilliant Fire: On the Matter of the Mind*. New York: Basic Books.

Ehrenreich, B. (1989). *Fear of Falling: The Inner Life of the Middle Class*. New York: Pantheon.

Emde, R. (1973). *Emotional Expression in Infancy: A Biobehavioral Study*. Psychological Issues Monograph No. 37. Madison, CT: International University Press.

Erikson, E. H. (1959). *Childhood and Society*. New York: Norton.

Faludi, S. (2011). *Stiffed: The Betrayal of the American Man*. New York: HarperCollins.

Florida, R. (2002). *The Rise of the Creative Class*. New York: Basic Books.

Fonagy, P. (2013). There is Even More Room for Doublethink: The Perilous State of Psychoanalytic Research. *Psychoanalytic Dialogues*, 23(1): 116–122.

Fonagy, P., Gergely, G., Jurist, E. and Target, M. (2005). *Affect Regulation, Mentalization, and the Development of Self*. New York: Other Press.

Forrester, J. (1997). *Dispatches from the Freud Wars: Psychoanalysis and its Passions*. Cambridge, MA: Harvard University Press.

Foucault, M. (1966). *The Order of Things*. English translation. New York: Random House, 1970.

Foucault, M. (1971). Nietzsche, Genealogy, History. In P. Rabinov (ed.) *The Foucault Reader*. New York: Random, 1984.

Foucault, M. (1983). The Ethics of the Concern of the Self as a Practice of Freedom. *Concordia: Revisa internacial de filosophia*, 6: 96–116. English translation. In P. Rabinov (ed.) *The Essential Foucault*, Volume 1: *Ethics*. New York: Pantheon, 1997.

Foucault, M. (1984). What is Enlightenment. In P. Rabinov (ed.) *The Essential Foucault*, Volume 1: *Ethics*. New York: Pantheon, 1997.

Foucault, M. (2006). *Psychiatric Power: Lectures at the Collège de France 1973–1974*. New York: Palgrave.

Frank, J. and Frank J. B. (1993). *Persuasion and Healing: A Comparative Study of Psychotherapy*. 3rd edition. Baltimore, MD: Johns Hopkins University Press.

Freud, S. (1895). Project for a Scientific Psychology. In *The Standard Edition of the Complete Psychological Works of Sigmund Freud,* Volume 1. London: Hogarth, 1956–1974.

Freud, S. (1900). The Interpretation of Dreams. In *The Standard Edition of the Complete Psychological Works of Sigmund Freud,* Volumes 3–4. London: Hogarth, 1956–1974.

Freud, S. (1905). Three Essays on the Theory of Sexuality. In *The Standard Edition of the Complete Psychological Works of Sigmund Freud,* Volume 7. London: Hogarth, 1956–1974.

Freud, S. (1910). Leonardo da Vinci and a Memory of his Childhood. In *The Standard Edition of the Complete Psychological Works of Sigmund Freud,* Volume 11. London: Hogarth, 1956–1974.

Freud, S. (1913/1930). Preface to the Hebrew Translation of *Totem and Taboo*. In *The Standard Edition of the Complete Psychological Works of Sigmund Freud,* Volume 13. London: Hogarth Press, 1956–1974.

Freud, S. (1925). On the Occasion of the Opening of the Hebrew University. In *The Standard Edition of the Complete Psychological Works of Sigmund Freud,* Volume 19. London: Hogarth Press, 1956–1974.

Freud, S. (1927). The Future of an Illusion. In *The Standard Edition of the Complete Psychological Works of Sigmund Freud,* Volume 21. London: Hogarth, 1956–1974.

Freud, S. (1939). Moses and Monotheism: Three Essays. In *The Standard Edition of the Complete Psychological Works of Sigmund Freud,* Volume 23. London: Hogarth Press, 1956–1974.

Freud, S. (1985a). *The Complete Letters of Sigmund Freud to Wilhelm Fliess.* Cambridge, MA: Belknap Press.

Freud, S. (1985b). *A Phylogenetic Fantasy: Overview of the Transference Neuroses.* Edited by I. Grubrich-Simitis. English translation. Cambridge, MA: Harvard University Press, 1987.

Freud, S. and Breuer, J. (1895). Studies on Hysteria. In *The Standard Edition of the Complete Psychological Works of Sigmund Freud,* Volume 2. London: Hogarth, 1956–1974.

Friedman, T. (1999). *The Lexus and the Olive Tree.* New York: Farrar, Straus, Giroux.

Friedman, T. (2005). *The World is Flat: A Brief History of the 21st Century.* New York: Farrar, Straus, Giroux.

Fukuyama, F. (1992). *The End of History and the Last Man.* New York: Free Press.

Gay, P. (1966). *The Enlightenment*, Volume 1*: The New Paganism.* New York: Norton.

Gay, P. (1989). *Freud: A Life for our Times.* New York: Norton.

Gay, P. (2002). *Schnitzler's Century: The Making of Middle Class Culture 1815–1914.* New York: Norton.

Gellner, E. (2003). *The Psychoanalytic Movement.* 3rd edition with an introduction by Jerome Brunner. New York: Wiley-Blackwell.

Gibbs, P. L. (2007). Reality in Cyberspace: Analysands' Use of the Internet and Ordinary Everyday Psychosis. *Psychoanalytic Review*, 94: 11–38.

Giddens, A. (1992). *The Tranformation of Intimacy: Sexuality, Love and Eroticism in Modern Societies.* London: Polity.

Gilbert, D. (2007). *Stumbling upon Happiness.* New York: Vintage.

Gilman, S. (1988). *Jewish Self-Hatred: Anti-Semitism and the Hidden Language of the Jews.* Baltimore, MD: Johns Hopkins University Press.

Gilman, S. (1994a). *The Case of Sigmund Freud: Medicine and Identity at the Fin de Siècle.* Baltimore, MD: Johns Hopkins University Press.

Gilman, S. (1994b). *Freud, Race and Gender.* Princeton, NJ: Princeton University Press.

Gladwell, M. (2008). *Outliers: The Story of Success.* New York: Little, Brown.

Gould, S. J. (2003). *The Hedgehog, the Fox and the Magister's Pox: Mending the Gap between Science and Humanities.* New York: Random.

Greenberg, J., Koole, S. L. and Pyszczynski, T. (eds.) (2004). *Handbook of Experimental Existential Psychology.* New York: Guilford Press.

Grünbaum, A. (1984). *The Foundations of Psychoanalysis.* Berkeley: University of California Press.

Habermas, J. (1968). *Knowledge and Human Interest.* English translation. Boston, MA: Beacon Press, 1971.

Hale, N. G. (1995). *The Rise and Crisis of Psychoanalysis in the United States.* Oxford: Oxford University Press.

Harris, S. (2004). *The End of Faith: Religion, Terror and the Future of Reason.* New York: Norton.

Harris, S. (2010). *The Moral Landscape: How Science Can Determine Human Values.* New York: Free Press.

Hoffman, I. Z. (1998). *Ritual and Spontaneity in the Psychoanalytic Process.* Hillsdale, NJ: The Analytic Press.

Hoffman, I. (2009). Doublethinking our Way to "Scientific" Legitimacy: The Desiccation of Human Experience. *Journal of the American Psychoanalytic Association,* 57: 1043–1069.

Horkheimer, M. and Adorno, T. W. (1947). *The Dialectics of Enlightenment.* English translation by E. Jephcott. Palo Alto, CA: Stanford University Press, 2007.

Illouz, E. (2008). *Saving the Modern Soul: Therapy, Emotions and the Culture of Self-Help.* Berkeley: University of California Press.

Israel, J. (2001). *Radical Enlightenment.* Oxford: Oxford University Press.

Jacques, E. (1965). Death and the Midlife Crisis. *International Journal of Psychoanalysis,* 46: 502–514.

Jones, E. (1953–1957). *The Life and Work of Sigmund Freud.* London: Hogarth.

Jurist, E. (2010). Elliot Jurist Interviews Peter Fonagy. *Psychoanalytic Psychology,* 27(1): 2–7.

Kagan, J. (1989). *Unstable Ideas: Temperament, Cognition and the Self.* Cambridge, MA: Harvard University Press.

Kahneman, D. (2003). Objective Happiness. In D. Kahneman, E. Diener and D. Schwarz (eds.) *Well-Being: The Foundations of Hedonic Psychology.* New York: Russell-Sage Foundation.

Kahneman, D. and Deaton, A. (2010). High Income Improves Evalutation of Life, but not Well Being. *Proceedings of the American Academy of Science*, 107(38): 16489–16493.

Kandel, E. (2005). *Psychiatry, Psychoanalysis and the New Biology of Mind.* Washington, DC: American Psychiatric Publishing.

Kandel, E. (2007). *In Search of Memory: The Emergence of a New Science of Mind.* New York: Norton.

Kandel, E. (2012). *The Age of Insight: The Quest to Understand the Unconscious in Art, Mind, and Brain, from Vienna 1900 to the Present.* New York: Random House.

Kant, I. (1787). What is Enlightenment. English translation. In Allen Wood (ed.) *The Basic Writings of Immanuel Kant.* New York: Modern Library, 2001.

Keller, B. (2005). *Class Matters.* New York: New York Times Publications.

Kernberg, O. (1975). *Borderline Conditions and Pathological Narcissism.* New York: Aronson.

Kets de Vries, M. F. R. (1985). The Dark Side of Entrepreneurship. *Harvard Business Review*, November–December: 160–168.

Kets de Vries, M. F. R. (1996). The Anatomy of the Entrepreneur. *Human Relations*, 49: 853–883.

Klein, G. (1976). *Psychoanalytic Theory: An Exploration of Essentials.* Madison, CT: International Universities Press.

Kohut, H. (1971). *The Analysis of the Self.* Madison, CT: International Universities Press.

Kohut, H. (1977). *The Restoration of the Self.* Madison, CT: International Universities Press.

Kohut, H. (1979). The Two Analyses of Mr Z. *International Journal of Psychoanalysis*, 60(1): 3–27.

Kramer, P. D. (1993). *Listening to Prozac: A Psychiatrist Explores Antidepressant Drugs and the Remaking of the Self.* New York: Viking.

Kuhn, T. S. (1962). *The Structure of Scientific Revolutions.* Chicago: Chicago University Press.

Lamb, M. E. (ed.) (1997). *The Role of the Father in Child Development.* New York: Wiley.

Lasch, C. (1979). *The Culture of Narcissism.* New York: Norton.

Lasch, C. (1991). *The Culture of Narcissism: American Life in an Age of Diminishing Expectations.* Revised edition. New York: Norton.

Lasch, C. (1995). *The Revolt of the Elites and the Betrayal of Democracy.* New York: Norton.

Laurent, E. (2011). *Lost in Cognition: Psychanalyse et Sciences Cognitives.* Nantes: Editions Nouvelles Cecile Defaut.

Lemma, A. (2010). An Order of Pure Decision: Growing up in a Virtual World and the Adolescent's Experience of Being-in-a-Body. *Journal of the American Psychoanalytic Association*, 58(4): 691–714.

Lévi-Strauss, C. (1949). The Effectiveness of Symbols. English translation by C. Jacobson. In C. Lévi-Strauss, *Structural Anthropology.* New York: Basic Books, 1963.

Lewis, M. (1989). *Liar's Poker: Rising through the Wreckage of Wall Street.* New York: Norton.

Lewis, M. (2010). *The Big Short: Inside the Doomsday Machine.* New York: Norton.

Lewis, M. (2011). *Boomerang: Travels in the New Third World.* New York: Norton.

Malach-Pines, A., Sadeh, A., Dvir, D. and Yafe-Yanai. O. (2002). Entrepreneurs and Managers: Similar yet Different. *International Journal of Organizational Analysis*, 10(2): 172–190.

Malcolm, J. (1981). *Psychoanalysis, the Impossible Profession.* New York: Knopf.

Masson, J. M. (1984). *The Assault on Truth: Freud's Suppression of the Seduction Theory.* New York: Farrar, Straus, Giroux.

McDougall, J. (1980). *Plea for a Measure of Abnormality.* Madison, CT: International Universities Press.

Miner, J. (1997). *The Psychological Typology of Successful Entrepreneurs.* Westport, CT: Quorum Books/Greenwood Publishing Group.

Mitchell, S. (1988). *Relational Concepts in Psychoanalysis.* Cambridge, MA: Harvard University Press.

Mitchell, S. (1993). *Hope and Dread in Psychoanalysis.* New York: Basic Books.

Molino, A. (1998). *Freely Associated: Encounters in Psychoanalysis with Christopher Bollas, Joyce McDougall, Michael Eigen, Adam Phillips and Nina Coltart.* London: Free Association Books.

Moyn, S. (2010). *The Last Utopia: Human Rights in History.* Cambridge, MA: Belknap, Harvard University Press.

Nietzsche, F. (1888). *Genealogy of Morals.* English translation by Walter Kaufmann. New York: Vintage, 1989.

Noll, R. (1994). *The Jung Cult: Origins of a Charismatic Movement.* New York: Free Press.

Nussbaum, M. (1995). *Cultivating Humanity.* Cambridge, MA: Harvard University Press.

Nussbaum, M. (2010). *Not for Profit: Why Democracy Needs the Humanities.* Princeton, NJ: Princeton University Press.

Ogden, T. (1993). *The Matrix of the Mind: Object Relations and the Psychoanalytic Dialogue.* New York: Jason Aronson.

Omer, C. (2000). *Parental Presence: Reclaiming a Leadership Role in Bringing up our Children.* New York: Zeig, Tucker & Theisen.

Onfray, M. (2010). *Le Crépuscule d'une idole.* Paris: Grasset.

Pascal, B. (1670). *Pensées.* English translation by J. Krailshaimer. London: Penguin, 1965.

Phillips, A. (1996). *Terrors and Experts.* London: Faber.

Phillips, A. (2002). *Equals.* New York: Basic Books.

Phillips, A. (2014). *Becoming Freud: The Making of a Psychoanalyst.* Yale Jewish Lives. New Haven, CT: Yale University Press.

Pinker, S. (1997). *How the Mind Works.* New York: Norton.

Pinker, S. (2011). *The Better Angels of our Nature: Why Violence Has Declined.* New York: Viking Penguin.

Polanski, R. (1984). *Roman by Polanski.* New York: Morrow & Co.

Popper, K. (1963). *Conjectures and Refutations.* London: Routledge.

Posmanik, S. (2009). The Theme of Akedat Yitzhak in Hebrew Literature. Unpublished doctoral dissertation, Tel Aviv University.

Prince, B., Ainslie, R., McWilliams, N., Thomas, N. K. and Axelrod, D. (2012). Division 39 Practice Survey: A Roundtable. *DIVISION/Review*, July. Available at www.apadivisions.org/division-39/publications/review/2012/07/practice-survey-roundtable.aspx, accessed April 7, 2015.

Pyszczynski, T. A., Solomon, S. and Greenberg J. (2003). *In the Wake of 9/11: The Psychology of Terror.* Washington, DC: APA.

Quine, W. (1978). *The Web of Belief.* New York: McGraw-Hill.

Randall, J. (1962). *The Career of Philosophy.* New York: Columbia University Press.

Rank, O. (1930). *Psychology and the Soul.* English translation by William Turner. Philadelphia: University of Pennsylvania Press, 1950.

Rank, O. (1932). *Art and Artist.* New York: Knopf.

Rank, O. (1948). *Beyond Psychology.* New York: Dover.

Reich, R. (2005). The New Rich–Rich Gap. *American Prospect*, December 12.

Reik, T. (1949). *Of Love and Lust.* New York: Farrar, Straus, Giroux.

Remnik, D. (2011). The Dissenters: Haaretz Prides Itself on Being the Conscience of Israel: But Does it Have a Future? *New Yorker*, February 28. Available at www.newyorker.com/reporting/2011/02/28/110228fa_fact_remnick, accessed April 7, 2015.

Ricard, M. (2007). *Happiness: A Guide to Developing Life's Most Important Skill.* New York: Little, Brown.

Ricoeur, P. (1965). *Freud and Philosophy: An Essay in Interpretation.* English translation. New Haven, CT: Yale University Press, 1970.

Rieff, P. (1955). *Freud: The Mind of the Moralist.* Chicago: Chicago University Press.

Riesman, D. (1950). *The Lonely Crowd: A Study of the Changing American Character.* New Haven, CT: Yale University Press.

Robert, M. (1974). *D'Oedipe a Moise: Freud et la Conscience Juive.* Paris: Calman Levy.

Rorty, R. (1989). *Irony, Contingency and Solidarity.* Cambridge: Cambridge University Press.

Roth, A. and Fonagy, P. (2005). *What Works for Whom? A Critical Review of Psychotherapy Research.* 2nd edition. New York: Guilford Press.

Roth, P. (2013). *Philip Roth: Unmasked.* Documentary. Directed by William Karel. New York: Cinétévé.

Rothkopf, D. (2008). *Superclass.* New York: Farrar, Straus, Giroux.

Roy, O. (2009). *Holy Ignorance: When Religion and Culture Part Ways.* New York: Columbia University Press.

Safran, J. (2013). Critique of Irwin Hoffman's "Doublethinking our Way to 'Scientific Legitimacy.'" *Psychoanalytic Dialogues*, 22(6): 710–720.

Said, E. W. (2003). *Freud and the Non-European.* London: Verso.

Samuels, A. (2009). Jung and Anti-Semitism. *Institute of Historical Research.* Available at http://sas-space.sas.ac.uk/4412/1/Jung_And_Antisemitism_by_Andrew_Samuels___Institute_of_Historical_Research.pdf, accessed August 18, 2009.

Sartre, J.-P. (1943). *Being and Nothingness.* English translation by Hazel Barnes. New York: Philosophical Library, 1956.

Sassen, S. (2000). *The Global City: New York, London, Tokyo.* Princeton, NJ: Princeton University Press.

Schafer, R. (1976). *A New Language for Psychoanalysis.* New Haven, CT: Yale University Press.

Schafer, R. (1983). *The Analytic Attitude.* New York: Basic Books.

Schorske, C. (1981). *Fin de Siècle Vienna: Politics and Culture.* New York: Vintage.

Schwartz, B. (2004). *The Paradox of Choice: Why More is Less.* New York: Harper.

Segal, H. (1988). *Introduction to the Work of Melanie Klein.* Enlarged edition. London: Karnac.

Segal, H. (1994). Interview. In V. Hunter, *Psychoanalysts Talk.* New York: Guilford.

Sen, A. (2006). *Identity and Violence: The Illusion of Destiny.* New York: Norton.

Shahar, G. (2010). Poetics, Schematics, Pragmatics and the Psychoanalysis–Research Dialogue (Rift). *Psychoanalytic Psychotherapy*, 24: 315–328.

Shahar, G. and Davidson, L. (2009). Participation-Engagement: A Philosophically Based Heuristic for Prioritizing Clinical Interventions in the Treatment of Comorbid, Complex, and Chronic Psychiatric Conditions. *Psychiatry: Interpersonal and Biological Processes*, 72(2): 154–176.

Shahar, G., Porcerelli, J., Kamoo R., Epperson, C. N. and Czarkowski, K. A. (2010). Defensive Projection, Superimposed on Simplistic Object Relations, Erodes Patient–Provider Relationships in High-Risk Pregnancy: An Empirical Investigation. *Journal of the American Psychoanalytic Association*, 58: 953.

Shedler, J. (2010). The Effectiveness of Psychodynamic Psychotherapy. *American Psychologist*, 65(2): 98–109.

Simon, B. (1988). *Tragic Drama and the Family: Psychoanalytic Studies from Aeschilus to Beckett.* New Haven, CT: Yale University Press.

Slezkine, Y. (2004). *The Jewish Century.* Princeton, NJ: Princeton University Press.

Sloterdijk, P. (2005). *Im Weltinnenraum des Kapitals.* Frankfurt: Suhrkamp.

Sloterdijk, P. (2006). *Zorn und Zeit.* Frankfurt: Suhrkamp.

Sloterdijk, P. (2009). *Du Musst Dein Leben Ändern!* Frankfurt: Suhrkamp.

Snow, C. P. (1958). *The Two Cultures.* Cambridge: Cambridge University Press.

Solomon, S., Greenberg, J. and Pyszczynski, T. (2004). The Cultural Animal: Twenty Years of Terror Management Theory and Research. In J. Greenberg, S. L. Koole and T. Pyszczynski (eds.) *Handbook of Experimental Existential Psychology.* New York: Guilford Press.

Spence, D. (1982). *Narrative Truth and Historical Truth.* New York: Norton.

Spezzano, C. and Gargiulio, G. (2003). *Soul on the Couch: Spirituality, Religion and Morality in Contemporary Psychoanalysis.* Relational Book Series. London: Routledge.

Stepansky, P. (2009). *Psychoanalysis at the Margins.* New York: Other Press.

Stern, D. (1985). *The Interpersonal World of the Infant.* New York: Basic Books.

Stoller, R. (1991). *Porn: Myths for the Twentieth Century.* New Haven, CT: Yale University Press.

Stolorow, R. (2009). *Trauma and Human Existence: Autobiographical, Psychoanalytic, and Philosophical Reflections*. London: Routledge.

Stolorow, R., Attwood, G. and Orange, D. (2002) *Worlds of Experience: Interweaving Philosophical and Clinical Experience in Psychoanalysis.* New York: Basic Books.

Stolorow, R., Brandchaft, B. and Attwood, G. (1987). *Psychoanalytic Treatment: An Intersubjective Approach.* New York: Jason Aronson.

Strenger, C. (1991). *Between Hermeneutics and Science: An Essay on the Epistemology of Psychoanalysis.* Madison, CT: International Universities Press.

Strenger, C. (2002). *The Quest for Voice in Contemporary Psychoanalysis.* Madison, CT: International Universities Press.

Strenger, C. (2004). *The Designed Self: Psychoanalysis and Contemporary Identities.* Relational Book Series. Hillsdale, NJ: The Analytic Press.

Strenger, C. (2008). I Accuse. *Haaretz*, September 28. Available at www.haaretz.com/print-edition/opinion/i-accuse-1.254730, accessed April 7, 2015.

Strenger, C. (2009). Strenger than Fiction. Blog available at www.haaretz.com/blogs/strenger-than-fiction.

Strenger, C. (2011a). *The Fear of Insignificance: Searching for Meaning in the 21st Century.* New York: Palgrave.

Strenger, C. (2011b). *Israel: Einführung in ein schwieriges Land.* Berlin: Jüdischer Verlag bei Suhrkamp.

Strenger, C. (2012). *The World Citizenship Project*. TEDX presentation. Available at www.youtube.com/watch?v—ArgTetQzd8, accessed April 7, 2015.

Strenger, C. and Ruttenberg, A. (2008). The Existential Necessity of Midlife Change. *Harvard Business Review*, 86(2): 82–90.

Sulloway, F. (1979/1992). *Freud, Biologist of the Mind.* Cambridge, MA: Harvard University Press.

Tiede, T. (2001). *Self-Help Nation: The Long Overdue, Entirely Justified, Delightfully Hostile Guide to the Snake-Oil Peddlers who are Sapping our Nation's Soul*. New York: Atlantic Monthly Press.

Wallerstein, R. (1995). *The Talking Cures.* New Haven, CT: Yale University Press.

Wallerstein, R. (2012). Will Psychoanalysis Fulfill its Promise? *International Journal of Psychoanalysis*, 93: 377–399.

Weininger, O. (1903/2005). *Sex and Character.* Bloomington: Indiana University Press.

Winnicott, D. W. (1965). *Maturational Processes and the Facilitating Environment.* London: Hogarth.

Winnicott, D. W. (1971). *Playing and Reality.* London: Tavistock.

Wittgenstein, L. (1953). *Philosophical Investigations.* English translation by E. Anscombe. Oxford: Blackwell.

Yerushalmi, Y. H. (1991). *Freud's Moses: Judaism Terminable and Interminable.* New Haven, CT: Yale University Press.

Zaretsky, E. (2004). *Secrets of the Soul: A Social and Cultural History of Psychoanalysis.* New York: Knopf.

Žižek, S. (2004). What Can Psychoanalysis Tell us about Cyberspace? *Psychoanalytic Review*, 91: 801–830.

Index